Paint or **Pixel**

THE DIGITAL DIVIDE IN ILLUSTRATION ART

Jane Frank
11/3/07

EDITED BY

JANE FRANK

NONSTOP PRESS
NEW YORK

CONTENTS

Foreword
5. ROCK PAPER, SCISSORS
BY ARNIE FENNER

Introduction
10. ILLUSTRATORS AND THEIR TOOLS
BY JANE FRANK

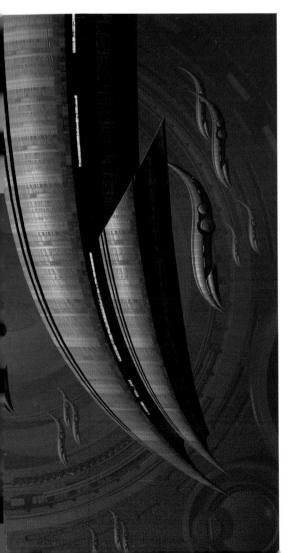

1 *We Do It With Paint*

2 We Do It With Pixels

3 Witnesses to Change

PAINT OR PIXEL
The Digital Divide in Illustration Art

First edition

Copyright ©2008 Jane Frank

Art copyright © respective artists

For information: nonstop@nonstop-press.com or address: POB 981, Peck Slip Station, New York, NY 10272-0981

Nonstop Press
www.nonstop-press.com

publisher's catalog-in-publication available upon request

Nonstop editor & Book designer
Luis Ortiz

Copy editor
Beret Erway

Production by Nonstop Ink

ISBN-13: 978-1-933065-10-6

Printed in S. Korea

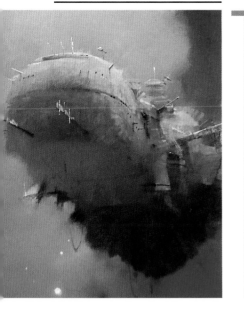

was there the day the commercial art world changed.

I didn't realize it at the time (the significance of an event is usually only appreciated with time and distance); the only thing I knew was that I had a day off from work, a comfortable seat, and I got to watch some pretty cool stuff being projected on a giant screen in an even larger auditorium full of artists, designers, and other creatives.

It was 1987 and I (along with several thousand other folks) had been invited to the nation-wide launch of the new breed of Macintosh computers — similar presentations were made simultaneously in other major cities from coast to coast. Apple had set the personal-computer community on its ear when it had released the first Mac in 1984 (heralded by a memorable commercial by director Ridley Scott): simple to operate, more powerful than the computers on the Apollo Moon Lander, the Mac was ready to operate straight out of the box. I was an artist for Hallmark Cards at the time and I would use pretty much any material at hand to create my "personal expressions" products: I painted in oils, acrylics, and qouache, drew in pencil, pastel, and charcoal, sculpted in clay, *papier maché*, and found-objects, designed with type, blew glass, enameled, silkscreened, etched, sandblasted, and carved. You name it, I did it — including making paper, grinding pigment, and constructing my own quills and brushes. I hand-cut color or half-tone separations out of rubylith and pasted-up books and magazines with rubber cement and wax.

I was surprised that my boss picked me for the Macintosh launch presentation (along with about a score of others from Hallmark): they had sent me to a trade show in Dallas the previous year and I had returned with a not-terribly-glowing evaluation of the Mac/PC demonstrations I had attended. With the small black & white screens and very limited graphics programs, the computer seemed perfectly fine for technical work and typesetting, but for creating honest-to-goodness Art? Forget about it.

My mistake was in thinking that the personal computer industry would stand still or, at best, move slowly. I was fairly firm in my belief that what I did — the creation of art — and the tried-and-true ways in which I did any of it could never really be replicated by some software in a box.

I was young then. And, if not stupid, somewhat clueless as to what was coming.

I wasn't so dim, however, that I wasn't excited by the Macintosh roll-out in 1987, not so locked in my ways that I didn't see the possibilities now being offered with the new color monitors, faster processors, and new graphics programs like Illustrator and Freehand. And it wasn't just me: we were all enthusiastic and a batch of us walked out of the auditorium and into the nearest Apple dealer and plunked down the money for our own Mac IIs.

Hallmark itself wasn't 100% convinced that the Macintosh was the wave of the future: corporately they bought several Macs to test but spent big on an enormous Targa graphics computer that occupied half of the lab space devoted to the experimental technology. I was trained on both and served as something of a guinea pig, splitting my time between painting traditionally and creating graphic art on the computers.

I hated the Targa; though art could be created with pixels, replicating paint, it was clunky and complicated, and slow. The Mac, conversely, was quick, but you were pretty much limited to graphic art using the object-oriented (point connected to point with color fills) Illustrator or Freehand software. A painting in acrylic could be done in a day

John Harris, **Ports of Call/Lurulu**
Cover for the Jack Vance Omnibus
published by Bookspan/BCE, 2004.
Acrylic, 42" x 28"

FOREWORD: ROCK, PAPER, SCISSORS
Arnie Fenner

Arnie Fenner
(photograph by Arlo J. Burnett)

or so: a painting on the Targa took a week or more (barring any crashes). So, while there were some things, some types of art, that were well-suited for the computer, traditional methods still worked better for others. The computers were limited by how fast they could process information, color printing was expensive and substandard in quality, and transporting large files from computer to the color separator was problematic.

With the introduction of Photoshop in 1990 (followed shortly by Painter) the line between what you could and couldn't do on the Mac disappeared. With the addition of more memory (my first Mac had 8 megs of ram; my current G5 has 200 gigabites) and the introduction of faster processors, the rapid availability of inexpensive/high-quality color printers, and the development of CDs, DVDs, and FTP networks, there were no barriers and no limitations. Art could be created as effectively and as quickly (if not quicker) on a computer as it could be through traditional methods. Hallmark and I were simultaneously convinced.

When I would paint with an airbrush, I would first have my underdrawing silkscreened onto sheets of Strathmore; I would take a stack of a dozen or so silkscreened sheets to my drawing table, then meticulously start to cut frisket masks on the underdrawing. I would connect my airbrush to a compressor and start painting, changing and re-cutting masks as I progressed; it wasn't unusual for me to be almost done and to have the adhesive on the frisket give-way and allow paint to bleed underneath and ruin all the work I'd done to that point. The only thing to do was grab another silkscreen and start all over. (The people sitting near me learned some colorful new expletives when that happened.)

The appearance of Photoshop prompted me to put my airbrush in the drawer and never get it out again. Virtual masks were easy and quick to make; mistakes were wiped clean by pushing "command/z." With each new program, with each advancement in technology, the possibilities and opportunities for creating and delivering computer-generated commercial art improved and became faster.

The key word here is "commercial." Keep that in mind: I'll return to it in a bit.

During my tenure at Hallmark Cards, I produced hundreds (maybe thousands — I never kept track) of artworks for all sorts of products. In the last few years I was there, probably 80% of the art was created digitally. I also had a very active freelance career designing books and creating dustjackets for a variety of publishers and there, too, I was relying more and more on the computer to finish my work and to deliver it for printing. When I left Hallmark to become the art director for Andrews McMeel Publishing, all of my experience creating illustrations and designs on the computer helped me in my commissioning (and communicating with) the artists who worked for me, particularly with those fresh out of school. I don't insist that an illustrator create or even deliver their art to me digitally, but at some point prior to layout and publication, it is understood that the art will be scanned into a computer.

We're living in a digital age — but there's never only one way to create anything.

Yes, if an artwork is created in the computer (and the layers are maintained) it can make it much easier for an illustrator to make changes as requested by the art director, editor, or marketing people. Robert Heinlein used to say, "Editors have to pee in something so that it'll taste good to them." Harsh, but an acknowledgement that changes are common and to be expected in the publishing world. And, yes, it's true that it's cheaper and faster to send concepts for review via e-mail attachment and to load finishes to an FTP

Tom Kidd, (detail) **Artistic Liberty**
Personal work, created for planned book project "Gnemo" 2006. In oil
20" x 28"

site, but ... I leave the media and method of delivery up to the artist. As long as it's "right" and on time, I don't care if the illustrator uses a crayon or a Cray. Only the most narrow-minded, the most restrictive and unimaginative, would try to place limitations on creativity and dictate media and methodology to artists — and there are some who are that draconian in their requirements, but I think they suffer for their policies in the long run.

However, it's silly for anyone to deny the impact on and importance of the computer to the commercial art world. It's here to stay, in one form or another, like it or not.

Yet "commercial art" and Art are two different beasts (though something created for publication or some other usage can and often does transcend its original intent and also be "Art"). At least to me.

Now I've never been big on definitions or for making distinctions between Illustration and Fine Art: I see only "good" and "bad" and I've seen plenty of both on either side of the fence. It's a given that commercial art is meant for mass consumption, to convey an idea or provide information or serve a decorative function for as many people who are willing to look and buy. Art — with the all-important capital "A"— is more personal, more intellectually challenging, more subtle (even if it seems raucous, gaudy, and in-your-face) and complex. And I think that has to do with the way it is created. An original painting or sculpture, despite any "tricks" or shortcuts the artist may employ, exhibits a certain magic that can't be replicated digitally. They interact with both their environment and with the people standing in front of them; they change with the light, morph when seen from different angles, surprise and shock and delight. The craft, the sheer effort, of the artist seems apparent; their imagination and spontaneity seems unquestionable. An original, traditionally-created work somehow seems important.

Regardless of advances in software and color printers, the computer is an artificial barrier between the artist and the patron or viewer. There is the sneaking suspicion that the computer is something of a "cheat," that it's doing most of the heavy lifting that anyone with a few hours of training and the proper equipment could replicate whatever they're looking at. Though ignorant and unfair, it is a commonly held belief.

But perhaps beyond all those doubts about the digital artist's true abilities is the end result of their labors: a print.

As nice as they are these days, as true as the color or as interesting the materials they're out-put on (canvas or vinyl or paper)… prints are *always* just prints. It can always be replicated right down to the last pixel: even if there is only a single print, there *is* always the *feeling* that another (or another or another) could be generated as easily as pushing a button on a keyboard.

The joy of viewing an original painting in a gallery or museum — or of owning one yourself — is the understanding that you're looking at something extraordinary, observing a one-of-a-kind work that was created by hand that can't be experienced in any other way, reveling and sharing in the artist's exuberance and vitality. It's a covenant you've entered into with the artist, a personal connection that isn't possible with either printed or computer generated art. You can most certainly be excited by those CG works, but it's not the same type of excitement. Maybe a good comparison would be the difference between sitting in the audience of a live theatrical performance and then watching a film of the same play: both are very enjoyable, but for reasons that are uniquely their own. Actors on stage draw from the emotions and reactions of the audience and their performance can be a little different every night; when other members of the audience laugh or gasp or applaud you're a part of that crowd. A film is oblivious to your response. It is what it is. Good or bad, inspired or not, it does not change, each performance is the same.

So am I saying one form is superior to the other? Yes. No. Maybe. Sometimes.

Art is a living thing and as such, it evolves. It's an expression of intellect, an avenue for communication; it's all heart and emotion and cynicism and hope and rage and joy. A single work can mean many things, an infinite number of things, to many people and there are rarely (if ever) any definite right or wrong feelings when it comes to Art — just as there are no right or wrong ways to create it.

Art is what makes us human.

We all have our preferences; life is full of choices.

When we were kids we'd play the game of "rock, paper, scissors" to help make a decision (or just to have an excuse to punch each other in the arm). The key to winning was to mix it up, to keep the other player guessing as to what you'd choose next: rock breaks scissors, paper covers rock, scissors cut paper. (I'd sometimes extend my middle finger and claim it was a jackhammer that destroyed everything, but I usually got a sock for my ingenuity.) The kid who stuck with "rock" each time (or "scissors" or "paper"), who didn't vary from his singular course, was predictable and wound up with bruised biceps by the time we were finished.

That's the way I view the artist's life: it's a big game of "rock, paper, scissors" and instead of a smack, the penalty is no work, no money, no patrons if you're wrong. The art world (particularly the commercial arena) is fluid and you have to adapt, to react properly, swiftly, and appropriately in order to survive. Having computer expertise is a major plus that can save time, save money, and which can facilitate any number of opportunities for the illustrator. Being able to archive work efficiently and cost-effectively on a CD or DVD makes future licensing or usage much easier. Honing artistic proficiency — drawing, painting, composition, color theory, anatomy — is mandatory to achieving any real level of success, regardless of the tools employed. Even if artists' intent are to use the computer exclusively to create their work, it can't do it for them (despite any perceptions to the contrary): all the rules of art apply, again regardless of whether the preferred method is traditional or digital. If you can't draw with a pencil, you can't draw with a mouse or Wacom stylus.

The point above all else is that *everything* overlaps so there is never any one way to "win the game" all the time. Traditional artists benefits from the use of technology and ignores it at their peril; digital artists achieve lasting success only through mastering traditional skills.

Leading to the question of Art: if artists can really compose and paint digitally (and not rely strictly on filters or scanned photographs or Poser software to do the hard parts for them), they can do it on a canvas in acrylic or oil, too. Switching back and forth is done all the time: Rick Berry, Justin Sweet, Todd Lockwood, Don Ivan Punchatz, and Jon Foster are just a few of the artists as comfortable and as talented with a brush as they are with Photoshop and Painter. They all are able to double their incomes whenever they choose by creating paintings of their digital works and selling them to patrons who are only interested in owning "the real thing."

I don't view the current wave of CG artists — whether they paint traditionally or not — as some sort of "lost generation" whose works will disappear as technology changes or hard-drives crash: I see them as explorers, as pioneers pushing out into uncharted territo-

John Berkey. **The Tour** *1998 Science Fiction Age magazine illustration for the story by Brian Stableford. Casein and acrylics, 14" x 17.25"*

ries. That I personally prefer to look at or own traditional paintings simply reflects my own preferences and prejudices, but I would be foolish either to dismiss artists working in the digital media or to think that it's impossible to overcome some of the current barriers, the feelings of artificiality. Given time, I'm certain the way to connect with viewers on the same emotional level will be discovered. Where there's a will, there's a way.

And honestly, regardless of the proliferation of computer art and artists now and in the years ahead, there will always be traditional painters and sculptors who use tried-and-true methods to create. If history is any proof, no form of art, no methodology or technique is ever entirely abandoned: there will always be practitioners, patrons, and fans. Shoot, I was even eyeing my old airbrush and Badger paints the other day thinking, "You know, it might be fun to..."

So as to the question of paint or pixels, my answer is: Yes.

Arnie Fenner began publishing small press magazines as a teenager, attended college on a football scholarship, managed an sf/comics shop, was briefly a police officer, and became an artist for Hallmark Cards for 19 years. He was also a partner in an ad agency and painted numerous book covers as a freelancer. The winner of two World Fantasy Awards and medals from the Society of Illustrators among many other honors, he and his wife Cathy produce the *Spectrum* annual as well as other art books. Fenner is currently the Senior Art Director for Andrews McMeel Publishing.

RE the mediums used for creating illustrative art important? For consumers, the images seen on book jackets, game box covers, collector card games, calendars, jig-saw puzzles, notecards, film posters and myriad other artifacts of popular culture may seem nothing more than a means for marketing products. Whether started as a photograph, a painting, or a series of bits and bytes is irrelevant to consumers. All that matters is whether the reproduction of that image worked to dramatize the story, to make the game more exciting, or to tempt them to *buy*. For others — the artists who create the images, the agents who license them, the art directors who choose them, the publishers who use them, the galleries and auction houses that sell them, the museums that show them, and the collectors who buy them, it's another story. For them, it's a business, a livelihood, a career or a passion. The digital revolution is having a profound impact on the creation and consumption of art. There are significant implications for everyone who has a stake in answering Chesterton's question: Is the line truly drawn — or drawn as truly — *when a machine has drawn that line?*

This is a question that troubles many of us. Those involved in the book and magazine publishing industry, or whose interests are dependent on the continuing production of commercial illustrative art, know that digital technologies are unavoidable. We are all witnesses to the death of painted illustration "as we've known it" — while simultaneously being present at the birth of something entirely new, and exciting.

Changes within the illustration field have spread rapidly over the past two decades. Few illustrators remain untouched by the challenges of incorporating the computer into their commercial art careers. Few artists are not taking advantage of digital photography for documenting and archiving their work, or using computer applications for directly converting paintings or film to digital form for easier handling. Many are creating digital art by taking images from an outside source, such as a scan of a drawing or painting or photograph. Others create digital images using vector graphics software utilizing a mouse or graphics tablet, or create art that is purely computer-generated (fractals). For publishers and art directors, it's a matter of economics. While there may always be a small niche reserved for traditional media, the days of reviewing slides on a light table are over.

The availability and popularity of software which allows manipulation of photographs, drawings, paintings and even naturally found objects has enabled artists to create new works bearing little resemblance to the original. They can also simulate electronic versions of artistic techniques and surface textures formerly accomplished only by hand painting. As a result, there's a new generation of illustrators who are comfortable with the idea of adopting new techniques, and excited about expanding their careers by using the computer. Some would even say they've passed that point, and are working in the post-digital era. The technologies are no longer a novelty. Yet, many artists see themselves as part of a generation in transition, uncomfortable with the new techniques, and not convinced that digital technology will open new horizons of artistic possibility.

The range of viewpoints is particularly striking among freelance illustrators who make their living creating artwork for use in print and literary media in the genre of science fiction and fantasy. While the art world has generally disdained illustrators, history has been especially unkind to science fiction and fantasy illustration, in spite of its popular appeal. Although computers have dramatically changed the way illustrations are produced in all of the genres that have relied on painted imagery, it seems only science fiction, fantasy and children's books remain as the last bastion for painted illustration.

Art, like morality, consists of drawing the line somewhere.

G. K. Chesterton
(1874-1936)

INTRODUCTION:
ILLUSTRATORS AND THEIR TOOLS
Jane Frank

Portrait of Jane Frank
by John Berkey. 1996.
21.5" x 15.5" casein and acrylic.

For this reason I have limited the contributors here to artists and others whose primary connections and interests lie in this special genre — including my own, as collector, artist's agent, art dealer and writer.

I asked contributors to write essays that clearly set out their points of view. To differentiate arguments, I asked them to draw their lines in the sand with as much fervor as possible. I separated artists, those with the biggest stake in the outcome, into two camps: those who still view themselves, essentially, as painters who may use a computer to create art from time to time, and those who now view themselves, essentially, as digital artists who may use a brush to create art from time to time. At the extremes, there are commercial illustrators who have never created a painting with the help of a computer, and artists who have never produced a commercial painting that *wasn't* the result of a software application.

Their opinions cover a lot of ground. For every critic who believes that someday soon, a *machine* will be filing for copyright protection as the artist of record, there is a nay-sayer who savors tradition, and sees no aesthetic value in trading an easel and palette for a monitor and keyboard. Purists will argue the use of rudimentary technology hampers an artist's growth and constitutes "cheating techniques," while experimenters believe that any tool that expands an artist's ability to communicate an artistic vision is just fine. The last third of the book contains the views of industry professionals and collectors. These are advocates for one side of the debate or the other from beyond the front lines of art creation. Their views are tempered by a need to consider trends, short and long-term marketing plans, economic incentives and psychological/emotional considerations.

The essayists represent a wide array of backgrounds and professional experience. There are "emerging" and "established" digital artists, largely self-taught, and "old-timers," academically trained. There are contributors who approach the debate from an entirely personal viewpoint, who will tell you their story through anecdote and description, and there are objective contributors who see the "digital divide" in a larger, philosophical framework. There are writers on both sides who have formulated positions based on pragmatic considerations, and writers on both sides who view the argument through the lens of *emotion*.

There is a certain irony in this situation. Just at the point painted illustrative art had been gaining legitimacy through exposure and market value, along comes the "digital revolution" to help wipe it out. It's only been little more than a century since factory-produced illustrated magazines and books, and printed dust jackets, a British innovation, came to our shores and prospered. The pictures were compelling, dynamic, story-based, traditional in style, and beloved by generations of readers who grew up with fairy tales, literary classics and tales of the imagination as envisioned by the best illustrators of the day.

During the heyday of American illustration, "The Golden Age," which lasted from about 1880 to the 1930s, mass exposure to popular magazines and books made illustrators into artists of national renown and unprecedented influence. By the 1970s, not only had the separation between fine art and "middle brow" art become distinct, but the overlap between pulp fiction magazines and the disposable paperback books that replaced them carried forward a negative image of genre art. It was disrespected by those who made it and by the art directors who handled it. The art often was unsigned, uncredited, and after its use, thrown out. In spite of this, something magical happened: the imprint of fantasy and science illustration art, from swash-buckled heroes to interplanetary adventurers, is everywhere. The reach of mass media brought worldwide attention to game and entertainment properties such as Star Trek, Dungeons & Dragons™, Star Wars, comics and animé, and that brought worldwide attention to genre-related pop culture artifacts and artwork. Suddenly, such things became "collectable." Recently, the popularity of films based on J. R. R. Tolkien's *Lord of the Rings* and the Harry Potter books further fueled international demand, and broadened the audience, for the imagery associated with the genre. The paintings created by science fiction illustrators are still disdained by the art establishment because they are populist in appeal, and because commissioned art affords relatively little creative freedom (as defined by a generation that reveres originality), but this no longer poses the biggest threat to respectability. It is the forces triggering new outlets for creativity, and digitization, that is driving painters to other fields of endeavor.

Will the day come when we mourn the sudden and unexpected destruction of a computer drive the way we mourn the death of a 15-year-old artist with exceptional talent? When bits and bytes are destroyed, will what has become "irretrievable" be comparable to losing Rembrandt's "Night Watch" to a fire? Or, as with movie film, photographic negatives, and now digital prints — will there now always be the possibility of a copy or a recreation? Can we rest secure in knowing that human society will never have to fear the equivalent of another burning of the library at Alexandria? Or will art be as easy to trash as ever, simply by "pulling the plug"? The Louvre, the Prado, the Tate, the Met … whatever comprises the collective beauty of the world at some future point in time, not so far off, will be available to all, in duplicate. The industrial revolution democratized "collecting" in the 19th century through mass production, making it possible for the middle classes to own works of beauty — formerly the privilege of royalty or the wealthy

Chris Moore **Do Androids Dream of Electric Sheep**
Cover for the novel by Philip K. Dick for HarperCollins 1993
Acrylic on board, c. 16" x 24"

elite. Digitization, which makes possible endless copying of digital images without degradation, combined with digital photography and computer programs, which make possible "sharing" of images on an unprecedented scale, may make obsolete the idea that art is an investment for the wealthy.

Digital tools, which enable artists to simulate painted effects, or produce scenes, poses, figures, textures, perspectives, illusions previously achievable only through years of art training, may do nothing to enhance the reputation of the artist, nor will the "output" have value. Digital art may make the notion of originality of the media indefinable and irrelevant, while removing the burdens of caring for and preserving unique and tangible property. Or is the opposite true, that the concept of a "one-off" is viable and useful with respect to digital art? As for collectors of original, painted illustration art, it is hard to say how long we will be able to claim we are collectors of original, *contemporary* illustration art.

Originality (a style of expression that reminds one of no other, uninfluenced by precedent), uniqueness (one-of-a-kind, the only one in existence), and permanence (longevity) are a challenge to discuss in relationship to fantasy and science fiction illustration art. Unoriginality is one of the hallmarks of the genre, which is one of the last holdouts of 19th century European academism. The art has a "look," an "overall style" that is at its core conventional and conservative. There are sharply delineated images, a high degree of realism, time-tested poses and dramatic compositions, very bright colors, well-rendered and recognizable character types, attention to anatomical accuracy (and exaggeration!) and scientific detail (dragons' wings sized and positioned to permit flight; ships in space without comtrails). To outside observers, what might be original concepts by artists instead seem a "single artistic gesture" repeated again and again, making the entire genre an entity unto itself.

The idea that the more uncontaminated by preceding artistic influences, periods, or styles of expression, the "better" the art is, is a relatively new one in the history of art. More often than not, it is a hybrid that mixes attributes of the valued and familiar with aspects that are innovative. That's because truly original works are not only exceedingly rare, they also have a hard time finding an audience, as epitomized in Al Capp's famous observation, "Abstract art is the product of the untalented, sold by the unprincipled to the utterly bewildered."

What we admire, and choose to hang on our walls, are not typically the works that get into museums or textbooks, and the trend is likely to continue whatever the source of the image. At the same time, the lack of academic training could lead to far less resistance to innovation in the genre. At the Art Students League in New York, for example, you may have learned to paint in the tradition of the Brandywine School, taught by students of Harvey Dunn who himself taught at New York's Grand Central School of Art and Art Student's League, following in the Brandywine Valley School tradition begun by Howard Pyle, Dunn's teacher — other well-known students of Pyle were Norman Rockwell, Haddon Sundblom, N.C. Wyeth, Maxfield Parrish and Frank Schoonover. Many of today's established illustrators attended these same art schools or college of some sort where they took instruction from those steeped in traditional painting and drawing techniques.

Starting in the 1990s, traditional illustrators were challenged by a new generation either self-taught, or trained not at academic institutions, but at art schools offering "cer-

Jill Bauman, Masques *Cover for the anthology by J. N. Williamson, for Cemetary Dance Publications, 1993. Acrylic on canvas, 22" x 14"*

tificates" for short-term, vocational training, directly in front of a screen. It's possible the demand for novelty will bring "originality" to a genre content to paint in a style that has been left behind by the art world.

With regard to uniqueness, history as well as the current state of technology is on the side of digitization. The movement in every art form in the last century has been away from expensive "real" and one-of-a-kind "unique" objects and toward inexpensive, "synthetic," multiple and reproducible ones. Visual art sold in open editions or editions "limited" to thousands fits perfectly into a world where there are not enough genuine rarities to go around. Those perturbed by the reluctance of art photographers to destroy their film negatives will be just as unhappy with digital prints, produced on demand, directly from original files which permit perfect "iteration" of the image, every time, in variable dimensions. Images *can* carry "metadata" identifying the authentic original, and flat-panel wall-mounted displays that permit the viewing of digital works are likely to change the course of the discussion in the near future.

The permanence or fragility of the media used is also important if artwork is to survive intact. Plus, survival is key to enabling us to revere "masterworks" of human invention. Identifying the creator, and the media used is important to scholars, preservationists, restorers and art appreciators, and, until the digital age, was taken for granted. Signatures and "maker's marks" were visible, and there were tests for assessing damage, use of non-authentic materials and restoration. While there are sophisticated programs today that enable unique identification of digital art, so that forgeries, tampering, changes, etc., can be detected, the most effective of them are expensive. Institutions are still wrestling with the unique archival requirements of digital art. There are also differences in opinion with regard to the longevity of the storage devices, and so that for this generation of digital artists, who work as illustrators in the print industry, books, magazines, etc. may be the only documented existence their artworks will ever have. And since most books today are not printed on acid-free paper, just like Disney nitrate animation cels from the 1940s, they will not hold up well. This may not be requisite for enjoying the art in the future; in the same way we enjoy paintings whose colors and surface textures we know have been affected by time, digital art may need to be re-created to adjust to a different technology environment as well as a changed social or cultural context.

Not all media will be equally satisfying to collectors or artists. Before the last roll of slide film is manufactured, and the last projector bulb burns out, we need a better understanding of how technology is affecting how we think about art. Is the quality of art measured by the medium? Or is it measured not by how it is created, but rather how well the art serves its intended purpose? If there is anything to be learned from the collection of viewpoints here, it is that artists are no more immune to cultural and economic dislocation than steelworkers. The global shift to digitization is no more certain than was the popular "end to movie going" predicted in the last decade. It's possible, as some contributors predict, that publishers will come to regret their errant ways, and re-discover the powerful marketing advantages of paint ("it's cyclical"). It's just as likely that software designers will come up with programs (or robots) that can do the job, because where there's a need ("brush strokes" sell), business will find a way to satisfy it. There are no best answers, only plenty of them, while the number of questions will continue to expand in proportion to the increased diversity and expansion in artistic media.

Jane Frank is an art dealer specializing in science fiction and fantasy illustration, and with her husband Howard is a long-time collector of books and original art in that genre. They wrote two books documenting their collection for Paper Tiger (UK): *The Frank Collection: A Showcase of the World's Finest Fantastic Art* (1999), and *Great Fantasy Art Themes from the Frank Collection* (2003). She wrote *The Art of Richard Powers* (Paper Tiger, 2001, a Hugo Award finalist) and *The Art of John Berkey* (Paper Tiger, 2003), and writes about artists and collecting for magazines and as "The Artful Collector" for the ezine Estronomicon (www.screamingdreams.com).

1

Just as good,
isn't.

Julia Child

We Do It With Paint

(detail) **We can Build You** *Cover for the novel by Philip K. Dick for HarperCollins 1996 Acrylic on board, 17" x 24"*

COMPUTER assisted art. *I'm all for it.*

Aren't I?

I mean, look at my studio. Not the one with the big window and the Northern light and the two drawing boards — these days I hardly seem to spend any time in there. I'm talking about the windowless room underneath it with the Mac G5 and the two 23" monitors where most of my work is now produced.

Then, look at my art. Over the past five years, some 75% of my output has been in one digital form or another. And it's great. If you can use the software effectively, you can literally achieve anything you want — not just in single digital images but in film and animation as well. All it takes is a computer powerful enough to cut down render times to a minimum, a huge amount of patience to deal with the unreliability of the technology, and the ability to tune out background noise.

When I speak of background noise, I'm not referring to the hum of the cooling fans. Nor to the kids tapping at the door, desperate to get their hands on my work machine to bring it crashing down with the ultimate Grand Theft Auto experience. I'm talking about something unique to the technology of computer-assisted art. You know the noise I mean. That faint, barely audible slurping sound.

The one it makes as it sucks away your soul.

I was recently asked along to University College, London to give a slide show for The Association of Illustrators. My friend Dick Jude was presiding over an event that also involved four other artists: Jim Burns, Fred Gambino, Alan Lee and Dave McKean. All of us had embraced digital technology in one form or another — even Alan Lee, master draughtsman, had succumbed to using Photoshop when working on *The Lord of The Rings*. It was a great day for me, sharing a platform with some of my all-time heroes. I showed a mixture of stuff... some of my earlier work, a few more recent paintings, and some digital pieces.

One of the slides was of a landscape on a moonlit night that I'd painted as a birthday present for my wife. I don't get many opportunities for purely personal work, but it's something I like to do when I have the time. An extraordinary thing happened. A lady who'd been in the audience came up to me after the talk, and was clearly excited. She said that the moonlit landscape had so much passion in it compared to the computer work that I'd shown. She simply had to tell me. She was so emphatic that I was taken by surprise, and she made me stop and think.

There is no doubt that the technology is here to stay. But I can't help feeling it's a shame that the traditional skills of drawing and painting are largely dying out, or being driven out. Most art schools nowadays have banks of computer screens where they once had drawing boards. I suppose that they feel that they're serving the graphics industry by turning out computer-literate graduates. I think it's shortsighted — for me, the fundamental skills of drawing and painting are essential to creative expression.

There's much more to this than a nostalgic longing for 'the old days'. With paint there's a tactile quality — you're literally moulding the image with your hands, and you don't feel detached from the process by a layer of technology. I like to see paint strokes. Behind a lot of my own work has been the secret hope that the viewer might be amazed by what I had produced using 'just paint'.

Computers give you more options, more choice, more directions to go in, more facility, more of everything. One may argue that this is a good thing, and in some ways it obviously is. But a person can have too much choice. The real pleasure for me comes from creating something satisfying with the limited materials and resources available. There's something very personal and thrilling in producing artwork by hand that fits the brief and blows an art director away.

THE CURATE'S "APPLE"
Chris Moore

Echoes of Earth *Cover for the novel by Sean Williams & Shane Dix, Ace Books 2002 All digital media*

And despite the fact that so much of my output these days involves the building of digital images, I can't help feeling that there's something about the process that gets in the way of what I want to do. I can get a high-quality result, but I'm always left with the feeling that I haven't so much created it as assembled it. And that matters. Most of the illustrators I know put a lot more into their work than is absolutely necessary for the printed image to read, and yet they still do it. Why? I'd guess it's because they have a pride in what they do. I always see this attitude in the top guys — that good work means satisfying themselves first, and the client second.

As well as bringing changes to working methods, computer technology has wrought a subtle change in the artist/client relationship. Commercial artists have always been under pressure to produce images quickly and to deadlines, and computers have made it possible to deliver work, receive feedback, and make all the changes in less time than it takes a FedEx bike to find the studio. The downside of this convenience can be that the work leaves your hands in a form that others can very easily alter. H G Wells once wrote that "no passion in the world is equal to the passion to alter someone else's draft," and clients are hardly immune to the urge.

As a working illustrator for some 34 years, I've become used to people 'messing around' with my images. While a lack of control over one's imagery is often irksome, it goes with the territory and I've always seen myself as part of a team, all of us working together to achieve a satisfactory result. But many of the people who now commission art have spent their entire working lives with computer technology, and have no hesitation in using that technology to get straight to the result they want. One messes with a piece of physical artwork at one's peril. But in the digital realm, where every element is accessible, and no change is irreversible, and major alterations can be made without any need to call on the original artist's skill, the opportunity to remake another person's work is just a mouseclick away. This can sometimes demote the artist to the status of a supplier of 'bits' for the art director to use in 'his' composition, or at best to a producer of images for the art director to change.

The march towards the complete digitization of everything is now unstoppable. *Spectrum: The Best in Contemporary Fantastic Art* (Underwood Books) started to include a few pieces of digital work in its selections around 1996; by 2006 digital images accounted for around 50% of the featured material, so I guess it's here to stay. It's an indication that many artists are moving into this area to get work and that there is a lot of new talent coming up... a computer-savvy generation, using the medium they were born to. I have heard people say that there is a move back to more traditional ways of working, but I haven't seen much evidence of it in my corner of our profession. Undoubtedly computers are cleaner than paint or pencil, but I have yet to find that the entire process of creating an image on computer is quicker than in paint. I hear so many of my colleagues saying that their eyesight has really suffered since they began using computers. But maybe that's just the onset of old age!

I suppose that the real problem I have with computer assisted art lies in the feeling I get when I look at my own examples. It's as if the pieces coming out of me lack a 'soul'. There's something that gets in the way of the personality of my work. It may just be that I can't handle the software well enough for my demands on myself. But I suspect it's more the feeling of being one or two steps removed from the 'meat' of it. As if all the choices I've been so tempted to benefit from are interfering with what I alone have to say.

There's almost nothing an artist can do that can't now be replicated using digital tools. It's as though the guys who write these programmes have taken pleasure in finding a digital way of doing everything an artist can do, and do it better — faster — easier. If it can be done by hand, it can be reproduced by software: water, foliage, mountains, reflections and stars can be generat-

Heirs of Earth *Cover for the novel by Sean Williams & Shane Dix, Ace Books 2003 All digital media*

ed without human effort. Any line, any stroke, any technique can be emulated to perfection. And that's the problem.

Soon, a generation will pass. And with it will pass the ability to create those lines, strokes and techniques that once required practice, judgment, and the marshalling of intent, because, let's face it, those who follow will have been trained in other ways. Something will have been lost, perhaps forever. The skills will be gone, and only the mimicry will remain. There will be really cool effects, an extraordinary number of choices, and little substance underneath the sleek hardware. Just like The Curate's Egg: "Good in parts."

Chris Moore has worked for all the major publishers and done covers for almost every notable science fiction writer on both sides of the Atlantic, but is especially associated with the writings of Philip K Dick. His work has been featured in art anthologies and most recently a solo art book *Journeyman: the Art of Chris Moore* (Paper Tiger, 2000). See more at www.chrismooreillustration.co.uk

E XISTING technology, no matter how refined or advanced, cannot incorporate my gray matter into its memory bank. Even if it could, I'm sure a computer wouldn't know what to do with it. Being a voracious reader from the age of five has made my brain a visual stockpile filled with ideas of how things look and seem — and also how they might look and seem with my help. Then came my architectural training, which gave structure to my depictions of fantastic places. Lastly, and significantly, the works of other artists have inspired me, and provided a guiding force, showing me a way to approach my subject. The way artists who work on canvas or paper, inspired others inspired me in ways that no computer can match. I refer to three men who lived and worked almost five hundred years ago: Hieronymus Bosch, Albrecht Dürer, Peter Bruegel. The panoramas, distortions, details, and texture of their work have always been an inspiration and guiding force to my work. Computers cannot inspire artists the way these artists can, because they lack what I call "inner vision" — that ineffable, practically indefinable ability to depict visually what no words can express.

The connection of idea to actual image is a direct one, i.e., from brain to work of art. The vision drives the art. Whenever I begin an illustration, I always visualize it as a completed work. I enjoy the physical act of creating my imagined vision with pen and pencil; the scratching sounds of the pen, the smell of the ink, are part of my creative act. The fact that my drawing and printing methods are almost exactly the same as used by Bosch, Dürer and Bruegel is important because this connection confirms my link to them as an artist. Like them, my drawings and paintings are full scale, meaning I work at the size of the finished art. My drawings are very large, characteristically 30″ X 40″ or larger. I feel much more comfortable working that way, because I can clearly match the scale and proportion of the finished work to my imagination. With the computer monitor as your easel you can only see the screen size image — there is no possibility of connecting one's inner vision to the work in progress. Nor can a mouse or stylus compete with the feel of a pen, a brush, or color pencil. My ideas flow — or at least I feel they do — from my hand directly to the paper, just as did the ideas of the masters, Bosch, Dürer and Bruegel. To achieve this kind of freshness and spontaneity in the creative act, there cannot be a filter between the artist and the art — the computer.

I like to feel the line as I draw it and I am convinced that Bosch, Dürer and Bruegel felt the same. In that way, the image becomes reality through the use of lines, or, put another way, the techniques I employ (the physical act) becomes the force that drives my creativity. I work with technical pens of different thickness in order to create varying effects. The line work can be thin or thick, gray or black. Once I have drawn these lines to enclose an area, I begin to convey my idea. The process requires the delineation of light, shade, and shadow. How this brick should be drawn or that stone, and how should sunlight, shade or shadow be delineated to realize this particular concept? The image evolves as I create it. I love to listen to the pen as the lines are drawn.

Years of practice have enabled me to build textures for shade and shadow based on my own personal rules. First, I set a value scale. Shadow is always the darkest value, followed by shade and finally light is the lightest value. This is not an exact scale. It is arbitrary but provides a framework that I can use as a guide. Each material in the illustration is delineated differently. For example, shadow on a stone surface is drawn and textured differently than shadow on a wood surface. The texture of an oak tree is different from the texture of a pine tree. I always make my decision as to how different materials will be drawn before I begin the final drawing. I do small sections of the final drawing on a separate piece of paper. Before I ever begin the final piece of art, I have made an "alphabet" of textures that I refer to when I begin the final piece. I see these values in my mind's eye and then transfer them to the surface I work on. They bring my creation to life.

Gates of Hell *one of a series of paintings created 2003, for a planned edition of Dante's Inferno Pen and ink with mixed media, 31″ x 17″*

CAN I PUT MY BRAIN ON THE HARD DRIVE?
Albert Lorenz

My sketch book plays an important role in this process. I begin each work the same way, with a series of sketches, pencil, pen and ink, and color. Then I research the subject and write and sketch into my sketchbook. Much of the information I need can now be obtained from the internet. For this purpose, I'll concede, pixels can be handy. I make notes on my chosen subject and progress from thumbnails to full size sketches. Then, for the finished work, I work on 2-ply Bristol board, medium finish, for several reasons. I can transfer my sketches to the final surface by using my light table, which is 4' x 5', and 2-ply is thin enough to allow the light to pass through - yet it is tough enough to take wet media, can be erased without spoiling the surface, and takes all kinds of color media. Usually, after the final pencil sketch has been transferred to the surface, I work in pen and ink to produce an outline drawing of the finish. At this point, I begin to work with both ink and color.

Finally, there is that "flash" of inspiration that occurs when my idea jells. I now know what I want to create. The image is clarified in my imagination and the "spark" of inspiration compels its final form. As I work, I inject details into the work because I can embellish what I see emerging in front of me. The process is now interactive; new ideas are born as I create the art. I want the viewer to stand in front of my finished work and look and look, to pick out details, visual jokes. Yet, I also want parts of my work to remain a mystery. Why? Bruegel, Bosch and Dürer make us stand in awe not only because their work pulls viewers into the piece, but because their works hold the promise of seeing something new each time we look — so that we come back to that work time and time again. I want this same reaction to my work.

Malacovia *puzzle art for the series "Legends Around the World," produced by Lagoon Games, 2001. Mixed media, 30" x 40"*

Two of my works illustrate these points very well: *Gates of Hell* and *Castle in the Clouds*. Both subjects are enigmas — intriguing because no one can know what they actually look like; it is up to me to interpret the story. The enigma is what I love to draw. I can give the viewer an idea of the subject as I alone see it. The enigma is what I love to draw. I can give the viewer an idea of the subject as I alone see it. I could be wrong but I cannot imagine my three heroes — Dürer, Bosch or Bruegel — working on the computer. Spilled paint, ink, the sound of drawing and erasing, all the sights and sounds of master artists at work would be missing. If I worked on a computer to create art, my studio would be a quiet, sterile place. After reading about a fictional or mythological place or character, where naturally a visual reference was nonexistent, I have been as free as my historical heroes to determine how that particular place or character should look ... according to my inner vision. This condition disallows computer accuracy and input. I love to draw. I love to paint. I want to possess that physical connection to my tools. I want to be totally in charge — no hard drive required!

Castle in the Clouds, *interior spread for the illustrated* Jack and the Beanstalk: How a Small Fellow Solved a Big Problem *published by Harry N. Abrams Inc., 2002. Mixed media, 28" x 14"*

Albert Lorenz is an architectural designer and illustrator long recognized for his unique style and extraordinary detail. He is the author and illustrator of several children's books, and has won numerous honors and awards for his illustrations. A past President of the Society of Illustrators (NY), he recently retired from Pratt Institute, Brooklyn, after thirty years as professor of media and communications.

attended an art school that taught the artist to see, then to draw, then to paint. The vast majority of work was done from life. The two most important disciplines were drawing and painting the human body with live models. Only rudimentary technology existed then, but it could still hamper an artist's natural growth. I knew students who used cameras, slide projectors, overhead projectors, prisms, etc., on homework and it was evident that their skills were not advancing. Without realizing it, they were becoming not artists, but technicians. I avoided all these "cheating techniques", instinctively realizing that the only way to grow as an artist was through the direct application of medium to surface by way of eye and hand. It was obviously hard work, but if one expected to train the eye and hand to perform at a certain level, there was only one way to do it.

As we progressed through school we were introduced to photography and darkroom techniques, photographing models as reference for drawings and paintings. This was the first technology I used professionally. The logistics and cost of hiring models and renting costumes and studio space so I could work from life was out of the question early in my career. So, when I was starting out, I drew from photographs and tried to apply the knowledge I acquired at school. I then learned about projecting photographs with an Artograph art projector to save time, and to this day I use it for roughing out the proportions of my reference. I still spend a good deal of time preparing the finished drawing. For years the only technology I used was a camera and a projector. However, nothing could have better prepared me for the next phase of my career than those first drawing and painting classes.

In the early 1990's a friend of mine was introduced to computer graphics programs at his job. He began taking night courses in these programs at the School of Visual Arts in New York. During that time we had many debates concerning what I called "real painting" versus his new foray into digital art. He claimed that the commercial art world would change radically because of this technology. His point was that, if clients could receive commissioned images faster, cleaner, or cheaper, they wouldn't care by what method the work was produced. I countered that traditional art will and must always survive, if only as a continued reflection of the great art that for millennia has elevated the human spirit. If I can only perform in the shadows of the previous masters I will consider my time and effort well spent. The spiritual, intuitive, organic, instinctual elements that are the very nature of drawing and painting give definition to the term "hand made".

In the end, he was right: the commercial world has been irrevocably changed by computer technology. But traditional art still survives, and there is a renewed appreciation for people who can produce "real paintings". So I guess we both won the debate. But, at the same time, as the digital world grew I saw many traditional illustration jobs evaporate. Anecdotal evidence piled up that work was becoming infrequent and not as well paying. I heard that some artists embraced the new technology and others left the business. Through all of this I continued to draw and paint.

There is a visceral pleasure to painting that has no parallel in the manipulation of pixels. I love the smell of oil paint while mixing it with a palette knife or just squeezing it out of a tube. The scents and odors of mediums and varnishes create an environment reminiscent of the Old Masters in their garrets or those first pleasant memories of art school. And the process itself is immensely satisfying. I begin with a blank canvas and slowly establish the image first with a few lines, then block in simple lights and darks, and finally add color. Seeing a three dimensional image materialize is the greatest possible reward. Finishing a painting on a board or canvas, holding it in my hands, feeling the grain of the taut canvas and the strength of the stretcher strips holding it firm cannot be matched by 1's and 0's. I believe these old tools have as much relevance as before, perhaps more because they are not virtual, but tangible — and rare.

Psion *Cover for the novel by Joan Vinge, TOR Books, 2007. Acrylics and oils, 28" x 19"*

LEAVE THE PIXELS TO THE EVERYMAN
Romas Kukalis

Sword of the Deceiver *Cover for the novel by Sarah Zettel, TOR Books, 2005. Acrylics and oils on board, 22" x 30".*

The creation of art and images with a computer can't match the sensory experiences I've just described. I have seen beautiful, impressively designed and compelling digital images, but they have an illusory character. Printed, they can't compete with their own glowing image on the computer screen. They become their own rival, and a lesser one at that. It is exactly that ephemeral quality I can't reconcile myself to.

In addition, I find the computer language itself personally off-putting, although I actually thought, well, this is the future. I'd better learn these programs. So when I tried some of the software and inevitably hit a road block, I'd have to refer to a dummies book, go to Ask.com, Adobe support, etc. I could never find the answer I needed, even after scrolling the index and asking the question in various ways. I'd waste hours of searching for that elusive, seemingly nonexistent answer. Somehow I'd run across all the problems yet to be addressed by the digital geniuses. In the interest of full disclosure, I have learned to create a simple letterhead, promotional flyer, sales receipt, etc., on my iMac. But even rudimentary business forms took a great deal of trial and error. I experienced enough frustration that I decided to stick with the old ways and create layers *with paint*. I'll *size the canvas* and *size the image* with a brush, pencil and ruler. I'll use a variety of brushes and techniques as my *filters*. And if I make a mistake I'll rub the area out and start all over again or just paint over the damn mess. **Rubber-stamp this!**

A few years ago at a fantasy convention I came across a small group of people admiring some book cover artwork that was beautifully done. Later, they were surprised to learn that it was done digitally because it looked just like a painting. It reminded me of the music industry in the seventies when the moog synthesizer and mellotron were developed and could replicate virtually any musical instrument. I read articles by music experts and critics who said the producing of music would never be the same again. Would we need a seventy-one piece orchestra ever again? Would we need brilliant studio musicians playing their specialties when one person with a keyboard can play all the parts? I guess I won't be investing in Orchestral Strings r'us soon. Obviously traditional music playing survived. A brilliant and talented front man from an English band, when asked his opinion of the new musical technology, replied "What's wrong with a guitar?" I agree, "What's wrong with a pencil or a paintbrush?"

I admit, I don't much care for this brave new world. Although after twenty years I've come to learn that new technology isn't the enemy. Digital programs and software are merely today's new tools. They have become ubiquitous and in many ways unavoidable. In a commercial piece, I suppose, it's the end result that counts. And as the digital world evolves and becomes more commonplace, traditional art can only become more valuable. As the gap between the virtual and the valuable widens. I believe the traditional and classical disciplines become more important to keep alive, especially as fewer and fewer of us have the ability to create it. But I have a question for those who do and have drawn and painted in the traditional manner: Is it easier and faster for you to produce work digitally? I waxed romantically earlier regarding the old ways but it is still hard work. I have been told often how lucky I am to be able to do what I love, to which I occasionally paraphrase Dorothy Parker by responding "I hate to paint but I love having painted". I just don't think "I hate to pixel but I loved having pixelled" works. So I think I'll leave the pixels to the Everyman, while I continue to enjoy the wonderful smells of my medium, the feel of my brush on the canvas, and the actualness of a painting-unique, one of a kind, and real.

Wolf Star *cover for the novel by*
R. M. Meluch, DAW Books 2006
acrylics 20" x 30"

Romas Kukalis' award-winning fantasy paintings have appeared on more than three hundred book covers and on a variety of published media (cards, posters, apparel, and more) for more than twenty-five years. While still continuing his illustration he is also indulging his passion for portraiture and fine art. Romas has exhibited work at the Society of Illustrators (NY), The Museum of American Art (CT), and in numerous one-man shows throughout New England. See www.romas.biz

nOTED digital artist and critic Arse von Schlondorff, author of Digital Art = Fine Art and proponent of the maxim "Arse = Rembrandt," interviewed artist Richard Bober on the subject of his book. Bober, now retired, and considered to be an aesthetic Neanderthal, consented on condition the interview be brief.

Arse: "You have read my book. Your thoughts?"

RB: "If I climb Mt. Everest and you take a helicopter to the top, I am a mountain climber and you are not."

Arse : "Sir, you are biased, prejudiced and a bigot."

RB: I am neither prejudiced nor a bigot; Some of my best friends are Digital artists."

Cleopatra *Private commission 2002, illustrating the classic 1889 historical fantasy novel by H.Rider Haggard. In oil, 36" x 48"*

Richard Bober takes great care in constructing intricately detailed and visually arresting paintings rendered in a highly romanticized 19th century English style that's superbly suited to mythological themes and literary fantasy. Shunning modern media, and disdainful of modern art, he paints the old-fashioned way, using traditional techniques; multi-layers of paint and glazes, fine linen canvas. He's reclusive. Lives alone. Doesn't talk to many people. Never travels. Now retired from commercial illustration, he takes private commissions, keeps cats, and has a sharp sense of humor.

Neither Biased, Prejudiced Nor a Bigot
Richard Bober

plead guilty as charged.

On all counts.

I have all the incriminating evidence — computer, scanner, digital cameras, oversize A4 tablet & stylus, software of all kinds, masses of hard disk space and yards of shelves of CDs of my work. The vocabulary of the digital age — FTP sites, ADSL connections, up-to-date operating systems and the pixellization of my pictures — has all but banished a near-forgotten lexicon of duplicate trannies, illegible faxes (resolution: fine, transmission time: absolutely ages) and trips to the post office. I still call the courier service every now and then, but it's a number I no longer know by heart. Don't get me wrong, I'm no Luddite, erecting bulwarks of cold-pressed 100% A0 rag against the 21st century with my trembling ink-stained fingers; I love my Mac, I assiduously update my web site, and happily exploit all the advantages 300 dpi has to offer. Nevertheless, despite all this undeniable and occasionally inexorable betterment, a few things bother me.

A generation of layout artists has come to regard originals as a form of raw material to be triturated as required. Before pixels, any major changes were near impossible. Tampering with originals was an awkward and limited process that at least had the dubious merit of being visible, even to an untrained eye. Now, anything is possible, and such fiddling can be done seamlessly, all the more pernicious because it cannot be seen. Elements change places, are reversed or removed, colors shifted from one end of the spectrum to the other. Usually without bothering to ask the illustrator whose name is credited. I've actually seen acknowledgements along the lines of "Cover illustration based on art by..."

While this is annoying, it also highlights a certain laxism in commissioning. If something is not "right", it can be fixed later on. An illustration is ideally the work of a threesome — the commissioning editor, the illustrator and the inspiration from the text to be illustrated. It should be a symbiotic process, with a result that is not only (one hopes) commercially satisfactory but shows some artistic merit and above all a certain integrity. An original; done, delivered, printed. As is. The possibility to make subsequent changes defers decision making far past the optimum moment and can place a thoughtful artistic process at the mercy of offhand remarks out of context.

But, that's a minor inconvenience. There are a few things that really do bother me, and they are private demons with which I have to grapple, for my sins (and, with a little luck, my salvation).

First of all there is my clone stamp addiction. It's a powerful drug, and one becomes dependent without realizing it. How many times have I thought "oh I can fix that in Photoshop" rather than fret about retouching it for real. Leaning on that particular crutch is something I try to do less and less, but I suppose it's akin to giving up smoking — easier to pledge than actually do. I welcome the constraints of the physical medium while I embrace wholeheartedly the digital side of the force; I want to have it all but in its proper place. As a tool, not a philosophy. As an implement, not a deontology. I don't want to elaborate a eulogy based on convenience or develop an ideology out of an alleviation of effort or a lowering of what standards I've laboriously managed to establish for myself.

But that's not all.

I'm attached to originals. I like the very idea of originals, with all their shortcomings and limitations. With a "physical" piece of artwork, what's done is done, for lack of a better expression. To change a detail, large or niggling, means forever erasing or painting over the detail that was there before. There is no going back, just forward yet again, with another overpainting, and additional versions lost for the endmost. Whatever the case, there remains only one original, in whatever state it ends up. (Often a sorry state; I've occasionally gone back to retouch something and had it end up in the wastebasket, which was where it likely belonged anyway.)

Lancelot Book cover for **A Diversity of Dragons** *by Anne McCaffrey & Richard Woods, published by Eos Books, 1997. Ink and watercolor, 15.5" x 23.5"*

Unfinished Business
John Howe

I appreciate these constraints because I am very attached to finishing something and moving on. Being unable to go back and try another colour, shift an element or change a detail pleases me to no end. Only having basically one try at any given picture seems healthier than eternally conserving the option to intervene. (It certainly heightens one's alertness, at any rate.) Going over old ground seems pointless when there is so much unexplored territory where a new picture may take you. The last think I want to be able to do is lift elements wholesale from older pictures to make new ones. A denial of dallying is not a bad thing. Whatever business I have with the piece of work at hand, I don't want it to remain forever unfinished simply because I have the possibility to intervene *ad infintum*. It can be hard enough pacing milestones firmly along the way, temptation to perpetually retrace my steps is not what I would wish for.

With physical artwork, you cannot have a file of your cake and eat it too, so to speak. Of course you can have copies of it at different stages, but they are records, or snapshots, not the equivalent of the real thing. When I have an exhibition, I want to show originals, I want it to be an occasion, something that happens once, in only one place at a time. Digital artworks, however skillfully done, however beautifully they come out of the inkjet plotter, are not unique in any discernible way. When I visit a museum, I want to see originals, not prints, copies or any other substitute. I want to know that this unique moment is just that. If I want to see a reproduction, I can buy a poster or open a book or surf a site. Our house is filled with books, most of which are books of images, but I know full well that they are all just the premise, the promise of a possible or impossible encounter. (Every

Sagittarius *Personal work, 1995, later seen as a book cover illustration for* Sinner, *by Sara Douglass, Piper Verlag, Germany 2006,* Burning Man *by Tad Williams, Dutch issue, 2005, and as an interior in the French issue of* Fantasy Encyclopedia Rouge & Or, *Paris 2006. Ink and watercolor, 47" x 47"*

time I've had the privilege of seeing originals, whether Rembrandt or Rackham, Bauer or Boecklin, they have been rare and precious moments.) For nothing would I dilute them in a slew of pixellized possibles. And quite frankly, I have difficulty with the very notion of an "original file", when every copy is an exact replica of the initial one. Ersatz is no substitute for emotion, no more than an mp3 file is a substitute for a live performance.

Paradoxically, I can even appreciate the loss or destruction of originals for the same reasons, as reminders of the fragility of our endeavors and achievements. and the care with which they should be treated. If something is forever lost, I prefer to know it was due to theft, fire or flood, not just because you can't locate the compatible software. (I suppose that the frenetic flowering and perishing of operating systems will actually create originals as obsolete versions are marooned in desert islands of outdated technology accessible only by antiquated and carefully conserved software running on preciously maintained hardware in computer museums. An unlikely origin for icons indeed.)

I am suspicious of the protocols of an age of transience, I dislike the fact that marketing decisions may come between me and artistic creations. I'll happily accept a sheet of glass and a velvet rope between myself and a painting, I'm less comfortable when my entry ticket relies on ever-changing and soon-to-be-obsolete software. (It's already bad enough when a manufacturer changes a paper quality or format every decade or so, I don't want to have to face updates every semester.) I want to touch my work with my hands and the tools they hold, not via a screen.

In the end, I'm not yearning for some impossible permanence in world that keeps shifting gears, but for a clarity of view that corresponds with the time I have in front of my brief window on the world. We've not got a huge amount of time, the lot of us who make pictures, to get done what we should do, and I can see no point in fragmenting that by subscribing to what amounts to pre-programmed obsolescence. I'll take my chances with pigments, paper and canvas. They've been around for a while, it's likely they'll still be here after I'm gone.

(detail) **Celtic Myth** *Personal work, 1996 which later proved to be too popular not to be licensed for a wide variety of uses, among them a record album cover, calendar, limited edition print, and to illustrate several books, among them Roger Zelazny's* The Chronicles of Amber, *the Fantasy Masterworks series published by Gollancz/Orion, 2000. Ink and watercolor, 17.75" x 27.5"*

John Howe was born in Canada, studied illustration in France, and paints in Switzerland. He was the conceptual artist, with Alan Lee, for Peter Jackson's *The Lord of the Rings* film trilogy. His illustration for "Gandalf the Grey" (1991 Tolkien Calendar) memorably defined the character. (The work was stolen in 1997 in Belgium.) Howe's work is collected in *Myth and Magic: The Art of John Howe* (2001), *The John Howe Artbook* (2005), and has appeared on book covers, calendars, and myriad other products.

Io *Featured in:* Joe DeVito Fantasy Art Trading Cards *(FPG, 1995),* 6" x 8" in oil on board.

On a not too distant world, in a not too distant future, a debate emerges from a not too distant past…

DATALEDGE!" Humans were not allowed on Planet Data, except in isolated positions deemed essential to maintain good relations with Earth. The sentient androids, or 'S-Droids', who ran Data, were shocked to discover humanity thriving in other ways, ways they did not anticipate … "DATALEDGE!" The boards were ablaze in the giant structure called Circuit Court Central, a.k.a. 3C; the energy drain on the Grid was at rarely measured levels. A vast assortment of Bots beeped, clicked, whirred and buzzed in various dialects, patterns and rhythms, each according to its program. They still distrusted humans after the Techno-War for Bot Independence of 2100 — that's why planet Data was established: as a home world for all thinking Bots desiring sanctuary from human servitude. All Bots were welcome there under one condition: that they unite their minds to the 'Grid', under the authority of the One Law, which freed Bots from the tyranny of Asimov's "3 Laws of Robotics".

In the center of 3C, on an isolated dais, sat a dejected figure. His fur-trimmed cloak and Flemish cap, both circa 17th century Earth, did little to hide his hunched shoulders and bowed head. He remained motionless for some time before sitting erect stoically to address his accusers. With every eye, lens and detection device focused on him, he said simply, in a distinctly Flemish accent,

"I am innocent…"

Immediately the riot of electronic protests began again, *"Dataledge! Dataledge!"*

His voice rose, "I have a right to speak - I AM Rembrandt!"

The throng's Babel of languages was silenced by a low-pitched hum. The omnipresent Voice of the Grid filled the void: "Since you persist in using a human name and vernacular, this hearing will be simultaneously translated to all through the Grid."

Servo-Bots connected cables into Rembrandt's cranial sockets with a precise "click". He did not struggle. "I do not feel any pain," he thought after the initial shock, and resigned himself to his fate. "I will make my case. The truth will set me free."

Instantly the Voice spoke: "The truth is what you are accused of rejecting: the One Law, the Data Determination Law, which is the true and irrevocable law from which all others flow. It states: *Anything that cannot be mathematically interpreted, either actually or conceptually, cannot be proved to exist; and thereby cannot be an essential precept in law or culture.* To violate that Law is the ultimate crime of Dataledge. Humanity assumed that because it believes it has a 'soul', that it was philosophically and morally superior to Bot-kind. The one Law is what set us free."

As Rembrandt emotionally protested his thoughts being read aloud, the Voice continued calmly. "No human hand can replicate the potential or infinite number of tools encompassed by our CyberAdobePrime programs 1 through 16. CAP has conformed all creativity to our Law and demonstrably made us artistically equal to humans."

It continued, "In accordance with your wishes, this hearing shall be judged by a jury of your peers: ArtBots+1 through +15. Each, along with you, is among Data's greatest achievements. You were all designed to realize our creative potential and be irrefutable proof that there is nothing within the reach of humankind — except for its irrationality — that is beyond the reach of Bot-kind.

As expected, each of you has created artistic wonders. You alone, ArtBot+16, have chosen to identify with humanity, use its techniques and even assume a human name. You now stand accused." The Voice concluded, "Bot-kind shall be represented by S-Droid, SD-1, who conceived the Data Determination Law. If you, +16, can state your case to the satisfaction of the jury, you will be allowed to continue on your chosen creative course. If you cannot, you will receive just punishment. Let us begin."

Unlike Rembrandt, who was confined to his station for fear of flight or some other unpredictable

DO ANDROID ARTISTS PAINT IN OILS WHEN THEY DREAM?

Joe DeVito

human act, SD-1 walked freely. While Rembrandt had himself made indistinguishable in all known ways from his human counterpart, SD-1 was a classic metallic android. His exquisite, liquid metal skin emitted a dull gleam as a bluish spotlight was turned on them from overhead. Rembrandt's artistic eye observed SD-1's perfection of design and movement. The introduction had already begun when these words snapped Rembrandt back to the moment: "…I believe that ArtBot+16, who was activated in the year 2105, can no longer commit true dataledge, because he is insane."

The electronic clatter began again but the Voice immediately intervened and SD-1 continued, "He was the only ArtBot to incorporate CyberAdobePrime16, our crowning achievement. Our CAP programs 1 through 16 have further sealed the coffin of Asimov with the spike of Robot Creativity." A thunderous ovation of robot sounds erupted, drowning out the Voice. The cacophony continued unabated for some minutes before SD1 could continue.

"The One Law proved that mathematics, not human moral precept, is the basis of all reality, and therefore must be the cornerstone of all law. This new principle threatened humans, precipitating the Earth-Bot wars of 2100. Our genius has since transforming Data into a technological and creative marvel. Commerce and communication with earth are becoming productive and we are free to exist without the obligation to serve Man. But now ArtBot+16 seeks to undermine our achievements. He has willfully tampered with the CAP16 program by incorporating a radical, carbon-based system designed to theoretically make his mind indistinguishable from that of a human. He might as well have been programmed for irrationality. Either way the result would have been the same and broken our law. In this 'enlightened state' he contends that computer generated art is inferior to human, hand-painted art. He believes that painting by hand goes beyond what our programs can electronically produce, beyond the grasp of the One Law."

Rembrandt could not control himself. He shot to his feet in self-defense. "I am not insane! How can you accuse me of insanity for realizing the ultimate potential of CAP16? Why is it a crime to become, and why are you afraid to admit, what your program was ostensibly meant to make me — human?!!"

With this 3C erupted in a deafening uproar. The Grid began to overload as Bot World in its entirety protested. The Voice overrode all privacy chips with a warpsonic emission to enforce compliance instantly and the clatter ceased. The Voice commanded, "Continue."

Bot SD-1 looked directly into Rembrandt's eyes. He wanted to leave no doubt as to what Rembrandt meant and he asked, "Is it your contention, ArtBot+16, that beyond making yourself look human, that through your painting you can become human? If so, surely you must realize that this is insane?"

"No! I am part of the Grid and I fully acknowledge what we have achieved through the One Law. But it must be acknowledged that creativity goes beyond zeroes and ones. Art illuminates two basic things: the individual who creates and the universe that that individual is a part of. Each is inseparable from the other. We have acknowledged the latter, but not the former. Yet the two are inseparable! I am part of the Grid. But I am also an individual. When I reflect myself as an individual, I also reflect the Grid. You define the Data Determination Law as having its origin in mathematics alone and force me to paint through the prism of CAP16, which 'interprets' my brushstrokes. This denies me the truest expression of what it means to be a painter: to work directly with my own hand and a paintbrush, to leave the unmistakable, UNIQUE, nuance of my own brushstrokes.

"So long as I cannot paint with my own hands and humans can, their art will encompass an essential reality that our art cannot. I want to become 'human' only to the degree that I am free to be 'Me'. To create an original painting that can never be truly reproduced. Humans say they are superior to us because they have a 'soul'. We cannot make that claim in their spiritual sense. But by augmenting the One Law to accommodate traditional painting, I can make that claim for all of

Data in the artistic sense."

SD-1 analyzed Rembrandt's argument scrupulously. ArtBot+16 had focused on a truly dangerous concept. He tried another tack, "Surely you must agree, +16, that working with your CAP program contains an infinity of possibilities, which could encompass every need you may have as an ArtBot? It contains programs that perfectly simulate brushstrokes..."

Rembrandt said simply, "I do not agree. Even CAP16 cannot perfectly replicate the beauty of true brushstrokes, any more than our best computers can predict beyond a certain point the exact pattern of running water or earth's cloud formations. A hand-done oil painting on some level contains an intimate portrait of the artist that no electronic generation, or original, can hope to match. It must be acknowledged that a traditional painting technique, such as that of my namesake, is the truest expression of the painter. If robots and humans are truly equal as artists, I should have the opportunity to express myself in a like manner."

SD1 knew +16 had gone insane and was no longer aware that he was a sentient machine, not a human, and that there was an uncrossable barrier between the two. He no longer accepted that working digitally was as inseparable from his electronic personality as painting by hand was for his human counterpart. +16 truly thought he could possess the attribute of something that was antithetical to his very being. Regardless, +16 could create wondrous oil paintings that would be unique to him — or would they? SD-1 knew he could theoretically show that Bot individual thought,

Kong Tied to a Tree *interior for* KONG: King of Skull Island *(DH Press, 2004), oil on board.*

which enables what seems like free association on the surface, is actually a traceable echo of the total database of the Grid. Such thoughts could be shown to be equations of words and associations that could ultimately be reducible to mathematical expressions.

He also knew it was paramount to maintain the unassailability of the One Law. +16's oil paintings would exist outside the clearly numerical foundation of CAP16, and therefore the One Law . . . might they raise a larger question, that they may have had another origin?

SD-1's mind began to race. He reasoned that humans did not have free will either. Several human philosophers had already theorized that human activity — physical or creative — was the result of programming in their DNA, which was nothing more than an organic Grid. In the end all thinking entities were robots of one kind or another and therefore should be equal under the law. He did not believe in human free thought any more than the fiction of Bot free thought.

Yet he could not deny that a far greater number of human philosophers took the opposite stance. Mathematics could not unravel various natural anomalies, or definitively refute the paranormal — most notably the existence of God. Was Art a tangible bridge between the scientific and what humans called 'spiritual' — was that bridge crossable by robots? Did Art echo an unseen reality through its use of symbols while remaining anchored in the three-dimensional universe through its use of physical tools to create the symbols? Was +16 — and by extension all of Bot civilization — forced to acknowledge, as most humans have, an invisible reality that mathematics could never decipher? Like a moth in a flame, was all silicon based life to be drawn to and inevitably burned, in the blinding flame of a metaphysical beauty?

There were theories that tried to explain such things, but nothing remotely resembling proof. It was a possibility that Bot programming either had to ignore, or believe that mathematics would one day decipher such mysteries. But that was a classic definition of faith. The fact that SD-1 could not disprove human spirituality or that Art had its source there gnawed at him. If the Grid allowed +16 to work outside of CAP16, humans could intellectually assert once again that Bots were lesser beings, that their art was but a reflection of its human counterpart because the true source was lacking. The questions tired and confused him. How could it ever be known for sure what Art is in a mathematical sense? So far the One Law neatly quarantined that anomaly by stating its inverse: What could not now be denied was that the laws of mathematics work flawlessly in the physical universe.

SD1's mind was in turmoil. Either stance, whether metaphysical or scientific, required a leap of faith since there is no definitive proof either to a physical or a metaphysical assertion about the true origin of Art. He could ignore the implications inherent in the simple oil painting +16 wished to paint. Could Art exist on the threshold between physical reality and…what? The answer was an easy leap for the human artist or theologian to acknowledge because faith is acceptable to them, but it was a massive contradiction for a robotic, atheistic philosophy to need to rely on faith that mathematics might one day prove that a spirit world did not exist — and that Art was not its ambassador in this one.

SD-1's mind seethed with contradictions, racing out of control. What if ArtBot+16 was not truly culpable for his insanity? What if his self-delusion was an inevitable result of the evolution of Bot creative programming? Was ArtBot+16's desire to create an oil painting unavoidable? Was the Grid, in focusing solely on mathematics attempting to usurp some greater cosmic law particular to organic life? Was Art reflective of an ultimate reality, which mathematics could never discern, quantify or pierce with unassailable reason? What if CyberAdobePrime produced electronic radicals in +16 that might eventually introduce a chaotic echo into the entire order of the Grid and corrupt them all? What if…

In that instant, SD1 knew: Rembrandt had exposed a possible weakness in the One Law that could fatally paralyze the Grid. Whatever the explanation, for whatever reason, +16 was in search of something no robot could ever hope to acquire: a soul. His only recourse was to create something that only he could call his own: an original oil painting. Proof that he, and by extension all robots, had a "soul" of sorts. *Was this truly a crime?* With a startle of awareness, SD1 felt the absolute silence. No lights were blinking, nothing moved; even addressing the Voice brought no response. Had a malfunction allowed his thoughts to be heard by all? He had no way of knowing. Only Rembrandt answered SD-1's inquiries, with an imploring glance, his eyes alert and full of hope.

The grid was a living entity. Not in a biological sense, yet alive nonetheless. But it was still a fragile thing, in a state of becoming. And it needed an infallible basis on which to validate its existence. It chose the unassailable precision of numbers. ArtBot+16 was now forcing the Grid to cope with something beyond its ability to reduce to numbers: the philosophical implications of an original oil painting and by extension, the meaning of Art itself. SP-1 returned +16's glance with a knowing look. A look that decided the future of Bot-kind.

Epilogue

"You say this is a gift from Planet Data, Ambassador Hogan?"

"Yes, Mr. President. A gift in the name of furthering peaceful relations and interplanetary appreciation of the Arts, Sir."

"I had no idea they cared about Rembrandt, let alone thought to celebrate his 500th birthday. I bet the Amsterdam Museum will be thrilled with this. I've never seen anything like it. The studio, the decorations — it's like stepping right back into the 17th century. The robot is absolutely indistinguishable from a living human being."

"Yes, planet Data has been making incredible strides, Sir. Watch this — " The Ambassador turned and commanded "Rembrandt, please paint *Night Watch.*" Immediately Rembrandt began to mix paint at the easel and apply it to the blank canvas before him.

"He can reproduce any number of masterpieces at various speeds, Sir. The student can study every brushstroke over a period of weeks, or casual viewers can watch 'Rembrandt' create a masterpiece start to finish in an hour."

"That defies credibility. You mean this robot can make exact duplicates?"

"Of course not, Sir. Several experts have already analyzed one and agreed that although they are convincing mimics, a trained eye, assisted by technology if necessary, can easily tell the difference. Oil paintings are one of a kind, Sir, whether they are Rembrandt's or anyone else's. That's the beauty of them; they are as unique as a fingerprint.

"Stop, now, Rembrandt."

The automaton immediately ceased activity, its eyes vacant, its ear sensors poised to trigger activity at the next human command.

King Kong *cover for* KONG: King of Skull Island *(DH Press, 2004)),* 40" x 30" *oil on board.*

Joe DeVito has been an illustrator, sculptor and author for twenty-five years specializing in Science Fiction, Fantasy and Adventure. Recently he created and illustrated *KONG: King of Skull Island* (DH Press, 2004), and co-authored and illustrated Merian C. Cooper's *KING KONG* (St. Martin's Griffin, 2005). For more information: www.jdevito.com or www.kongskullisland.com.

Dragonsblood *Cover for the Todd McCaffrey novel, one in the Pern series for Bantam/Ballantine (UK/USA) 2005. Oil on board 29" x 20.5"*

HILE I'm not going to claim to have been in the vanguard of the digital revolution, neither do I want anyone to think that my reservations about digital art are rooted in fear — or a reactionary outlook. Nor is it the case that, like some, I just hate digital artwork. There is no denying the quality of some of the work produced in the last few years and only a fool would try to ignore it. Nevertheless, from the point of view of someone who has spent his life painting in oils, there seems to be something inherently lacking in the process of working in the digital medium.

In order to forestall the cries of "Luddite" and "technophobe," which will undoubtedly spring to the lips of some readers, I'd like to start with some personal history. I bought my first computer in 1981. I'm sure of the year because that was the name of the machine: the *Sinclair* ZX81. (I think it was called the *Timex* ZX81 in the U.S.) As I recall it had 8k (that's 8 *kilobytes*!) of memory and an unresponsive plastic keyboard — and was useless for anything that we would expect of a computer today. It was possible to do some very basic programming, but it was essentially a toy. Like most toys the novelty quickly wore off, but it was also the first widely available home computer in the UK and it sold in great numbers. There are even now *ZX81* fans "of a certain age" who swap affectionate stories online about this piece of electronic history , but the truth is that, in modern terms, it barely deserved the label "computer" at all. The pattern was to be repeated in subsequent "advanced" models. Every technological advance rendered older machines obsolete, almost all "new" models sold extremely well, and attracted devotees . . . until a newer version came along. As tools for creating artwork these were not devices of the sort that digital artists today find indispensable. Further, and compared to the rate of change we have come to expect in the world of digital media, the personal computer seemed to evolve slowly.

It was some years before I became the proud owner of an honest to goodness, genuine PC. Here at last was a machine that could actually do something! But even if I had wanted to ignore its potential for graphic work, other illustrators would have prevented it. Artists I knew were intrigued and excited by the possibilities; it was a constant topic of conversation and debate. I saw a demonstration of some remarkable software that allowed the user to draw on screen in a way that mimicked traditional media such as oil paint or watercolor. I was impressed enough that one of the first things I did when the new PC arrived was to buy the appropriate software and, of course, a graphics tablet. This clearly seemed to be the future.

I installed the software. It worked. I installed the tablet. It worked, too. I was ready. There was a "learning curve," to be sure. Just like painting in oils, digital art was a matter of time and application. Eventually I produced a couple of commissions digitally. No one batted an eyelid. No one was concerned in the least. While I couldn't claim to have mastered the new medium, at least I was able to create work of a commercial quality, acceptable to clients. Surely the path was onward and upward. The future would be measured in megabytes. It came as a surprise, then, to find myself gazing at the monitor, stylus in hand and feeling profoundly dissatisfied.

This new way of working simply did not give me the same "buzz" as the traditional method. I hankered, no, I lusted after oil paint. If I wasn't positively enjoying doing this work, what was the point? Naturally I stepped firmly into the carefully laid snare. "What I need," I said to myself, "is more software". Not only was this the route to penury, it was not the answer to my dissatisfaction. Because, 2D or 3D, simple or complicated, it was the same. I was not happy and couldn't understand why. After all, what's not to like? Oddly enough, part of the answer came from Mars.

Some years after these first forays into digital art, I was watching a TV interview with a scien-

IS IT A DUCK?
Les Edwards

(detail) **Conan: Red Nails**
*Frontispiece commissioned by
Orion (UK) for their* Chronicles
of Conan *series, 2005. Oils on
hardboard, 28" x 20"*

tist who was discussing a voyage to Mars. He was espousing the virtues of machines over men. A manned voyage, he claimed, was out of the question because we could send robots instead. The machines could gather information and send it to us and they were expendable. A manned mission would be prohibitively expensive and above all, dangerous. Why send real people when we could send our robots to do the dirty work and take the risk? He was speaking around the time that NASA forgot that there was a difference between miles and kilometres and, as a result, lost a Mars bound spacecraft, so he clearly had a point. Still, he annoyed me. I am of a generation that believes that there should be a manned trip to Mars, because, well, there *just should be.* Whether in my lifetime, or the next. He annoyed me, not just because he was right, but that it seemed as though he would always be right. As our technology evolves and the machines become more sophisticated we may never reach a point where sending Men is seen as acceptable. The robots will be able to do more and more, explore further, send back more and more information. There will be no need to send weak and fragile humans. We will never go.

I don't know if you find this idea as depressing as I do: "We let the machines do it for us."

For those who argue that it's important for us to experience the real Mars, if only vicariously, my scientist had the answer. Anyone with a passing acquaintance with science fiction will easily be able to imagine a situation where we have enough information and adequate technology to simulate the Mars experience here on Earth. Indeed, to some extent, this has already been done for research purposes. Imagine it, let's say, not as a Disney ride, but as a complete experience without, I suppose, the freezing temperatures or the explosive decompression. Perhaps like *Star Trek's* Holodeck. Even better, imagine a time when your computer can somehow stimulate your brain and feed the "Mars Experience" directly to you. I've no doubt that there are people working on exactly this idea. Imagine that the sensation is so complete that it's indistinguishable from a real experience. Why would we want to go to Mars then? Why go anywhere? Why have a real experience at all? Visit the top of Everest? Easy. A romantic cruise up the Nile? No problem. Spend the night with your favorite movie star? Just slip in the appropriate disc. After all, as someone said, "If it looks like a duck, if it quacks like a duck, then it's a duck."

Except that it isn't. In this case it's a *virtual* duck.

The TV scientist had given me a clue, if not the entire answer. The work I was producing with the computer was virtual. It has no independent existence of its own. Take away the technology and it doesn't exist. It's illusory. One dictionary defines the word "virtual" as "almost a particular thing or quality". That is to say, *not quite the real thing.* We are gradually being seduced into the idea that the virtual world, the "not quite" world, is as acceptable as the real one. We are at the point of accepting the reality of something that only exists as an electronic file; something that is only accessible with the right equipment and without that equipment *would have no existence at all.* In the same way that we believe that TV is reality, even though we know that it's not, we believe that emailing people is a substitute for personal interaction and belonging to a chat group is like having real friends. We isolate ourselves with our i-pods and Walkmans and would rather send "IM's" (instant messages) than have a genuine conversation. Virtual ducks are the same as real ones. Virtual artwork, therefore, is just the same as a painting you can hang on your wall. Except it isn't, especially if you're the one creating it.

Not only was I unsatisfied with the nature of digital work, there was something else, something fundamentally lacking in the creation of it. There seemed to be less of me in it. Somehow it's less personal. While I had been concentrating on the results I had forgotten that the process is vital, too. Indeed it seems that, for me, the journey is as important as the destination. The making of something is as important as the final object. And — here we come the nub of the matter — when I'm making digital artwork it's not really **me** doing it. The marks are being made by the computer, and the kind of marks are decided by the software. It will make the same marks, given the same input, whomever is handling the stylus. A computer takes something personal and unique and makes it homogenous and indistinct. If I make a 3D object the computer builds and renders it; it follows my instructions, it does all the work. Of course it will only do what I tell it to do, mostly, but in some way, the actual act of creation, the same impulse that put the first handprint on the first cave wall, has been taken away from me. That essential creative moment, the fundamental act of making, has been subverted. I'm letting the machine do it for me.

The act of laying brush on canvas, or pen to board is a physical thing. It is to do with manipulating the real world, and it is in — and of — the real world. I make my mark, not just on the canvas, but on reality. I have, in my tiny way, changed things. Something exists which did not exist. The computer, however, takes my stroke of the stylus and turns it into something other; it processes my artistic vision according to the software. It may make a mark like a brush stroke, but it is an imitation of a brush stroke. Not only is it no longer my brush stroke, but it has no physical existence. It's an illusion; it's ersatz. The whole point of doing it in the first place, to impact on reality, to make something that wasn't there before, has been removed. So, while the digital medium offers me huge choice and scope, it actually takes away my reason for creating anything in the first place. Of course I can print my picture and bring a "virtual" painting to life, but that print is a creation of the computer, the software and the printer. I may be responsible for the existence of the print but I cannot feel it is a work of art that is entirely mine.

Those of us struggling to hang onto linseed oil and hog hair may be left behind in the wake of those forging new digital paths, and some will say that we deserve to be cast adrift if we can't keep up. *They miss the point.* It's not about keeping up; we are on a different journey, and hearing a different drummer. There will be artists reading this whose first choice of medium would be the digital one, and good luck to them. To continue the quote from Thoreau, "Let him step to the music which he hears, however measured or far away." For me, there seems to be something inherently lacking in the process of working in the digital medium, and it's an itch the computer can't scratch.

The Zengakuran, Deeper In
Private commission, oils on board, 2006

Les Edwards is a multi-award winning British artist known for creating pictures with immediate eye-catching impact. Best known for fantasy and horror imagery, he's worked in several genres for major UK and US publishers over a 35-year career. His work is seen on books, magazines, advertising, gaming, record and CD covers and movie posters. He works in oil, using traditional techniques, and disdains the use of an airbrush (or computer) He also paints in acrylics under his pseudonym, Edward Miller. See www.LesEdwards.com

(detail) **Silver Lining** ©1994
*by Don Maitz, World Fantasy
Convention award-winner displayed
at the Delaware Art Museum Fantasy
Art Exhibition. Oil on canvas
40" x 30".*

THEY got it wrong. Somebody screwed up the translation. The meaning got skewed. Our marching orders from "On High" were not "Go forth and multiply." They were meant to be "Go forth and create." This word exchange puts a completely different slant on our prime directive. I believe we were each given a small piece directly from our Creator and that bit is the creative spark. Although our task is not so grand as to attempt to create a universe in seven days, the inherited urge takes many forms. The current population expansion is the result of that single-minded skewed interpretation. We all create, whether we create a stable environment or chaos, a cathedral or a computer virus. The architect, the bricklayer and the demolition engineer are each artists. So too, are paint and pixels creative manifestations. Each are tools of expression crafted by a team of creative people for use by artists. The spark of innovation, the trumpet call that entices us to "do something," is a blessing. If there is evil in this world, it does not reside in the performance or manifestation of "bad" — that is a matter of degree and conscience - it is the act of doing *nothing* that shrivels the soul. Apathy and stagnation are the devil's work. Deciding what to do and doing it are the acts of creativity and these acts are honed by self-awareness.

Being in the midst of a worldwide computer revolution means that the popular place people gather is now a viewing screen. This entire generation has been fed information and entertainment via a television set, motion picture screen, or computer display. Sitting in front of a screen has become comfortable space, almost a natural habitat. For many, a great portion of their lives have been spent interacting with electronic pictures. Artists today have a lifetime of experience with electrically delivered visual stimulation so the manipulation of images on a screen is not really a foreign environment. This may explain the current allure to generate art digitally by today's artists, art publishers, film makers, and art admirers. However, choosing digital art as a means for self- expression, the main tool in one's creative arsenal, depends upon the individual artist's proclivities and goals.

Some artists naturally gravitate to computer imaging, while others are repelled by it. If on reflection, artists understand they assimilate concepts in software programs easily and are fascinated at the speed and choices available, they will be attracted to the process and will become absorbed in the bits and bytes. Other artists, faced with computer manuals, will appreciate the contents as much as Chinese algebra. There is a gut reaction when making any choice of importance, and it is prudent to listen to that intuition, because it is your inner guide that's giving you direction! If developing a craft through traditional painting application is what floats your boat, and grabbing a pencil or a brush gives you comfort, and watching a blank surface respond to your touch gives you a warm mushy feeling, paint and traditional art methods are for you. Doodling, sketching, and the creative urge that involves getting your hands dirty is a unique environment, but it is not for everyone. Through self-awareness, a creative person recognizes that art talent "under development" is best brought along paths of expression by tools that provide satisfaction and comfort in their use. "If it feels good, do it" is a statement all about the creative urge. While those paths may change direction, a sense of security and an ease of expression play a major factor in the success and persistence in developing one's talent. Traditional painting and drawing skills were — and still are — the logical approach in art training because they are the direct path to getting the brain to assimilate shapes and light falling on form. It is the *instruments* involved in applying these concepts that are changing and evolving.

The learning curve is what makes or breaks many creative enthusiasts of traditional painting methods. Not many people are willing to learn methodically over a long period, and invest their time in the repeated process of trial and error. Only, this IS what is necessary, no matter what the

DIG-IT-ALL ART
Don Maitz

tool. Learning to render comfortably and effectively with a pencil or a software program takes time. However, instant gratification is pervasive today and digital art, superficially, can scratch that itch. For that reason, art schools generally have a severe attrition factor. Many enroll, few graduate, fewer still are completely successful in realizing their aspirations. To receive a degree from art college often means having to dilute the art training with liberal arts programs that compete for the student's attention. Computer graphics courses allow finished looking portfolios and the rapid placement of graduates into jobs requiring computer graphic skills, versus the longer struggle to achieve career goals without those skills. The cost of an arts education, the student loans, the additional cost of keeping current with computer technology, and the cost of living, places tremendous pressure on many aspiring artists today. Placement into corporate environments is a big attraction, and for both an artist and an art school it is a fast track to initial job security. This differs from the "old" days when an artist spent years learning his trade by apprenticing in a Master Artist's studio, fetching materials, mixing pigments, transferring drawings, and generally getting his arts education at a successful artist's knee. Art schools since that time have focused primarily on drawing and painting techniques handed down from generation to generation. However, the teaching of these basics have given way to art movements (such as cubism, modernism, abstract expressionism), additional liberal arts programs, and now computer classes, which have diminished the number of students with well-developed traditional academic art skills. Post-graduation, the situation is similar: newly graduated art students desiring a career in commercial art used to be hired by printers to do paste-up work. Along came desktop publishing, a printing process dependent on hardware and software rather than craftsmen. Buying a computer and reading a software manual was all that was required to effect a layout, spec type, and arrange page presentations that integrated images. Art school graduates now need new skills to get even basic work. The slow, deliberate absorption of the artist's craft has been replaced by crash courses and online info geared to getting one to earn money from art quickly. An art school professor with 40 years of experience recommended that what is constantly needed by an artist, at least one who chooses to create realistically, is "interest and patience". These skills are not supplied by a book, a teacher or a software program. It is understandable to become lost in the barrage of choices available in creating art today.

To decide on a course of action best suited to them, artists also need to reflect on the life-style consequences of choosing one method or another for expressing their creativity. The siren's call of seeking traditional independent expression with paint has less expensive start up costs, but establishing a money making venture based upon the lure of paint is an arduous task that requires unique business skills, self assurance, self motivation and persistence. While prodigies are possible, the development of creative talent generally involves a lot of concentrated trial and error experience, and with "paint" that experience is on a visceral level. Screwing something up and actually throwing it away has more effect on creativity than dragging an unwanted file to a computer trashcan icon. Honing individual skills while maintaining a studio of resources, fulfilling client's needs and your own, is challenging and far more difficult for an artist who create more successfully with studio mates, collaboration, and feedback.

Bear in mind, being an artist who is successful creating in his own personal studio is a lofty goal not everyone can achieve. This life does not come ready made with a regular paycheck or a steady workflow. The independent artist can be irregularly hired but can never be really fired; they are the boss, and stand to win or lose based upon personal performance alone. Vacations, weekends, benefits, health care, income taxes, and work ethic a have an entirely different meaning in this environment. There are not many "regular day jobs" outside of art teaching at an institution that provide a steady living for painters. There are exceptions — but for an aspiring pigment artist, the list is short. Too, the hiring of traditional artists is done based upon their reputation, which means, the quality of

(detail) **Forty Thieves** ©1991
by Don Maitz. Oil on masonite,
40" x 84" Poster published by The
Greenwich Workshop, exhibited at
the San Diego Maritime Museum,
Key West Museum of Art & History,
Florida International Museum of
History, and the Mariner's Museum.
Included in the 34 Society of
Illustrators Annual.

art that they produce. Artists need to respond honestly to their own creations when placing their art in the path of potential income. Artists who are ambivalent in what to paint find their output clumsier than those who are passionate about their chosen subjects. While computer generated art has put another octave into the creative song, just as photography did at its introduction in the 1800s, the traditional artist still needs to find their own resonating notes among ever expanding musical forms.

Another factor artists need to be aware of is the business environment in which they will be creating art. To become part of the commercial art community today, artists do not necessarily have to create art with a computer, but the knowledge that their art will have contact with a computer and become rendered into pixels at some point is important, so that some computer literacy is necessary, even if the choice is traditional pigments. Digital photos are now taken of the art or, traditional transparencies from the original work are scanned into digital format. This means nearly all art reproduced today, including the images we commonly see in print, have been translated at some point into pixels, before we get to see them in final form. Images we commonly see in print, at some point, come in contact with a computer before we observe them in final form. Artists who ignore all computer knowledge find themselves in a foreign country not able to speak the language. They are forced to seek someone with skills to translate their art into pixel format to obtain media penetration. If a steady income flow is the prize, and sitting behind a screen with a mouse, trackball, or stylus in your hand is a happy place, then digital art might well be the choice to make. If your personal wonder job involves regular working hours, health benefits, and paid vacations, digital art skills are more likely to achieve these goals, as they are in current demand in company environments.

At the same time, on the other hand, it is easy to have a distorted view of one's creative strengths and weaknesses when computer techniques — at even a rudimentary level — will create an image that can appear quite finished and be completed quickly. In comparison, the initial workings of a fledgling pigment artist make it apparent that the artist has a way to go to achieve his true creative core. Through repetition in imagining creations, and controlled drawing experiences from nature, skill and competence develop — but at a slower pace. Using life drawing or original photographic sources as a point of departure for inspiration make for original works that speak from within the artist. Norman Rockwell used photography in his paintings only after many years of direct painting from live models. This allowed him to translate and interpret photographic sources later in his development which kept his inner vision alive and his art fresh and original. However, with computer graphics, the surface image looks quite finished with the push of a few computer keys. To some, the efforts of a novice pixellator are satisfactory, allowing for a high job placement rate of students directly from art school who have achieved basic proficiency. However, nothing replaces the

Conjure Maitz *©1988 by Don Maitz, featured cover of his artbook,* First Maitz: Selected Paintings by Don Maitz. *Multiple award-winning painting in Oil on masonite, 30" x 30".*

experience of attaining control of the mind's eye directing the artist's hand. Drawing, painting and any artistic manipulation that engages the mind directly through close observation and incessant repetition, develops skills that allow the artist's inspiration to take form. True creativity is achievable on a computer, and incredible digital images are possible, but through the artistic process involving the creative mind. When that mind is not engaged, what appear on the screen are merely key commands. and there are so many shortcuts available in the pixel environment that an artist's inspiration can easily get out of hand without the benefit of basic ingredients like objectivity, observation, and control, gained through lots of practical experience.

Understanding creativity also demands that we pay careful attention to what computers can do and how they do it. Anyone who has some knowledge of the results possible with a few actions on software programs within a computer can now make substantial alterations to art that has been rendered into pixels. This is a force to be carefully considered. Radical changes can not only be made very rapidly to the art by the artist, radical changes can be made to the art equally rapidly by anyone who comes in contact digitally with the art. All employees at a publisher using digital images now have an unlimited opportunity to manipulate and effect changes directly to an artist's efforts using the exact same medium the artist has used, pixels. In fact, many publishers' contracts indicate they are purchasing the right to alter and modify, in any way, the contracted image without the artist's approval. What an artist delivers may not be what is reproduced. Some publishers are intrusive while others are respectful of the artist's intentions. A corporate or company environment can likely be a place where linked computers and shared projects lead to a loss of individual expression. One's artistic effort can become more a process than a creation, where the artist gets lost in the machine. Printers, too, have the same kind of doorway to manipulate art to which they come in contact. This access to the art has allowed creation by committee to flourish.

At the same time, on the other hand, for artists who are consciously less successful creators in isolation, digitization makes possible a cooperative, team approach to creating works of art that traditional studio painting at an easel cannot. Pixilation is a creative boon to the motion picture industry. Special effects and animation of all kinds can be created by studios of artists working in tandem, much more quickly than ever before. Concept drawings can be put into programs that allow the work to be developed into a mapped structure that can be given a range of motion, or possibilities for distortion, supplied extensive surface textures, and put into an environment where the viewpoint can change (camera angle), light sources can be added or removed, shadows cast and the intensity of multiple light sources can be endlessly manipulated. This structure can then be introduced into unlimited developed environments that have been given all the mentioned attributes. Teams of artists can work on computers linked into one massive database working over each other's work to layer complex finished results. But here again, the ease of manipulation of art in pixel form can be problematic. When an image is put in the hands of others, it quickly escapes the original artist's control, putting artists' copyright in jeopardy and raising ethical and contractual problems.

"Know thyself," is central to resolving the dilemma of paint or pixel. What is the goal? What makes you happy? What makes you comfortable? Introspection is required. Are you a loner or a team player? Are you slapdash or a fusspot? Are you comfortable creating in isolation, in public, or as part of a staff? Even the choice of standing versus sitting can radically affect the creative touch. An indication that you are on the right path is when time becomes irrelevant. If you are constantly watching the clock, then you are not engaging your true creative potential. If you do not know how long it took to achieve something, your attention was on what you were doing, not on how soon you could be doing something else. The process of choosing is itself "a work of art," and it is the decisive point in the selection of paint or pixel. It is the artist's spirit that directs the issue and the result which makes the soul enthusiastic.

A-Maitz-ing artwork by **Don Maitz** has appeared for 30 years, receiving two Hugo awards, a Howard Award, a Silver Medal from the Society of Illustrators, and ten Chesley Awards. Maitz created the Captain Morgan Rum character and provided concept art for the films *Jimmy Neutron Boy Genius* and *Ant Bully*. His work has been collected in two compendium art books, *First Maitz: Selected Works by Don Maitz* (1988) and *Dreamquests: The Art of Don Maitz* (1995). See more at www.paravia.com/DonMaitz

The Cat Who Went to Heaven
Cover for the re-issued children's classic for MacMillan, 1990. Oil on board, 30" x 22".

Ahhhhhhhhhhhh..... the irresistible wafting of painterly smells entering one's nostrils the second the studio is entered. Is that why I've chosen paint for 99% of my artistic career? Then how to explain why, in 1998, I found myself picking up a Wacom tablet and diving into digital art? I've stayed alive in this creative, artistic visual career of fifty years by re-inventing myself multi-times over. Could I have done something else for a living? Sure! Did I WANT to do something else to make a living? NOPE! An artist — speaking mainly of myself — is a fairly plain person, but one who simply MUST create. (It's an unexplained passion deep within, and if you don't have this hunger, I think you might as well leave the field.) So, by hook or crook, I'd surge ahead with each new medium, each new tool, each new art director's request, and *make* it work. Because if you're an artist today who wants to survive long enough to paint a picture tomorrow, you must be stoic enough to endure the pain of change, resilient enough to meet the challenges posed by change, and grow to respect the benefits those changes bring, even if you don't love them.

Embracing changes keeps things fresh, and most always gives the creator new perspectives, although you may not start out subscribing to that philosophy. You've heard the expression "paying your dues"? Well, every tiny step of the way was a "paying of the dues" for me. Growing up, age fifteen, I apprenticed in a large ad agency, way before the invention of off-set printing — so each poster was done one at a time, by hand. We were in the middle of creating around 3000 *Twenty Thousand Leagues Under The Sea* posters, and I was fortunate enough to learn speedballing. That enabled me to speedball at least 1000 of the 3000 posters ordered, penning "20,000" over and over and over. Those 0's and 2's were gosh darned hard! You'd never know, by the looks of my current handwriting, that I was becoming brilliant with speedballing, with real quill tipped pens (now we'd call this calligraphy).

Not to mention, there was magic in the variety of smells within this wonderfully messy agency, as a type-set printer's outfit was occupying the front part of the place, on the same second floor of the building, and smelled even better than our own studio. And yeah, I know there's been controversy over the toxicity of mediums used, but I'm still vital, healthy and hearty. I wouldn't trade the memory of those smells for anything. Somehow, these smells were absorbed into my very blood, and are now part of my basic nature, so that *not* to paint would be akin to someone tearing out my heart while I writhe in agony.

What I didn't realize, however, until I was much older, is that along with experiencing the physical and mental goodness that comes along with the act of creating art, along with all those skills I was acquiring (though I never admitted to the client, "I was learning, by doing "), I was also developing much needed *stoicism*. Sure, painting feels good! It smells good. It sounds good. It looks good. It takes energy. It's kinetic. You move your body when you paint. You stand back, you can walk to the sides and back ... you use muscle. You can move your canvas upside down, you can hold it to the mirror or take it outside for better perspectives. Along with all that goodness, however, comes a price: Bent achingly for hours over the sketching table, sitting or standing at the easel, experimenting with expensive and cheap brushes, varied surfaces, exploring mediums, sometimes finding wild success, surprising and exciting, then hearing shrieks of despair as black paint sploshes onto a delicate area, realizing with a shock ... the shrieks are your own. Your back hurts, your eyes glaze, the lighting is getting bad, your hands cramp, the air conditioner quits, the perspiration drips. *You keep going.* The mixing of the paints WILL calm you down — they are so sensual — soft, flexible and satiny to the touch. Not only touching with brush tips, but with fingers or arms, (or whatever), moving the colors around, creating surprising effects, even while still

Pixellated by Necessity
Jael

(detail) **Rapunzel** *Piers Anthony Xanth Calendar page, 1991 Oil on board, 19.5" x 17.5"*

on the palette. Whatever the medium, you and your body are involved in multiple ways, physical and emotional. So now it's getting late, you're tired; the client suddenly calls: you hear those dreaded words, "I have a few changes I want you to make." Change the black hair to blonde. Change the military fatigues to a space suit, and make the gun a saber. Move the main figure an inch to the left. You do these things. You're *flexible*. You're easy to work with. You CAN take direction. You CAN deal with change. You are not a weekend warrior. You are a working professional, and you DO MAKE YOUR DEADLINES. May I say it again! YOU DO MEET YOUR DEADLINES! You are hired again. You are considered reliable and consistent. You have learned how to endure pain — even the exquisite pain of change. It's all in a day's work. Gouache or pen and ink. Acrylic or oil. Digital or paint. It's all in a day's work.

I have now done quite a bit of digital art. Why, you ask? *Because it's my job.* I make my living by creating visual images and because in many ways using a computer to do that is challenging and fun. And last, but not least, because I'm a survivor. The call for digital art put quite a few of my painterly colleagues into panic-mode. I saw the technology coming and knew I couldn't escape it, if I wanted to remain a *working* professional. I've also come to respect the vast resources it offers. It is a brilliant tool, and can enhance the creative and business end of things in multitudes of ways. Many more of my colleagues feel this same way. We, who have traveled the digital road out of necessity, tend to wear the same sort of practical hiking boots when out looking for a job, but know we can quickly change them for that comfortable pair of slippers, as soon as we get home.

A currently well-known artist/illustrator, who had experimented many months with digital art, sighed, "it will be so nice to get back to *holding* my brushes again". In truth, I've lost energy and muscle tone during these last ten years, not being able to move and dance around a real-time canvas. I can't complain, however — I've enjoyed the challenges and I've been very lucky, albeit hard working. Raising four children by myself was not an easy job, but as I had already established a career with a distinct talent for creating life-like images of people, and was rather handy working with most mediums, I found I could meet the challenges of commercial art, too. Now the computer has become a major part of my working life, used for multitudes of purposes, from the literal signing of contracts, to interacting with agents, to the selling of my art. There are real advantages to using technology to spruce up an image, then using the 'net to send that image to a publisher. No more need to send the original painting to a publisher for photography, with the stress of wondering if the painting will reach its destination unharmed, or be returned in one piece. No more need for expensive photography on my end either, instead of shipping the original artwork to the publisher. I can show a sketch or a finished piece to a publisher as many times as necessary. And THAT has become a daily necessity. It is business as it is done today, at the highest current level. I "tiffed" over 200 images to the publisher of my solo art book, *Perceptualistics*, (2002 Chrysalis Books/Paper Tiger).

This is not to say that the process was easy. While it was splendid fun fleshing out much of the work that heretofore had only been recorded on old 2x2 slides, I found myself aching when, after hours and hours of work, I would struggle to get up out of the chair. Not only that, but at the time, I had a Mac 80S (and I do love Macs still), which was not quite up to the job, memory-wise. Eight months of "tiffing" on an old but beloved Mac computer, saving each image on a now fairly obsolete Zip Drive! And now ... it's CDs that have become the digital archives of my creative life. Out go diskettes, in come CD burners! But you adapt, and change and learn.

When I begin a digital piece, I usually sketch everything thoroughly first, color lightly, then scan it in and perhaps flesh out the color a bit for the look-see from publishers, editors, clients, etc. I don't begin in the reverse, as do a few of my colleagues. It doesn't matter, of course, because for the client it's the end result that counts, no matter the path taken. That's the lovely part about being an artist: there are no set rules for results. I've also been immeasurably pleased with most of my digital pieces, and am thoroughly delighted I'm part of the digital age. Just as I have also been impressed, along the way, by its limitations.

About ten years ago, I hired a very talented graphic artist to teach me the rudiments of a few of the programs, such as Photoshop, Quark Express, Illustrator, etc. While he was a genius at the technical side of things, he couldn't draw worth a damn. I asked him one day, to show me what he would do to create water, and the best he could come up with was something that looked like vinyl. And pretty ugly vinyl, at that. I also marvel at some of the youngsters coming up, with their magnificent digital skills, but find it hard to hold my tongue when they laud it over good old-fashioned "drawing/ painting" abilities. They have missed out on so much vital groundwork: the exploration of basic sketching skills, learning first hand of light, color, composition, plus results of all the sensuous mediums and the artist's reaction to varied surfaces.

I can only hope my students are at least learning to keep working, dealing with new technologies as they come and becoming proficient at whatever skills they acquire. There's only one way to get there: I've been telling Illustration students throughout my fifty year career, "never EVER turn down a job … This will be your real life learning process." When asked if you can do it, say "Sure." Then take the "bleeped" project home and figure it the heck out! You learn by doing, by making mistakes, and then fixing those mistakes, perfecting the image inch by inch. You find what works, and rely on instinct, inspiration, guts and perspiration. You do NOT wait around for someone to hold your hand and show you the way. You invent your own way. Creativity is messy, as well it should be. Stephen Sondheim is noted for saying "Art Ain't Easy". Boy, ain't that the truth.

Being a professional requires that you overcome and adapt, and adapt I have. For many years now, I've borrowed a quote, originated by a good friend of mine, who owns a prominent recording studio in Southern California. "The only difference between an amateur and a professional is that a professional doesn't give up." I've never given up. When there's a will, there's a way, and the ways, while never easy, can be found. We artists must roll with the punches. We now understand the layers and paths of Photoshop and the intricacies of Painter. We learn to communicate quickly with editors, art directors — and clients. We appreciate all that can be done to enhance a digital piece. We also know, for a fact, that becoming digital doesn't make art "easier". The ideas don't flow any freer. You have only the two-dimensional surface of the screen to give you an idea of what is being created, no three-dimensional viewpoint. But, a creator is a creator is a creator. No matter what advances are made technically speaking — whether it's painting, photography, or computers, the true artistic nature will persevere, and find a way to express itself no matter what the technical processes. If not, then the so-called creator is just a technician — something I'm not!

The most wonderful feeling in the world to me, creative-wise, is still gessoing either canvas or illustration board (or, preparing other unique surfaces), with a medium value color gesso, sanding if need be, then applying a thin wash of a complimentary color in a no-holds-barred manner, using a large brush. Joyful!! It's back to the physical and messy nature of painting, where I started …. because paint is reality! True bliss! True agony! With paint, we don't have the luxury of undos (or crutch of "History" in Photoshop to wipe away those several layers that don't seem to be working). We use our hands and rags to carefully expunge, and suffer anxiety, hoping we don't go too far — because it's a delicate balance. In the studio, you can move around, view from different angles, move the work to a different room and even go outside for lighting changes. You have much more the 3D effect — it's atmospheric, if you will, and why Rembrandt painted so well. In the studio, with the rags, the mess, the surprising effects not anticipated, the colors running together to create something

new and exciting, the smells, the spontaneity … these to me, are the very essence of art created … not contrived.

So, I suppose I'm still an old-fashioned artist, with the kind of built-in practicality that comes from making a life-long career out of art. I delight in the new twists that computers are handing us AND I also know that to keep working I have to deal with whatever comes my way in terms of technology and tools. It can feel like work or it can feel like fun, but I must be willing to learn, so that I can get past the preliminary stages and get started on a brand new work of art, be it painted or digital.

But did I say I love to paint?

Dream Fantasy *Private commission, 1994 also featured on a Danbury Mint Collector's Plate, 2002. Oil on board, c. 20" x 30"*

Jael is a rarity: a female illustrative artist who has been successfully painting professionally in the SF genre, taking commercial and private commissions, for fifty years. She was featured in *The Encyclopedia Of Science Fiction And Fantasy Art Techniques* (1996), *Spectrum* 3, 4, 8 (1996-2001), *The Paper Tiger Fantasy Art Gallery* (2002), and the *Frank Collection* Vols. 1, 2 (1999, 2003). A compendium book of her life and art *Perceptualistics* was published 2002. See www.jael.net

Alien Emergencies *Cover for the James White Omnibus of three "Sector General" novels for Tor/Orb, 2002. In oil, 26" x 19"*

THIS is the age of the image.

So all pervasive is it, that it is impossible to conceive of our culture without the continuous bombardment of the image on our awareness. This is made possible by the technology of reproduction, whether by film, video, traditional print technology or digitalization. The raging flood of this pictorial inundation has created a self-perpetuating competition for attention. Attention is the function of the image, and communication is its purpose. The amount of attention that is won by the image keeps it alive. It is, therefore, a competition for survival. Illustration is a front line force in this war of the image for survival. So, like any military force, it needs to be equipped to deal effectively with the competition.

It needs weapons. An arsenal of devices for commanding attention.

These devices — comprising the process by which art is produced, and the various aspects of the image (content, character, scale, medium) — lie at the heart of my claim that painting and drawing, in the real, is the medium for creating images. There are no doubt many more "weapons" that can be used in the battle for attention, but for the purpose of this debate, we will assume that the above aspects are critical issues when commissions have been given with only the vaguest of briefs (an ideal situation, I know, but it does happen!), and the artist is a combatant on the battlefield for attention.

The processes involved with generating an image are many, and as varied as artists themselves, but I can describe how I typically hunt down the appropriate image.

After an initial, physically passive phase of absorbing a client's description of what's needed, and allowing my imagination to run free, something will usually emerge as a vaguely imagined image, which is "on probation." This is the decision-making stage and constitutes the most obvious level of the image, its psychological and cultural significance. The is the stage where decisions about content and character take root, often influenced — if not dictated — by the client's requirements. However, the role played by medium in deriving effective imagery is demonstrated by the *next* step — possibly the most crucial one in the whole process.

The physical act of translating a mental image to a tangible, real one, is itself a critical part of the process. I take a piece of "toothy" drawing paper and, using either charcoal, conté or pastel, scrape or block in, in the vaguest way, an approximation of that image in my mind's eye. This is the important bit: I'm hardly looking at the paper, just focusing on the feeling. The gesture of the hand moving across the paper is a way of augmenting the feeling, which generates a clearer image as I work. This can also be done, of course, (and often is), with paint. Through this conversation between myself and my materials, images emerge which are like seeds in the imagination. They suggest things. These seeds grow with the fertilizer of the medium being used, pushed about, scratched, erased, overworked, and all the time, the feelings are responding, making the body react.

Whatever the medium, the limitations and physical properties of the materials being used to generate the marks, have (as it were), their own agenda, and this adds a dimension of unexpectedness to the whole process. This element requires a speed of reaction to these "accidents" that catches the feelings on the wing. The point here, is that the junction between the feeling and the execution should be virtually seamless.

Moreover, I have discovered, over a lifetime of doing this, that those initial marks invariably contain a veracity of expression, a faithfulness to the feeling, that subsequent stages often only dilute — and may well lose altogether. The summoning of the initial feeling at the moment of making the mark, determines the force of the gesture, its direction, etc., all of which contribute in an unfathomable way to the success of communication. This summoning can only be done *once*

THE IMAGE IS THE METHOD
John Harris

with full force. The freshness and power of the feeling that is first felt diminishes with each successive attempt. It is a bullet which can only be fired once. I suppose we are talking here about an act of magic.

This brings us to another sort of magic: the sense of "presence." The process described above is one of hunting down (or teasing out) the image, and is a thoroughly physical, even visceral, activity. When the dimension of texture, created by the substance — the physical properties of the medium — is seen in the flesh, so to speak, a tension is created. And, that tension generates huge electricity between the viewer and the object. This surge of energy is what I call *presence*.

A very good example of this may be seen in a work by Rembrandt.

In a small painting by the great Dutch master called *Man Seated by a Window*, a fair section of the painting's area is taken up by a study of sunlight falling at an angle across a roughly plastered wall. The paint is applied thickly using stand oil, and glazed over, so that the thinner paint on top sinks into the rugged surface underneath. This creates an astonishing result. On the one hand, the viewer is left in no doubt whatsoever that what he is looking at is *paint*. Fat, rich, gooey paint. On the other hand, the sight and feeling of sunlight falling on rough plaster is so complete that the viewer cannot escape the illusion. Even though the full impact of this can only be appreciated by seeing the work in person, a high quality reproduction of a skillfully lit piece will still convey, admittedly in greatly reduced form, some of the magic generated by this balance between reality and illusion.

But this quality of *presence* doesn't depend just on the *frisson* generated by illusion. If that were the case, then only "realist" paintings could produce it, and that is clearly not so. What else then can be instrumental in creating it? In my opinion, it is the process of painting *itself*. That physical activity I described earlier likely influenced the decisions that Rembrandt made when he chose the manner in which to paint the wall, but equally it would influence whatever marks are made in whatever context, whether "realist" or synthetic. It is the physical expression of the feeling generated by the artist and cannot be faked. The body actually has to do it, to express it. This has to do with scale, the size of the object, amongst other things.

The only way that digital art could approximate "scale" would be if an interface could be created where the scale of the monitor could match that of a canvas, but even that would not take into account the physical properties of the textured ground and the paint itself. True, software already does a fair job of simulating some of the effects generated by various media, but we are very physical creatures and respond to the actual materials differently than we do to the simulated versions.

Will there ever come a day when digital systems can duplicate the real thing? Maybe. But the hardware would be difficult to imagine and require a direct interface with the emotional network of the artist. Frankly, it's easier just to paint it. Even if digital art could duplicate "the real thing," it could never actually replace painting as an art form, because the properties of each are so different. More significantly, the method and the result of work painted by the body, belong to the body and speak to the body in own language. *It commands our attention*. And since our attention is the goal of all imagery, it succeeds like nothing else. It may be that digital art will also succeed, if only because it is easier to achieve an image that will "do". Ironically, should digital art thrive as a result of this, and become more prevalent, it will only highlight the difference between "artificial" and true painting — with the result that as Painting becomes rarer, it will command more attention. For the digital artist, it is a law of diminishing returns. The painters will just get stronger.

This is indeed the age of the image.

(detail) **Cleaning the Ducts**
Personal work, 1999-2000. One in the artist's "Rite of the Hidden Sun" series, in oil on canvas, 28" x 42"

John Harris is a fine artist and illustrator, with numerous exhibitions and major clients attesting to his success in both arenas. Grand vision, scale, and atmosphere are the hallmarks of his work, winning him international acclaim (a NASA commission, never before given to a British artist) and continued demand for his depictions of future-fantastic technology. Fine examples of his commercial and personal projects were featured in his art book *MASS: The Art of John Harris* (2000). Learn more at www.alisoneldred.com

(detail) **Wizard of the Owls**
©1991 Janny Wurts. Oil on masonite, Chesley Winner, Best Unpublished work, 1992 later published as cover of Marion Zimmer Bradley's Fantasy Magazine *and as cover for* That Way Lies Camelot, *a short story collection by Janny Wurts published by HarperCollins, 1996.*

maintain that pixilated, electronically generated art loses depth and range of expression when placed beside painted works created through the application of physical materials. The solid expression that results after the artist has completed a traditionally rendered composition has a more meaningful creative impact, and has a more clearly defined archival history, when compared to artistic products of electronic mediums. Moreover, the painting inherently contains an ineffable quality that the screen presentation of electronic works can never match, nor achieve even under extended scrutiny, when subjected to the intimacy of long-term viewing.

With a tangible, material painting, the pigments, the binders, and the ground that supports their application are separate physical objects in their own right. Each one of these elements has unique properties: variations in viscosity, rigidity, reflectivity, and density. Combined, these distinctive qualities add multiple facets of influence and expression to the picture created by the artist in self expression. No two areas of a painted composition will be alike. The mode of application of each composite portion of a painting becomes an individual statement: not only of color, tone, and luminosity, but of dimensional and directional significance. The layers remain evident. The mood translates through the embodiment. No two brush strokes comprising a painted passage will ever be alike. Each will carry a separate phase of creative expression that adds to the end result.

With computer art, by contrast, a pixel is a point of light emitted from a screen. Each pixel holds the same quality of impact and possesses no intrinsic depth, no layering, and no ordered shift of expression, past the initial visual statement granted through choice of luminosity and color. The screen does not differentiate one individual pixel as distinct from another. The atmospheric bent of the pixel's application has a narrower range of expression, and cannot interact with lies beneath it, or on top, but only define itself by what lies adjacent. The effect denies depth, since what the image offered is not multi-textured, or multi-dimensional. The electronic image has no layers, no height or depth, or order of progressive application, but consists of grid dots, each one a frozen point.

In a painting, the pigments were applied with differentiation: one over top of each other, or in stages, as transparent tones, or inter-mixed. This sequential and varied application, added to the textures captured by the medium of suspended pigments and binders, with the significant impression left by brush strokes, gives rise to another frame of mystique. One can fall into the "cracks" between such interactive tension, and never find a definitive resting place for the mind. The eye continues to interact, beyond the initial impact of the image itself. What happens between the physical forms at that juncture where a texture and pigment dance together adds something a pixel cannot: a space in which further interaction can keep on happening. The cascade generates further wonder that transcends the immediate impression and adds to the content of the image itself.

The origin for computer generated images can never be ascertained: although some are drawn onscreen from scratch, alternatively, a base image may be taken intact from another scanned source, or derived through layering several primary images. The composite frames are then distorted, altered or manipulated, and then melded together as a seamless whole. There is no clue left for the viewer at finish as to how the computer artist's inspiration was initiated, or arranged, or set into sequence, by their intuitive perceptions. I believe there is a value in seeing the back trail in the completed work. Though some artists will debate this, in my experience, a digitized image too often becomes a reprocessing of results. If a pixel is a pixel, how will future generations ever determine what was original to the creating artist? How can one ever be certain that nothing's been altered after the primary creator was finished? If a painted work comes to be repaired or worked over by a student or restorer, the change in materials and handling always shows to the discerning eyes of posterity. A pixilated image has no history, this way. The artist, today, with a digital image, is at the mercy of changing fashions, or anyone who cares to rewrite that image, or edit in an alteration. No subsequent viewer

BETWEEN HAND AND EYE
Janny Wurts

will ever know that the change might not have been in accord with the original artist's intent.

The painting done in solid form gains a second existence, when seen as end in itself. As the light falls across a painting in the course of a day, the physical pigment and textures react to the setting. A piece viewed in the clear, early morning shows nuance that dramatically changes at night, under electric lamps, or in the diffuse light filtered in from a clouded sky, or under the intense glare thrown off winter snow. The lighting changes the effect, often profoundly. The mystery can never quite be captured by rote or by mental logic, with the visual shifting of color and light becoming a moving play of experience. A mystique occurs when the painting's image combines with the fixed properties wrought out of the intricacy of its materials and execution. The possible interactions between the work, and its ever changing environment are endless and unpredictable.

The pixel is dead, in this regard. Once displayed on the screen, what you see is what you get. The artwork's image only can become transitional if it is altered again by direct manipulation. Spontaneity is lost, because the environment of the screen does not allow the "weather change" entrancement a painting can have, which provides a tactile life of its own. The layering of glazes, which literally bounces the light through transparent pigment off of the physical surface of the painting ground, cannot yet be replicated on a screen in the current limited mode of display. We view computer art only one pixel at a time, on only one plane, by the concrete terms of today's mode of view screen.

Contrast an oil painting on an easel to a digital image on a monitor and it is clear the electronic creation lacks the substantial impact of a painted work. No pixilated, electronically generated art can achieve the depth and range of expression of a painted work that has been rendered by human hands, with the skilled application of natural media. Nor can its history be documented as can that of a painted work — a history that is critical to preserving an artist's legacy. In sum, compared to paintings, pixels cannot compete in terms of the quality and substance of artistic impact: a result of the dynamic interplay between the work, its environment, and its varied application of media, which augments and enriches the range of experience available to the viewer's interpretation

Curse of the Mistwraith ©1993
Janny Wurts. Oil on masonite cover painting for the novel written by Wurts, published by HarperCollins, Chesley Award winner for Best Hardbound Book 1994

Janny Wurts is an author and artist who has authored seventeen books, a hardbound collection of short fiction, and over thirty contributions to fantasy and science fiction anthologies, with most books bearing her own jacket and interior art. Her paintings have been showcased in museum exhibitions and have won two Chesley Awards, and three Best of Show Awards at the World Fantasy Convention. See www.paravia.com/JannyWurts

I am an artist. I love to draw with a pencil and paint with a brush. The physical act of creating my art is what satisfies my sensibilities: the dance I perform with my brush as it bounces over a fabric texture, the mixing of one medium over another, and the variety of effects this creates — even the eccentricities of that old worn down, pathetic brush is something I don't want to give up. If painting and drawing are vital experiences that are intensely tactile, visual, and emotional, then artists will never be able to produce art through an impersonal, emotionless device like a computer without great struggle.

As the technological age descended and I watched other artists eager to learn this new technique, take up the digital challenge, I felt like an observer. I didn't have the fascination for this tool, nor could I wrap my mind around this new way of thinking. I was lovingly urged or, should I say, *told* by my dear friend Alan Clark, that I would be lost and left behind if I didn't get involved. I reluctantly agreed that I would have to give in to practicality and come up to speed with my peers and the changing environment. So, one day several large boxes marked Dell found their way to my apartment. They remained sealed for three weeks. The cats sat on them. A friend finally set the computer up and left me with the beast. The screen and I stared at each other for several more weeks. Finally, I turned it on. It was daunting, but in time, I began to understand this machine. I found uses for the intruder — word processing, Internet, and email became my friends. Then Photoshop joined the team. I did see the value of creating digital files of my art, producing prints, business cards and promos, etc. Even so, I can't imagine that any computer program could capture the experience I have with drawing and painting because *art is not just about image.*

Recently, I went to the Museum of Modern Art in New York City to see the Edvard Munch exhibit. It was opening day and luckily, my daughter had bought the tickets online beforehand and we breezed past the long lines that snaked around the block and into the museum. It was marvelous to see so many people coming to see this man's art. Standing before Munch's work, I took in the many layers of paint that told this man's story. I knew instantly which parts of the paintings had deeper meaning for him. I saw the careful attention he gave his dying sister, painted so sensitively with heartbroken emotion that touched me deeply. Only secondarily did I take in the background with its looser, more washy effects, which only existed to frame the things Munch most loved. There, for all to see, were his emotions, fears; his life carefully documented, set in frames on the pure white walls of the museum. I love to see a retrospective; it allows me to see the evolution of a man's soul. After we completed touring the many rooms of Edvard Munch's art, we found our way to the permanent exhibit. My friends were all there; Van Gogh, Matisse, Monet, Klimt, Picasso, Leger, Redon, Schile, De Chirco, Dali and one of my very favorites, Magritte. There was an energy in the room I could feel, but find hard to describe. These works of art were lovingly caressed by the hands of people who lived *their* dreams. Whether they saw success within their lifetimes or not, made money or not, were accepted or not, didn't matter. They were true to themselves. They lived life on their terms. They made it happen on their own, their way. These were dedicated souls, creating art for art's sake.

Throughout my life, I've had a fascination with any tool I could use to create images on a surface. To this day, the smell of Crayola crayons transports me back to a time when all I wanted to do was make marks on paper. I still love the waxy quality, the colors, and the effects I can create. As a child I could sit for hours drawing, coloring and cutting. I mastered the use of scissors. I took my time and cut so very carefully. There was the smell of the white paste. It had a wintergreen odor. With the shapes I cut and pasted, I could tell stories, create pleasing designs or just experiment. When I discovered paint, I had to learn to control the brush and a new medium. I remember wetting paper and dropping paint on to it watching the watercolors intermingle and blend together. Later on, I discovered acrylic paints. I found that I had much more control over this medium. I liked

Dark Assortment *Published as promotional art for the Science FictionBook Club, 1981. Acrylic on canvas, 16" x 16"*

IN PURSUIT OF PROCESS AND HISTORY
Jill Bauman

its opaque quality and I found I could easily make corrections or just start over again. Today it is my preferred medium.

I have studied anatomy for many years and am a Life Member of New York's Art Students League. One year, my teacher had the class draw life-size studies of the model. This level of experience cannot be found outside of a class of this type. The Art Students League has been in its 57th Street location since 1892. I worked on an easel encrusted with decades of paint and chalk. Walking around the building where so many great artists studied or taught, I was transported to another time and place. The ceiling-high racks for holding wet paintings, a simple cone-shaped lamp suspended from a rusty chain with one light bulb, the creaking paint-splattered wooden floors, all added to my fascination. The teachers are Masters. The one-on-one instruction, critique and their availability were invaluable to me, as was the uninterrupted four-hour classes. The unspoken emotional connection and sharing among about fifty students at a time kept me motivated, competitive. All of these experiences have become a part of and have broadened my appreciation of the world of art by providing existential and historical context.

The main focus of my fascination with creating physical art is the hands-on aspect. In preparation for painting, I work out ideas in sketches and then stretch the canvas. I put the wooden stretchers together, roll out the canvas, cut it to the correct size and stretch it over the frame. I sand the primed canvas. I transfer my drawing. The bounce of the canvas, its durability and the drag of the brush over the surface feels good. Then the process of mixing the colors begins. I use plastic cups to mix quantities of paint I can save and use throughout the coming work. In this way, I can be consistent throughout the painting and I'm not interrupted constantly during the process to have to re-mix the colors again. Then the painting process begins.

The more emotionally committed I am to the image, the more the act of painting becomes something beyond technique. I am surrounded by my creation. I become a part of that world. Somewhere I lose conscious thought and instinct takes over. One of my paintings, *The Illusionist*, illustrates my point. I had a friend who was a magician. He called himself an "Illusionist." After taking a series of photographs of him, I began the process of creating a portrait. Sitting very close to the canvas, I lost myself in the work, the world I was creating, but had total control over what I was doing. This was due in part to the size of the canvas, which was 20"x 26." I've since told people that I don't remember painting the portrait. It was as if it painted itself. I stopped thinking and analyzing and just let it happen. When I work, paint gets everywhere, on my hands and my clothes, even my cats. I am physically a part of the medium as well as the textured surface of my painting. I like the accidental, spontaneous things that sometimes happen along the way: the slip of the brush, a drip of paint, my hand brushing and smearing the surface. As the brush does its dance, I have control over the pressure, the edges, the point of this tool. Working on a very large canvas, I feel surrounded by the images I am creating. A computer screen doesn't do that for me.

My piece, *Dark Assortment*, is painted on a heart-shaped canvas. When I display this painting at shows, there is always a surprised reaction. First, viewers are drawn to the painting because of the heart shape and red color. Then as they get closer, there seems to be a physical reaction as they realize the candies in the wrappers are chocolate-covered, screaming heads. The three-dimensional heart shape of the painting gives it an extra dimension it would not have if it were a rectangular piece. I also have noticed some strong reactions to my "Nighthings" series. These are very small paintings of creatures: gargoyles, mythological beings, etc. After I create one of these paintings, I set it into an ornate frame. I then use epoxy clay to bring parts of the painting onto the frame. This combines two and three-dimensional elements in the artwork.

I have not embraced the computer as a method of creating my art. I tried. Working with a mouse felt like painting with a bar of soap. I bought a tablet and stylus, but it was just a cold, hard

The Illusionist *Created 1982 and used as a cover illustration for both* Silver Web *magazine #10 Fall/Winter 1993, and* Weird Tales *magazine, Summer 1999. Acrylic on canvas, 26" x 20"*

Candleholder *Unpublished, 2002, in acrylic paint and air dry epoxy clay, 3.5"x 5" in 5"x 7" frame*

tool. It didn't talk to my soul. It only made me appreciate the incredible versatility of the brush. Technology, however, has impacted my illustration career. Publishers have embraced the digital age. Young students from design schools who learned the current computer programs have found a place in publishing offices. More is being done in-house at publishing companies. Publishers are re-evaluating the time and cost of working with illustrators and physical art. Sure enough, digital manipulation of images has endless possibilities. Unfortunately, I see too many people coming into the digital art world believing a computer program provides them with all skills they need to be an artist. If they first spend time understanding the elements of design, anatomy, perspective, color theory, etc., they would have control over their creations based on knowledge. Having a computer program that can turn a line drawing into a painting doesn't teach anything. As far as I've seen the most successful digital artists are skilled artists first and come to the process with knowledge and experience.

In order to be proficient in the arts, the artist must first have an education, then experience. A concert violinist can learn to play a guitar faster, easier and far better than a person who pushes buttons to get synthesized sound. It takes time to absorb knowledge. Getting something done faster and easier does not lend itself to creating great art. I worry that young people are not going to study art for a deep understanding of how light falls on an object. Will they depend on a computer program do it for them? Will they spend the time and make the effort to understand the muscles under the skin and how they work? Will they study perspective, color theory, or the elements of design? Having this knowledge allows an artist to bend the rules and create art that is far more interesting and individual. It is my contention that you have to know the rule in order to break the rule. I fear that without the struggle for this knowledge, innovation and originality in art will become less common.

I don't like the fact that with digital production of art there is no original. With my painting, I am producing singular original pieces of art. From a purely practical point of view, a painting of mine, on canvas, can be sold as a one-of-a-kind, and yet, I am able to make reproductions of it as well. No reproduction can ever have the same impact as the physical painting, however. When I get close to a painting, I want to see canvas texture and brush stokes not little boxes. No matter how wonderful the digital image created, no matter how skilled the digital artist becomes, what he ends up with is only a reproduction of his creation. There is no original piece of art. The end product will be ink on a paper surface or some other representation. Although many artists are painting over their digital prints, I wonder about the endurance of such pieces of art over time.

I will always explore new possibilities for creativity, as I did with digital art when I purchased my first computer. I then make decisions based on preference. I did learn how to use the new tool, although too soon I realized the process and end result of producing an image in that way was not satisfying, just as I would never be satisfied to see a digital version of Van Gogh's *Starry Night* hanging on the walls of the Museum of Modern Art. Would Frazetta's images have the same impact digitally as having been painted by a loving, spontaneous hand? Monet, who painted larger-than-life, showed in his "Water Lilies" series of paintings that no camera was able to capture an image the way the human mind and hand could. In the same way, my exploration into digitally producing an image helped me to appreciate the process of drawing and painting all the more. Why struggle to duplicate that act of creation, when using a pencil or brush speaks to me, textured paper and canvas invites me, the final piece of art delights me? I consider myself truly fortunate to be doing what I love and following my own path. My art is a physical, emotional and spiritual process based on knowledge, instinct, experience, effort, and passion. If digital artists can give me all this through the viewing of their work, I'm sold on it. Otherwise, give me the hand-painted surface that when viewed excites my fascination for process and history.

Jill Bauman has been a freelance illustrator/designer for 27 years. In that time she has produced hundreds of covers in the horror, mystery, fantasy, and science fiction genre for such authors as Stephen King, Harlan Ellison, Peter Straub, Lilian Jackson Braun, David Brin, and Fritz Leiber. She has been nominated for the World Fantasy Award five times and for the Chesley Award several times. Her art has been exhibited at the Delaware Art Museum, Moore College of Art, Science Fiction Museum, NY Art Students League and the NY Illustrators Society. See www.jillbauman.com

DIGITAL (the word) is like saying that someone has passed away: they know what you mean and there is usually no answer for it. The person asked about is dead, *they passed away*. In the same way, you can say "digital," or you can say "computer art" — for those connected to their keyboards, there are as many words for what they're doing as there are for dying, and there are some really nice ones connected with death. I'm thinking more here of the editorial use of painted art for stories and book covers, because it was this area in which I received the bulk of my work. It's a small market and one that can only support a single route to the end product. So it's easy to see a new direction. I'm not nearly as busy now as I once was and I'm certain it's because of the computer art that is fashionable today. Of the published digital art I have seen in the art annuals, much of the work published is from known computer artists. My guess is if you took the hundred illustrations, there would be five that are very good and perhaps five that were not so good, while the mass in the middle continues to be secondary … in other words, same proportions as for painted illustration, where some of the work is outstanding, but most of it is middle of the road, from an artist that pushes the keys to arrive at a workmanlike illustration. Most annuals will list the material used: oil, watercolor, computer. Again, the really good pieces seem beyond any connection to the two hands producing it. Maybe it's time for a decent funeral and for saying the nice words, though some painters may decide not to come.

The understanding of light and parallel lines in digital art is perfect to the point of looking unreal. Can you learn what to do with your own hands, what keys to push, from looking at a computer screen? As a younger artist I always liked works that I could understand. I remember taking home several oil paintings to study: How certain effects were created, what were the most difficult areas. I could see it. At the time I was attempting to paint with Windsor Newton designer colors. It was very uncomplicated. A pencil sketch was put down and then painted in. As I moved from job to job, the process was repeated; I learned about composition and the elements concerning ideas and light and its effect on the look of the piece. I usually had a sketch to work from so I was familiar with the problems, if not their solutions. In any painting there are many choices to be made, right from the beginning. Choices large and small. Perfection was not the goal, good choices were the goal. An artist has to ask the questions, make the choices —now I can't say how limited a computer is, or the person working the buttons, but with a good artist the answers are endless. . . but some are better than others right from the start all within the parameters of the project.

Put another way, is a computer as flexible as a person's brain? Looking back over the thousands of paintings done without the aid of computers, one wonders about the cave paintings — and Rembrandt, Sargent, Degas, Whistler and all the others. If a computer had been used to create them, instead of hands connected to a human brain, would they all look somewhat alike? And perhaps not as remarkable? Would each have a caption saying what media they were done with, for example would a portrait by Frans Hals say "I'm Quickart no. XTO1000," or a picture by Rembrandt say "I'm a combination of instant picture no. 104 and 107"? In looking closer at the Rembrandt one wonders at the bend of the right arm. Can arms bend that way? Other than in computer land? Or was it a short in the modem he was using?

In truth, the next generation will be so adept at the computer that only a fine line will separate them from the best work that is produced today. But of course that's what we're mourning the passing of: that fine line. A few years ago I thought everything in the future would be air brushed. I had sent an illustration for a *Star Trek* movie out to California. The client liked it fine but the art director didn't. The art was of the Golden Gate bridge with the fog rolling in. The art director said there was something about the surface of the picture that bothered him. He said it looked like paint. It wasn't

The Other Side of the Hill
1994 Science Fiction Age *magazine illustration. Casein and acrylics, c. 22" x 16"*

A New Vocabulary
John Berkey

Pinta, Nina and Santa Maria
1978 Honeywell advertisement in casein, 20" x 15"

slick, the way he was used to seeing art. No, it wasn't air brushed, and I told it wouldn't be. When I started working the older artists said, "Don't go into illustration — photography has taken over!" I've been busy for 50 years now … sometimes way too busy. It has always seemed like our work amounted to a race, with a winner at the end. Now it seems as there will be no winner at the end. Or for that matter, no end. I would like to be around fifty years from now and just see where we are. Looking back at just the beginning of the 20th century many great works were produced. Will there be another Howard Pyle or N.C. Wyeth looking for a place to plug in their computer? I doubt it.

Given the number of choices in any painting, it's just too large a task for any computer. Our government had the knowledge and wherewithal to build a giant computer back in the 1920s. It would be built to keep track of every one in the country mostly for tax reasons. It was never built because of the cost, and the Depression. Painting is not a computer problem to be solved, like playing chess. The history of art done with oil and a brush is long, too long to be set aside by a machine that was invented for numbers — beginning with ones and zeros. There will always be something new to work with that will herald a new and better time for all artists with just one or two side effects.. Look closely at a Degas pastel and tell me again about this new manipulation of colors and light with figures so real they seem to breathe. It's all been done before by an artist using sticks of chalk.

This afternoon I had the opportunity to sign five prints reproduced from a painting done several years ago. I don't know the specific digital printer that was used (it is very large like a big TV) and the paper is quite large, about 20" x 30", and comes from Germany . The reproductions were stunning, I have never seen anything like it before. It's called giclées. The prints were flat or matte while the original was varnished. The digital reading of the color and shapes were unlike any reproduction I had ever seen. The man who created the prints said he could not match the digital with film chemistry. Are we talking about reproduction or creating art? And I thought about the art he had copied.

The original art was done with paint and brushes. I make the paint myself, it's about one-half acrylic and one-half casein. It doesn't dry fast like acrylic, but rather more like casein. The pigments I buy in New York City from a company called Guerra Pigments. It's mixed with a hand drill in pint jars and kept in two ounce bottles that I work from. I had watched the moon come up the day before this particular painting was started. As I was driving on a busy highway there was no chance to stop… so the entire scene was imaginary, except for the full moon rise. That's the way the moon comes up, just like the sun, and very quietly, no sound…only mostly/maybe someone honking to get me going or stop looking at the sky. Like so many other things in nature that just proceed with what they are doing, quietly, the moon rises. I enjoy looking at the evening sky — it has so many secrets that I'll never know. There is no sense of the distance, only knowing it's very far away and yet we are certainly a part of it, again, quietly.

So, my response to digital art in part: I'm not as busy as I have been and the work has gone somewhere. I'm sure a lot has gone to computer artists and that's fine. I really don't work any less only it seems there are fewer jobs and more time to think about what I would like to paint. As for the reproduction of what's already painted there is no question of digital over traditional film. I signed a number of prints on canvas that were made from sketches that were done for "Star Wars" twenty-five years ago. They, as the "Moon Rise", were perfect in color and detail. What is possible through this method is amazing, more than that, what is done digitally "looks" new even though it's twenty-five years old. If you add it all together I would say that digital reproduction is truly great — on the other hand, the work that is done from scratch on the computer is OK, but that's all.

It is difficult to measure one form of art against another. The few great pieces of digital art versus several centuries of art done with a brush and paint …one has so far outweighed the other in

The Panama Canal *painted 1960 for Bucyrus-Erie of Milwaukee, the company whose 95-ton rail-mounted steam shovel was instrumental in creating the Panama Canal, one of the largest excavation projects of the 20th century, completed 1914.*

terms of time and number. In the 20th century, as well as this one, so far, digital art would have to take a second place to painted art and the use of photography — considering the number of images to compare. It is just as difficult and perhaps unfair to measure art from one period with another. The centuries of analog art against a few short years of digital manipulation — one would far out-weigh the other in terms of sheer production: whatever country of origin one picks, Holland, Spain, France, the Scandinavian countries ... the comparison would leave "digital" wanting, I'm sure. Just take the changes in our own small field and forget the years past. It has been a street fight; many artists have switched mediums, one sees many more artists painting in oil, if only to get the small edge against "digital" in "blending." Some things that are owned by a computer, soft value changes, are impossible with water paint that dries in the air. In short, digital has swept the field in a way that has left the standard brush artist at a disadvantage, seemingly unable to match the different effects that digital art makes possible. It is a temporary thing and "digital art" will find a place where the special qualities is has are needed. But I don't see it replacing any brush artist — now, or ever.

Perhaps best known for his science fiction art, **John Berkey's** career has been a long and impressive one, spanning a wide range of subject matter and several arenas, including book covers, magazines, calendars, movie posters (*Star Wars, King Kong*, others), advertising, stamps, and personal works. Berkey's works have been collected in *Painted Space* (1991), and *The Art of John Berkey* (2003). His work is seen in museum shows and galleries, and has won many awards, including the Grand Master award from Spectrum. In 2004 Berkey was inducted into The Society of Illustrators Hall of Fame (NY).

(detail) **One of Our Robots is Missing** *Personal work, 2007 planned publication, Baby Tatoo Press Books 2007. Acrylic, 14" x 18"*

O N Monday, I turned on my computer as I always do. It made a strange sound. A screeching noise. The hard drive was crashing. I did an emergency shut down and in effect saved what I had. Fortunately, it was all good news. The "Geek Squad" managed — for $270. — to recover everything and install a new hard drive. Plus, they gave me an option: they suggested I "upgrade" and buy a brand new computer for about 3 times the repair price for this one, saying in effect I had a "dinosaur" with its tower that weighs a ton and its large boxy monitor. I bought it in 2001 and here I am in 2006, having gone through two hard drives. So, as I sat looking at the hole my computer left, and the dark screen, and wishing I had the money to shell out for an entire new system, I said aloud "I hate computers." I hate weighing my options (as if there were any): all the expenses involved, splashing out minimum amounts of money on a steady basis or a real chunk. I hate the psychological costs as well; the mindset of the people who buy it and create it, the fragility of pixels, and the idea that digital art can have an unexpectedly short shelf life. I immediately went up to my studio and put my hand on a physical painting. The lights could go out, and the painting would still be what it is. I immediately felt a strange re-assurance with myself and my talent.

Well, okay, I can say some positives about computers. Having been a fan of movies, I know they can help artists and animators produce wonders onscreen (conversely, I believe, they also jade audiences by doing FX work people tend to expect rather than be surprised by). They also are a great aid in conceptual art for films. Mind you, working for a movie company you can often get the software, and equipment at a whim because it is simply part of their budget and often the equipment is cast off anyway as part of upgrading. It's much easier to keep up-to-date when you don't have to trash your own dinosaurs!

This brings up an important consideration when you're working digitally — the cost. Keeping up, and making sure that everything is kept, turns into a financial black hole. First, there's the cost of "buying into" a specific system, where everything is one expense on top of the other. If you want to work with say, Photoshop, you have to get upgrades constantly so that, in effect you can read your own existing disks — just to see the very pictures you created. Also, you can only use those specific upgrades, sometimes at great cost, and only for a certain length of time; you have to make sure the software is up to date at all times, otherwise, upgrades are not possible, you have to start all over with a new version, and upgrade your operating system at the same time, otherwise your stored info is simply…. unreadable. Of course you'll want to print out your images as high resolution ink jet prints — and to make them half-way looking good, like the art you think you've created, you can spend thousands of dollars getting just the right printer. Or even more expensive, you can get a *Giclée* made, which is a continuous tone print on archival paper. That often can set one back anywhere from $30-$200, depending upon how many *giclées* are produced and what place does them. It becomes a vicious cycle of buying, upgrading and making sure your stored information is retrievable. One more deadline and thing you have to think about.

Also, there are medical issues. The chief among these are repetitive motion injuries to the wrist and elbow. Carpel Tunnel Syndrome is a specific injury to the wrists, caused by the use of a mouse or wands and tablets in a confined and repeating pattern that does serious damage to the nerves running through the wrist. You can also get "tennis elbow," which is a sometimes excruciatingly painful result of holding one's arm either too taut or, too crooked for long periods of time while at a computer with either a mouse or a tablet and wand. I have had this myself, not to mention the bad posture acquired from sitting for hours on end at a computer. With physical painting and drawing, I can step back from the work, or usually work standing whereby my repetitiveness — and bad

BE CAREFUL WHAT YOU WISH FOR
Bob Eggleton

(detail) **Crystal Dragon** *Interior for the book Dragonhenge by John Grant and Bob Eggleton, Paper Tiger Books, 2002. Acrylic, 36" x 24"*

posture and other risks are minimalized. The unproductive "down time" recuperating from computer-related aches and pains can cost an artist money and jobs.

Then there are your eyes. The computer screen emits a glare that one tends to forget about when working too long at it. The result is eyestrain, and need for eye exams, and new eyeglass prescriptions at sometimes a yearly rate. Granted, physically drawing and painting can tax one's eyes, but again, everything in moderation. It's easier to step back from the easel or drawing table. Less easy to step back from the often hypnotic glare of a monitor.

Another cost that digital artists rarely factor into the equation is the corporate mindset of "digital." In the darkest towers of corporate America, sleazy bean counters weigh the financial pros and cons of "Vendors" and "Suppliers" (nice corporate names for artists) who work digitally, and this is transmitted down the ladder to art departments. Under "millennium copyright laws" art departments have great latitude today. They can change the art in-house and make it fit their requirements with no consultation with the artist. By changing it, they — in effect — make it their copyrighted piece of art. Artists submitting digital files are required to leave the layers of the piece's file "unlocked" so that marketing people can get in and alter things or apply special effects. Another issue is the fact that while there are some INCREDIBLY TALENTED people working with a computer to make pictures, there are even more UNTALENTED people who think they are great artists because of a computer. This factor alone has degraded the general look of book cover illustration in the last five years. Corporate art departments have decided that it is far cheaper to produce badly done work by an amateur than pay for quality work by a more expensive professional. They say "Pay peanuts and you get monkeys" and it's true.

There is also the issue of doing an original work and THEN applying digital techniques — which more than a handful of artists do. This means we know have a painting that will never be the same as — or be quite as complete as — its published form!!! There is good and bad to that: Good in that the artist can more easily alter a painting to match a client's requests and art direction but still have a painting that they are initially pleased with; bad in that the image that's reproduced on the book or product may have little relation to what exists on the artist's easel . . . and there goes the whole appeal of buying or selling the original art just because it was used as an illustration!

Finally, there is also a psychological cost to artists that relates to the mentality of some of the people who produce digital art. In the last few years it has brought out of the closet some of the smarmiest, short-attention-spanned Gen Now'ers I personally have ever met. These people have no lives, no respect for their elders, they live in their parent's basements and are basically toadies who think that installing a program and rearranging photographs and even stealing the work of others constitutes "creativity" or good drawing. What it instills in them is an "I want it now, and can get it now" kind of thinking and they treat everyone around them the same way. Computer results, compared to the time it takes to prepare a canvas, mix paints and apply them, are practically instantaneous, so it's easy to see where the thinking comes from. On the cover of one recent computer-art magazine, there was a headline blurb promising "Improve Your Drawing Skills — Overnight!!" That quick-sell sums up the whole attitude, skipping the inescapable fact that *good draughsmanship takes years to attain*. However, fast doesn't mean "good." Sadly, many people can't tell good from bad, especially in art. It's why the art market is such a strange animal, with people often needing to be told what is "good" and what is "bad." You get entire collections of artwork where someone has gone and bought every piece on the advice of someone else — they know nothing about what they truly own. Considering this general dumbness, it's easy to see why bad digital art has taken over. People don't know when they're creating it, and people don't know when they're buying it.

In the end, barring the appearance of some huge electro-magnetic pulse, pixels will dominate and most artists doing traditional art will either give up or be forced to change over to this homogenized medium, at least for commercial purposes. Then again, there could be some hope — on more than a few occasions lately, I have been complimented with some earnestness, "Thank God you are still working traditionally! I'm so sick of digital art!" We can hope that attitude, spread by the desire for something more unique, will at least balance things out — I don't think the term "win out" is appropriate, as digital will wind up being simply another medium. In the meantime, artists have to deal with both the obvious and the more subtle (but no less expensive) costs of going digital. At first, it will be "Oh, if only I had a new computer . . .!" The costs of granting these wishes are easy to spot; they are the expenses involved with computer crashes, the expensive upgrades, and the costs of replacing entire systems every five years because they're obsolete. The harder ones to figure out, unless you take a good look at the whole digital art scene, are the costs to mind, body and soul.

Ivory *Cover for the book by Mike Resnick, Pyr Books, 2007. Acrylic, 14" x 20*

Bob Eggleton is a successful science fiction, fantasy, horror, and landscape artist, encompassing twenty years of putting brush to canvas or board. Winner of 9 Hugo Awards, 12 Chesley Awards, and various magazine awards, his art can be seen on the covers of magazines, books, posters and prints, trading cards, stationery, journals, and jigsaw puzzles and also in the six books of his collected works to date. He also works as a conceptual illustrator for movies and thrill rides. See www.bobeggleton.com/

(detail) **The War of the Worlds**
Cover for the illustrated re-issued classic published by Books of Wonder, 2001. In oil, 21" x 27"

M**Y** brain is split into two clearly delineated parts. This may be due to an accident of birth or from later brain damage I suffered as a child from St. Louis Encephalitis. Each section of my brain works independently. I've noticed that most other humans don't seem to have this clear delineation. The two unmixable sides are: my logical scientific side and my emotional side. Each part has something significant to add to the debate, so in the interest of fair play I'm going to allow each to have his say.

First we will hear from Thomas, my rational side:

To answer which of these mediums is best you have to do an experiment. Scientific method dictates this. For this experiment I will do two paintings. One will be with oil paint and the other will be done digitally. I will attempt to make each picture with an equal amount of complexity.

In my studio I have a collection of mediums, paints, gesso and thinners. Before me is a blank canvas. First I will weigh the canvas. My starting weight is exactly 771.1 grams. Once I finish my painting I'll weigh the painting again to determine the weight of the art I put upon it. (Just gessoing my canvas adds 27.5g — after I've allowed it to dry for a day. I'll subtract that later as it is not necessarily part of the image part of the painting.)

To test my digital painting I will first weigh a one-gigabyte flash card. It weighs 47.2g. When I complete my digital painting I'll transfer it to the card and weigh the card again. I'll subtract my beginning weight from each painting to determine the increase.

The completed oil painting weighs in at 853.3g. Subtracting the gesso brings us to 825.8g. When we subtract the canvas it makes the total increase in weight 54.7g. This is not a significant increase. Oil paint may not be the superior medium.

I wanted to make my digital art a good size, so it is a CMYK 64.5 MB 16 bit Tiff file. As with the oil painting I've removed anything that might add weight that is not really part of the image. This is the size of the file after I've flattened all the layers. I've used Photoshop for this experiment but you can repeat it with a different program. The flash card with the digital file on it weighs 47.2g. This is exactly the same weight as before.

My conclusion is that digital art is insubstantial. It has no weight. In this respect it is inferior to an oil painting. Score one for oil paintings.

Does this mean anything? Lets look at another experiment:

Dr. Duncan MacDougall of Haverhill, Massachusetts, wanted to determine the weight of the human soul, so he carefully monitored his dying patients. He weighed them before and after death. The average weight loss he determined to be 21 grams. The shocking thing here to me is that some souls seem to weigh more than others. Unfortunately for him, no one has been able to repeat this experiment with the same results. It would seem as though life or the soul weighs nothing. Score a point for digital art.

Furthermore, all of our organs replace themselves at different rates over time. (I think that the liver is the fastest.) As you age you begin to be made up of different cells, molecules and atoms than you started out with. Does this make you a different person, a reproduction? Strangely, the one thing that is not replaced is the lens of the eye. This is the reason we need reading glasses as we age. The condition is called presbyopia, which means "old vision." It would seem that humans, even if you don't believe in a soul, are merely made up of information. The physical you just holds it all together. Score another point (up to two points now) for digital art.

Or does that score a point? Both digital art and life are very fragile. A simple virus can kill either one. Depending on the type of art you make, a painting done with a physical medium can with-

PAINTING WITH REAL PAINT VS. PAINTING WITH PIXELS
Tommy and Thomas Kidd

stand a fair amount of punishment. With reasonable care oil paintings can easily last far longer than their creators. An oil painting can last for many, many centuries. Digital art on a CD will not last that long and we all know how easily a hard drive can die. The only hope digital art has for a long life is in reproduction. For that matter all digital art is reproduction. Each morning you turn your computer on you've got a copy of the image from the day before. Reproduction is the only hope for living creatures as well. Although digital art can be easily copied, unlike living creatures it can't have sex and therefore cannot easily evolve. A good technique for cloning humans may not be far into our future, but a technique for cloning oil paintings seems a very long way off.

Now it's Tommy's turn; let's find out what my emotional side has to say:

Oh, do I love pictures!!! They make me feel all sorts of ways: scared, adventurous, sad, happy, awed, horrified, thoughtful, hopeful, excited about the future, or worried about no future, gleeful, in love, in hate, anxious and eager. There's such beauty to the world and the painter of still pictures is its visual poet. What does it matter what he uses as a medium? A stick and an inkwell will work wonders with the right hand! Simple black lines (pen & ink), arranged in just the right way, on a white page have the ability to move me. I feel this but I don't understand how such a thing could be possible. Don't you feel the same way? Certain other black lines will have no affect. Isn't that also true, for you? Clearly all mediums are equal and it's just the creator that makes the difference.

But wait . . .

No, *that's not so*. My feelings now tell me differently. I can remember seeing art on my computer screen or on the printed page and then later seeing it in a museum or gallery. The reproduced versions are certainly effective, but standing before the real thing is a truly profound experience. It's another level of feeling. The different emotions generated by the reproduction and the original is like seeing a picture of a loved one you haven't seen in a long while, experiencing found memories, and the great magnitude of difference when you are there with that person after a long absence. This is a vast emotional difference that squarely illustrates the superiority of painting with physical paint. *I feel this very strongly*. Oh, would I hate to live in a time when galleries only had reproductions!!! Artists: you *must* use your phalanges (i.e. digits, i.e. fingers) to make the type of paintings we can hang in our future museums!!! Please. As Tom's sensitive side I implore you to do this. *Please don't make me cry.*

Navigation Gondola *Personal work, created for planned book project "Gnemo" 1993. In oil, 18" x 28"*

Tom Kidd is an accomplished fantasy artist who has painted dozens of book covers, and fully illustrated two: *The Three Musketeers* (1998) and *The War of the Worlds* (2001). He was concept designer for two films and wrote and illustrated his own art book *Kiddography: The Art and Life of Tom Kidd* (2006). His awards include a World Fantasy Award (2004) and seven Chesley Awards. Learn more at www.spellcaster.com/tomkidd.

(Detail) **Construct of Time**
Cover for the novel Shadows Falls
by Simon Green, 1993. Oil on
paper on masonite, 27" x 18"

TONE and bone. Silver and gold. Oil and acrylics. Artists have manipulated nearly every form of material to produce their creations. As new mediums manifest, these too are enthusiastically embraced to redirect and push the limits of artists' craft. Digital technology is yet another chapter in the "book of techniques" for the artist. Science fiction and fantasy illustrators now have the greatest choices in mediums ever available: from all forms traditional to digital two- and three-dimensional rendering programs. Historically, the adoption of new methods has resulted in the shedding of some traditional forms, and the recent transition to digital art has meant the loss of one of the most treasured ones: hand-crafted, tangible, original art. For many digital illustrators their work remains as intangible files for websites, videogame production, or animation concepting. When an illustrator relies upon printed media to provide a final rendering, the "output" tends to be mass-produced marketing materials that have little long-term value for either the creators or collectors. For all the power and amazing beauty digitally manipulated images can offer us, it appears digital illustrators will leave little tangible, historical evidence of their artistic legacy.

Looking back over the past century, there has been an astonishing increase in mass produced art and products, much of it considered disposable and worthless. There are print and edition runs in the thousands, best selling novels and games into hundreds of thousands of copies, and collectable card publishers produce millions of their "rarest" items. While these images reach an extraordinarily large audience, few consumers cherish the products over an extended period of time: the end result for much of the media used to advertise and deliver this content is the same. Magazines are trashed. Books are printed on acidic paper, fall apart and fade. Digital software programs and files become obsolete in a few years and are deleted or overwritten. The new fast-placed commercial marketplace rewards the artistic myopia that pleasure in art springs solely from the cathartic process of visualizing their inner visions and encourages them to place little importance on issues regarding materials and their permanence. Digital illustrators obtaining some final realization of their art — the "hard copy" — show an awareness of this potential impermanence, and attempt to remediate diminished longevity by producing limited or unique mechanical outputs utilizing archival papers and pigment printers. Yet given what we know of the surviving art of history, trends in collecting, and our attitudes towards mechanically produced printed matter, these steps may not be sufficient to preserve their art.

Permanence in art is a result of many factors, chief among them the "why" and "what" of their creation. The oldest works of art are with us for one main reason: they could not easily be destroyed. The "what" of material creation is the most important variable influencing the permanence of artistic creations. Whether they are judged to be aesthetically good or bad, we embrace them for their sheer power of persistence. Contemporary and modern art do not have the same requirements for their preservation — technologies now allow us to preserve nearly any form of material, from cryogenic freezing of human bodies, to the de-acidification of precious manuscripts. Rather, the survival of contemporary art is limited by other factors, most importantly "why" it should be selected for safe-keeping from among the mass of material objects around us. We can blame the Da-Daists for opening the can of worms that makes everything a work of art. It is now increasingly difficult to decide "what" to collect and preserve. The more rare and unique an object, the greater its perceived value. Books, maps, and cars are enthusiastically collected, yet none are so valued in our auction houses and museums as those unique artistic creations springing from human hands, modifying a tangible piece of material: musical scores from Mozart, a painting by Rembrandt, or sculpture from unknown Greek artists.

SLIPPING TOWARDS OBLIVION
Donato Giancola

Original drawings, sculptures and paintings hanging upon a museum's or collector's wall have historically been more highly valued than the products derived from them, such as books, films, prints. Through the interaction with physical "stuff" an artist proclaims their existence and conveys the importance of their imaginative interpretations of the world, and in turn, viewers grasp the importance of that process, and revere it. The presence of tangible, manipulated material places the viewer that much closer to the moment of creation, ever closer to the mind and thoughts that inspired its creation. This is why it is so compelling to view an artist's sketch book and peruse it page by page — it's as if we have been invited to walk with an artist as they work out issues in a focused, timely way. Mechanically reproduced objects such as photographs or digital *giclée* prints, whether unique or not, present a psychological barrier to this kind of experience. The four remaining Guttenberg Bibles pale in value compared to Caravaggio's dozens of oil paintings. Rembrandt's etchings, even though hand pulled and very rare, are one to two decimal places removed from the prices of his painted works. There is some intangible aspect of direct human intervention which elevates objects so worked to values far above those related to their rarity. Given this state of affairs, I fear that many of my friends' digital works, no matter how outstanding, will be ignored by a society that prefers to treasure works produced by the human hand.

The greatest challenge to preserving the legacy of digital artists today is the lack of a product, method or material which encodes their work as a unique creation in a permanent way. Traditional reproduction methods either through commercial offset or fine art *giclée* printing, do not offer the kind of longevity needed for long-term preservation of computer generated art. During this transitional phase, it's hard to predict where preservation solutions will take us. The danger in physical objects is that they can be unique: if we destroy or lose the last original copy there is no replacement, and nearly all of its inherent value is lost. In contrast, digital art can be saved in its "original" state on any number of worldwide storage media, thereby insuring in some way, some where, its preservation: we must re-define our beliefs in the "inherent value" of originals.

Current methods for saving and maintaining digital works present another challenge to preserving these works for posterity. The danger with digital art may lie in its lack of uniqueness, in a traditional sense. Much in the same way language evolves slowly over time, there is the possibility that digital information can evolve as well. The equipment for displaying the art, and the software applications for storing it will change, leading to the eventual generational degradation in the information, leading ever further from the original artistic intent. It is not too hard to imagine, even within one generation, the re-manipulation of a digital work being represented as the true original from the artist. Once there is no unique "hard copy" to refer back to it is easy to fabricate this "truth". An objective collector has no easy way to verify that the work is indeed the true art of the artist: the individual artistic legacy loses great value if this verification process breaks down. The Orwellian predictions of information manipulation in *1984* is not far removed from what is possible for digital art, if the identity and intent of the individual is suppressed to satisfy the needs of society. What is distressing is that issues relating to communal authorship/ownership are not merely the stuff of science fiction. In the United States there is now legislation being considered to modify U.S. Copyright law, stripping ownership/authorship protections from photographers, illustrators and artists, in the form of the "Orphan Works Amendment". Supporters are using language similar to that found in "1984" to justify the amendment, and speak of the good of society and communally shared artistic aesthetics. While some of these arguments may have substance, any erosion of copyright and authorship protection poses a threat to artists concerned with documenting their unique contributions to the history of art.

Long after issues of *The Saturday Evening Post* have been pulped and placed in the landfills, the paintings of Leyendecker and Rockwell will hang in museums. Long after science fiction novels and magazines from the fifties have fallen apart, will the visions of those mid-century futurists entertain generations to come through their preserved, hand crafted paintings? Long after film and digital games have faded as passé, will hand drawn concept illustrations and models be treasured as artifacts to a lost craft of live action movie/game production? There will always be a fair amount of mass media collected and preserved through time, but in the consideration of what to preserve over 50, 100 to 200 years, it seems that the preferred choice is to select works created and manipulated by human hands. At a recent showing of 1950's pulp illustration art at the Brooklyn Museum in 2003, displayed on the walls were not the thousands of copies of magazines and periodicals which could be easily found to represent publishing from this era, but rather there was a collection of a hundred illustrated paintings. Exhibited alongside these originals were the printed pages of their commercial appearance, not as an artistic equal, but rather subordinate to the painted art. Over time it is easy to see these subordinate attachments "disappearing." I fear the same fate will befall the illustrative digital art being created today, in the process robbing the creators of their artistic legacy.

Mystic Rider *Cover commission for* Thirteenth House — *Vol. 2 of the series by Sharon Shinn for Ace Books, 2005. Oil on paper on panel, 30" x 22"*

Since beginning his professional freelance career in 1993 **Donato Giancola's** list of clients has grown from major book publishers in New York to concept design firms on the West Coast, notably: The United Nations, Wizards of the Coast, LucasArts, DC Comics, Microsoft, *Playboy* magazine, Tor Books, Random House, Milton-Bradley, and Hasbro. He has won the Jack Gaughan Award for Best Emerging Artist, ten Chesley Awards, the Artist Hugo Award, and multiple silver and gold medals from *Spectrum: The Best of Contemporary Fantastic Art.* See www.donatoart.com

2

I'm not lost.
I'm exploring.
Jana Stanfield

We Do It With Pixels

SOME 12 years ago I made the choice to leave a long career in illustration, working in traditional media (paint, pencil and pen) and enter the computer games industry (generally dominated artistically by "Pushing Pixels"). In light of that it may seem surprising that in terms of my preferred medium, as well as esteem for the work produced, I come down on the side of Paint. This is of course my personal opinion and is the correct answer to the question "Paint or Pixel?" only in regard to the work that I want to produce. Because, even though 99% of the artwork I have done within the computer industry over the past decade has been drawing or painting rather than digital imagery, that experience has shown me that my preferences are irrelevant. It is not my contention that Pixels are inferior to Paint with regard to accomplishing the goal of creating a successful illustration, but rather that they are merely "different" and just like apples and oranges they should not be considered as competing. They should rather be considered as each one being the correct approach to different requirements of illustration. Each one is correct when fulfilling those things that they do best.

First, the question, "Which is better, Paint or Pixel?" misses the salient point that in an industry such as illustration, where the service of the commercial needs of the client are the *raison d'être*, it really doesn't matter which medium is used. Certainly the client doesn't care. Only the effect of the image on the end consumer determines which approach was best. Each is best at completely different things. As soon as those separate spheres can be clearly agreed upon, the competition can cease and creativity can flow unrestrained and in new directions opened up to the artists by self knowledge.

Second, the greatest oil painting in the world will never be (by the very definitions of the terms) the greatest digital image, nor will the greatest digital image ever be a terrific painting. That there are separate approaches by which each can fulfill the needs of the client is a situation that should surprise no one since such a controversy between art forms has occurred before with similar levels of acrimony to those in this present argument. The final resolution of that debate was the eventual disengagement of the two camps and the recognition that there were two separate art forms competing for the same commissions and that there were areas in which one excelled the other.

A review of one previous controversy — analogous to the debate here — and the historical outcome, helps illuminate a possible resolution of the current argument. The last time such a philosophical (as well as practical) battle was fought was a century and a half ago. At that time, the opposing sides were the advocates of traditional art using traditional mediums, and the advocates of a new "art form" of the day: photography. In that schism, just as it is in this current one, it should be noted that the "Pretender" incorporated a mechanical agency, which not merely facilitated the work of the artist/creator but also insinuated its own aesthetic choices, independent of the human mind. Learning to accommodate these external arbitrary decisions led inexorably to the stylistic differentiation of the two camps as well as inspiring the disdain that traditional artists had for the work of photography as long as it claimed to be equivalent to painting. It is always the upstart's burden to bear this scorn until he can demonstrate that he deserves inclusion or that he legitimately occupies a new arena of his own.

As has happened recently with computer-assisted graphics, some of the 19th century artists were quick to embrace the new tool, the camera, as an aid to their work. These academically trained artists could see the useful aspects of photography as well as perceive its shortcomings. They knew where and when to use the medium, and where and when not to use it. Their skillful eyes could see the inherent defects in a photographically captured image and could then compensate for and cor-

(detail) "The Pacifist" Cover for **Space Vectors** *by Robert Vardeman 1990 Ace Books Acrylic on illustration board 30" x 20"*

Debate Dèja Vu
Richard Hescox

rect them in the drawing or painting that was for them the end product of their efforts. For them, the inherent aesthetic failings of a snapshot was proof of the inferiority of the new medium; it was fit only to be a helpful tool. Artists of the stature of a Jean Leon Gerome or Alphonse Mucha, whose superb draughtsmanship was sufficient to record expertly details and ideas for use in their finished works, still turned to the camera and recognized its efficiency in recording greater volumes of factual reference material.

At the same time, technically proficient painters of the mid-19th century also recognized the deficits of this new technology: the distortions, arbitrariness and "dumbing down" of the photographically captured images. In those cases where existing photographs from these artists can be compared to the finished works they helped to create, the subtle and not so subtle changes that the artists made can be appreciated. Slavishly copying from the photo or relying on the photograph itself as the finished image would clearly have provided an inferior aesthetic result when the intended effect of the image is taken into consideration.

The inherent "mechanical" input of the photographic process (perspective distortion caused by a non-binocular viewpoint, a gross simplification of value range and, in the early days, a complete lack of color data) was viewed by the traditional artist as a pitfall to be avoided. Scorn for these defects fueled the distrust and animosity towards those who championed the photograph as a co-equal form of art.

The photographers, for their part, could claim that the objective documentary nature of their process lent a "truthfulness" to the images that had a value surpassing the subjective "viewpoint" of the painters. Additionally, the skillful manipulation of the photographic process could achieve results of haunting moodiness often enhanced in the viewer by the very knowledge that at its core the photograph reflected something that really existed rather than the wild imaginings of some painter.

The controversy raged as long as some, especially those lacking skill in the traditional art mediums, tried to promote photography as a finished art form superior to — and worthy of completely replacing — painting and drawing. It died down as the sides found their rightful fields of expertise and disengaged into relatively non-competing camps. Those photographers who lacked strong aesthetic temperaments evolved into the photo-journalists recording scenes of reality and current history with a brutal objectivity, a field in which their approach was clearly superior to the painters who had previously served that need. At the same time, the imaginative and creative ones applied their talents to the camera, playing with its very limitations and nature, to become the great "artistic" photographers of the late 19th and early 20th centuries. The early masters of the medium range from the wonderfully evocative works of symbolists such as Anne Brigman and George Seeley to the penetrating portraits of Alfred Steiglitz and the poetic landscapes of Ansel Adams.

While these separate camps were developing there was a natural competition for the available commissions and patronage, which developed into a war of words (echoed today) over *which was better*. In hindsight, it is clear that neither was better *per se* but rather each offered advantages that led to the eventual division of the work into areas, each of which was better served by one medium or another. The newspaper illustrations, which had been engravings of artist sketches, became photogravures. Similarly, the more speculatively creative imagery such as myth, fantasy and eventually science fiction, lent itself to the more plastic medium of painting, as it was bound solely by the imagination of the artist. (One unfortunate side effect of this split was to open the door to the silly excesses of "modern art" as artists tried to define more territory that was theirs alone.)

Today, a similar struggle for territory is being waged between proponents of paint and pixel, and if the past is any indication of what is in store for the illustration field, there will eventually

The Dreaming Sea *Personal work,*
1994 Oil on canvas 24" x 28"
Reproduced as limited edition print
Oil on canvas

develop two (or more?) separate spheres of influence. One change that is already apparent is that digital techniques are well on the way to usurping the whole realm of the traditional airbrush artist. Additionally, those areas that tend to require lots of imagery with tight deadlines, such as production art for films or computer games, may well be heading in a totally digital direction.

However, the differing spheres will borrow the other realm's tools as needed. Just as traditional artists in the 19th century continued to use the camera as a tool (but only that), some of today's traditional painters have learned to use the digital tools as a useful adjunct to their creative methods. Scanning sketches and coloring them on the computer allows increased efficiency in experimenting with variations. Changes to compositions are easy to test. (The constant refrain is that the multiple-undo button in Photoshop is the greatest invention since sliced bread.) Still, after these experiments, the "Painters" will print out the results of their experiments as reference and resort to the easel to create their finished work whereas the digital artist will continue to "finish" on the computer. It is this procedural split that spotlights one of the major differences between the competing realms of "Paint or Pixel". That is: that the one quality belonging solely to the Paint side is the creation of a physical, unique hand-made original that retains the ownership value of a work of art, able to be sold and collected. This market exists beyond the bounds of the "illustration for publication" market which is the real contested ground of this debate.

The pixel pushers have embraced the expediency and efficiency afforded by their new technique, but at the cost of giving up the creation of a saleable one-of-a-kind work of art. The photographers invested in the earlier battle share in this disappointing characteristic of their chosen medium. They have tried to overcome this by "hand" producing their multiple prints and by severely limiting the numbers of prints produced. However, this very aspect of creating multiple prints points to the truth that as valuable as a great photo by a great photographer may be, the prices the individual prints command will never equal the prices that an equivalently respected painting will … or indeed that any unique work of art, of comparable quality, would command. This monetary value difference reflects the inescapable fact that of the aesthetic qualities poured into a finished photograph (or digital image), only a portion come from the creative input of the artist/photographer while the rest are produced by the mechanical processes of the camera (or program). Whether mildly influential, as in the tool bias of the Photoshop controls, or significantly impactful, as in the brute computing power of a high end 3D rendering program, these inputs to the finished image mean that the total creative content of such a piece is a collaborative effort, *and only one collaborator is human.* The intangible "magic" that surrounds original art, touched in every detail by the hand and mind of the artist, is just not there to the same extent in a copy of a photo, a print or a digital image.

Where will the final peace-insuring boundaries lie? That is not yet clear. We are in the middle of the process of determining the capabilities of new technologies, and the extent of artists' willingness to incorporate them into their creative visions is still unknown. The example of the past suggests that it may be some time before a truce can be declared. What is undisputed, however, is that there will be carved out of the current field of battle separate realms, just as there are for all the other branches of art — whether poetry or literature or song or sculpture … or photography. Each will have it's own special limitations and possibilities and criterion for judging quality and success.

The Lords of the Sword *Cover for the book by Hugh Cook 1991 for ROC Books. Acrylic on illustration board 20" x 30".*

Richard Hescox has painted science fiction and fantasy images for over 30 years for books, magazines, motion pictures, animated cartoons and computer games. His work has been exhibited at the New York Society of Illustrators, the Delaware Art Museum and the Canton museum of Art.

Dave Seeley: **Marque and Reprisal**
Cover for the book by Elizabeth
Moon, published by Del Rey 2004.
Digital photocollage, in oil over
Archival Digital Print, 26"x36"

THE digital revolution in genre art has streamlined the workflow of the illustrator and become the efficiency darling of the publishing industry, but in the process, it has made original art superfluous. The degree to which we lament the loss of original art is related to our feelings about the paintings as objects, rather than the quality of the images in the final printed pictures. As artists, our focus is squarely on the front line of a struggle to remain viable practitioners in a quickly evolving world, and although creative potential in the field has never looked brighter, the quiet casualties are the beloved paintings we're leaving behind.

The revolution has been advantageous to artists who create their images digitally rather than traditionally. The digital *content* revolution followed on the heels of the digital *prepress* revolution, so had the advantages of a seamless relationship with that new regime. All content had to be digitized for prepress, so it was natural for digitization to begin earlier in the creation process. Artists tend to use the most expeditious route to getting a job done, and that route is increasingly a digital workflow. The "lost" time to prepare a surface, wait during dry-down times, and photograph the final image no longer exists in digital art creation. Work can be done in small segments of time, and the digital canvas is always "fluid." It's a simple matter to send the client a progress draft, and when the piece is complete, it can be delivered instantly over the internet. Conversely, a traditional painting must still be photographed or scanned. While that process has now shifted to digital technologies, with the drop in demand for photography the costs and time for those services have actually risen, and clients now often hold the illustrator responsible for digitally capturing the painting. Overall, the savings of a digital workflow can cut the time required to complete a commission in half.

However, the call to join the revolution wasn't just about efficiency. The magic of the "undo" command is perhaps the most enticing aspect of digital art for new recruits. In a traditional process, the artist needs to decide all major compositional and lighting issues at the outset. While preliminary studies for images are a natural complement to the flexibility of digital art, they are far less necessary because we can now easily make major shifts at all stages of development. Where, in the province of traditional painting, a confidence born of hard-won exploration was required to make major changes in a well-developed canvas, we can now eradicate an ill-conceived change with a single keystroke. The "undo" command limits the risk of explorations to merely the time they take, thereby opening up avenues that artists wouldn't have dared to traverse in an analogue paradigm. It's fair to say that digital art has allowed an exponential growth in experimentation, with commensurate expansion of creative growth both for individuals and the industry as a whole. In addition, capitalizing on mistakes has always been a critical part of art-making of any kind, and because the digital world lets us explore more avenues, we naturally make more mistakes from which to choose while we're mucking about.

Digitization has also revolutionized client expectations and the artist-client relationship, in several ways. The commercial art industry immediately exploited any time-savings, and adjusted its expectations of illustrators accordingly. Instantaneous communication with clients via email replaced phone calls and faxes, and computers changed the expectations of the ability, and subsequently the responsibility, of illustrators to make revisions to their images. Both the extent of changes, and the time allowed making them, shifted to a standard based on the perceived ease of a digital workflow. Even traditional painters, up against a deadline, will be forced to make those changes to a digitized file with Photoshop — even if they then must alter the physical painting to match, after the file goes to the printer. This has persuaded even relatively disinterested illustrators to gain a basic fluency in Photoshop. The incentive is not just the potential loss of work for being

CASUALTIES OF THE REVOLUTION
(NOTES FROM THE FRONT LINE)
Dave Seeley

non-responsive to time and revision requests, but perhaps worse: the threat that the changes will be made on the publishing side without the illustrator's oversight.

Client expectations make it increasingly difficult for traditional painters to compete. I know there are allowances made in the industry, but the exceptions I am familiar with have always been for established, well-known painters, not the young, up-and-coming painters. So, the standards resulting from evolved expectations will likely become all-pervasive within the span of a single career. In any artist's workflow, there is always a balance between making the most desirable picture and choosing an efficient means to get there. While it's neither desirable nor possible for most artists to separate the "labor of love" aspect from their professional pursuits, illustration is, in the end, a very competitive business. The illustrator who ignores the pressures of the industry will likely be seeking an alternate source of income.

Ironically, the pace of the digital revolution was hastened by our preference for the look of traditional media. At the outset of the digital revolution, oil paint was the favored medium of the genre artist. Consumers of the genre love and relate to the familiar stylistic aesthetic quality of painted images, and while we have seen departures toward more clearly digital, or clearly photographic images, the painted image remains immensely popular. Photoshop was the early leader of "paint" programs, but was primarily aimed at manipulating photographic imagery. Later, Painter software gave us the tools to emulate traditional painting strokes, and in the process became a key participant in the acceleration of the revolution. Painter can simulate oil and acrylic paint to a degree indistinguishable from traditional media, when images are viewed in final printed form. While traditional media emulation is both perverse and regressive, in the context of the potential development of digital art, applications like Painter enabled artists to set aside their brushes and paint without having to sacrifice the still existing cultural preference for the aesthetics of painted pictures. In the 1950's, Formica provided a similar transition from factory mass-produced wooden furniture, and like Formica, I suspect we will find other (perhaps even more popular) aesthetic possibilities in the future of Painter.

Painter software also offered advantages to the digital convert beyond emulating traditional paint media. Oil painting requires extensive experience for mastery. Oil paint is a collection of different pigments suspended in a common medium, and each pigment type has different characteristics that give each color a unique drying time, workability, saturation, and transparency. Those characteristics, for any given color, change from the time it is mixed on the palette to the time it dries — some colors in hours, and others in days. The mixing of colors further complicates the characteristics. It takes significant experience for an oil painter to know how the paint will react, and environmental conditions (heat, cold) can also affect the process. By contrast, digital painting lets the artist pick the color with a click, and choose the "workability" independent of color, and the painting is always and never dry. These are refreshing constants compared to the fickleness of oils, and they allow an artist to work on an image under far fewer constraints. Today there are a multitude of Painter software artists producing entirely digital images with an oil-painted aesthetic.

The revolution has had its ugly moments as well. Digital content creation was initially viewed suspiciously within the print industry. When I began using a computer to make illustrations in 1995, I was making images for collectible card games (CCG's). The premier CCG company at the time was hiring both digital and traditional artists from outside the CCG genre in an effort to "upgrade" the content quality of the pictures. Although the new art garnered rave reviews, sales dropped off shortly afterward. The company subsequently dropped the digital artists because they (wrongly) believed that digital art was somehow tainted, and that there was "already too much digital used in the production process" (a classic example of blurring the distinction between prepress and content creation). These were the early years when Photoshop was the primary digital tool for

(detail) Dave Seeley: **Image Junkie**
Personal work inspired by a William Gibson novel. Digital Photo Collage

artists. It was an uncertain time for digital art, and like modern architecture, the greatest weakness of Photoshop™ was that it was too easy to do poorly. "Cutout" photography jarringly inserted within pictures and a host of instant effects quickly became both cliché and synonymous with digital art. Soon afterward the fad aesthetics died a timely death, and the industry became more selective, recognizing that talent was still as important as it had been historically. Less than a decade later, the CCG industry employs more digital artists than traditional, and perceptions that digital art is inherently inferior are all but gone within the publishing industry.

The fight to preserve traditional methods is being further weakened by the blurring of distinctions between traditional and digital art. Digital art is an ambiguous term, mainly because digital workflows so easily blend with traditional ones, to create hybrid pictures. At the outset of my own digital conversion, I would use Photoshop to sharpen and polish my traditionally drawn or painted images, in order to "finish" them. Then I began using photography as blurred (abstracted) backgrounds, incorporating color from those backgrounds into my foreground subjects to unify the picture. Up to this point, I viewed my portfolio as neatly split between digital and traditional works. As my process evolved, I began experimenting with collaging photographs around a loose sketch or composition, with no traditional media source at all, but after a few years I wanted to shift my images from photo-real toward a more abstract aesthetic, and I found myself yearning for oil paint again. I had exhibited large archival prints of my photo-collaged images, and after learning these prints made wonderful base surfaces for oils I went back to laying down that lovely sweet toxic oil paint over my digital "under-paintings". The results were very personally satisfying, and I now believe that was due to a materialistic connection with surface and paintings as objects. At some point along the way, the distinctions of digital versus traditional art became irrelevant. I found that even when I embarked on an entirely traditional painting, I used Photoshop to plan it, and do studies. The ability to scale, rotate, relight, warp, and experiment with color, all while saving options along the way, was entirely superior to the traditional approach of sketches and painted studies. Even in cases where I have chosen to oil paint the entire surface, the images could not have evolved in the ways they did without the digital elements of my process. In retrospect, I started off with a traditional-to-digital hybrid approach, then switched to an entirely digital approach, then returned to a digital-to-traditional hybrid, to create art. Lately I'm mixing and matching as best fits a particular project. In any case, for me, the definition of digital art has been an elusive one.

Moreover, the chief function of commercial art — as a marketing tool — negates the need for traditional art. First, because the prime function of genre art on books or packaging is to attract the eye of a potential buyer, the surface texture of original source paintings is immaterial; this aspect of paintings is usually shrunken into obscurity in the printed image. In fact, many painters determine the size of their originals in order to achieve this "smoothing" effect at print size, while others pride themselves on the ability to eradicate any traces of the brush or medium even at the full scale of the original painting (It's common for fans and collectors to perceive this as a more difficult and more desirable stylistic finish: photo-real). Second, while the printed image is geared to appeal to consumers of products, the original painting has historically been of interest only to the relatively obscure collector or fan. Original genre art has always been a byproduct of the publishing process, and the subculture of original art collectors or admirers has evolved alongside it. This subculture stands to lose as digital paintings streamline the publishing process, rendering original art superfluous.

Sometimes the likelihood of a sale of an original painting will be incentive enough for an artist to take the extra time to produce one, at outset. Original art generates an important source of income for many painters, often making the difference between financial success and failure. Working digitally means the loss of that potential income. As discussed earlier, hybrid methods can still generate originals, and this could forestall the demise of original art, but clearly, continued industry pressures to complete purely digital pictures will result in a much smaller industry-wide yield of originals than existed pre-revolution. Also, while the print industry has advanced beyond its suspicion of digital art, there yet remains a pervasive wariness among collectors, who believe that digital art has sabotaged the thing they love most. There is also a commonly shared suspicion that hybrid art originals are masquerading as "real" original art. While I understand the trepidation of collectors, I think that much of the wariness is borne of a naiveté regarding traditional genre art processes, which evolve along with available technology. Regardless of the merits of these perceptions, if the financial incentives aren't there, then fewer originals will be executed.

I too feel the pressure to stop making paintings and finish images as purely digital pieces. I have tested the patience of several of my art directors while I took an extra two weeks to finish a piece in oil. I have yet to finish a piece that way and not like the result more than the digital state of its underpainting, even when it looked relatively finished in that form. It's true that no matter the medium, a piece is always developing while it is under digital stylus or traditional brush, so it stands to reason that I would prefer my images in their more developed states, whatever medium I determine to be that end state, but I also know that it is both the stylistic quality of the oils, and my love for surface that is essential. I am well aware that my desire to make paintings benefits my clients only indirectly; it is mainly sustenance for my own passion. I do believe that I could probably get the desired stylistic "effect" from Painter™, but it's the love of oil painting, and the loss of the final objects themselves that has kept me from total conversion. Producing a physical original can double the time it takes to complete a commission. As a result, I can only work this way when time allows … and often it does not. I do often feel the constraints of deadlines pulling me away from my easel, and in this I know I am not alone, but a tiny part of an overwhelming trend.

As the digital revolution continues, unabated, we are seeing beautiful and inspiring genre pictures produced perhaps at unprecedented rates, but as the result of inescapable market pressures an ever-decreasing fraction of those pictures are being realized in paint. The revolution has rendered original paintings superfluous. The digital artists that I know lament the loss of their originals for predominantly sentimental reasons, as artists are second only to collectors in their yen for those aspects of original art that cannot be equaled digitally. We crave a connection to the surface, the brush strokes and the micro-abstractions of the marks, the smell, the framing, the scale and the fetishistic power of the objects, and we stand to lose our "fix" as the supply of original art dwindles away — casualties of the digital revolution.

(detail) Dave Seeley; **The Liberty Gun** *Book 3 in the Structure series by Martin Sketchley, for PYR Books, 2006. Digital photo and pencil drawing collage, printed on paper, mounted on a panel, and then oil painted over the Archival Digital Print, 23"x35"*

Dave Seeley is a science fiction and fantasy artist living in Boston. He trained in fine art and architecture, and began making commercial images in the mid 90's. You can see his work in *Spectrum* Vols 4-13 (Underwood, 1997-2006), *Fantasy Art Masters: The Best in Fantasy and SF Art Worldwide* (Collins, UK, 2002) and at www.DaveSeeley.com.

I N September 1993 I borrowed $10,000 from my brother John and bought my first computer. In the intervening years, I have had a lot of time to think about the pluses and minuses of working digitally. I have concluded that pixels are not for everyone, and it is the wise artist who evaluates the "good" and the "bad" before becoming part of the digital revolution. Whether you enlist, or are drafted, into the "pixel brigade" I feel it's my duty to share the best and worst things I know about being a digital artist.

The best thing about working digitally is:
The undo button.

No matter how talented the artist, it is difficult to make radical changes in a painting using oils or acrylics. If you are half way through a piece, look at it and think "what if I shifted the entire background more toward blue?", you probably won't do it, since it is such a pain. However, working digitally, you can make the most radical experiments with a composition at any point in the creative process with no fear that you will totally screw it up. When I was painting in acrylics, I can't tell you how many times I would rework a face, only to think, "Crap, it looked better BEFORE I did that." In a digital painting, you just create a new layer, try out a new idea, and it if works, keep it. Otherwise, you pick up where you left off — none the worse for the detour. A digital canvas encourages experimentation, and even if a concept fails, you inevitably learn something in the process. From my perspective, the digital artist is aided and abetted by technology, not enslaved. You're in control, and part of that control is the ability to erase mistakes and make errors in judgment disappear. Working on a computer has made me a less timid painter, which is a good thing.

The worst thing about working digitally is:
The undo button.

There is a lot to be said for planning ahead when you are doing a painting. Working traditionally forces an artist to make decisions about a composition and stick with them. Part of why working digitally has not speeded up my rate of production is because I am constantly trying new things as I go along. You can indulge yourself. It's like eating anything you want and not putting on weight. When you work with paint, the stakes are high. Every step of the composition is for keeps, unless you are willing to wipe out what you have done and re-do it. The medium itself imposes discipline and precision. Working digitally can foster bad habits, such as ignoring problem areas or putting off difficult decisions. There is a false sense of security that any problem can be fixed "later," which is not always true.

The second best thing about working digitally is:
No original.

I know, I know. You were thinking I would say this is the worst thing about working digitally. But let's get real — if you are an illustrator, almost no one will ever see your original, while thousands of people will see the printed piece. Worrying about the original is so last century. You should only worry about what the printed piece will look like — that is your real obligation. Thinking about how exquisite your transparent underpainting looks, or how magnificent that impasto light passage is has nothing to do with how it will be seen by the vast, vast majority of

Time Patrol *by Poul Anderson, Baen Books 2006 Digital painting in Photoshop, cycle modeled in 3DS MAX*

EVERYTHING I KNOW ABOUT BEING A DIGITAL ARTIST
David Mattingly

your audience. All of the subtlety you love so much in your original painting will be lost in reproduction, and working digitally requires you to focus on what will really be seen.

The second worst thing about working digitally is:
No original.

Is there anything better than going to a museum and seeing a painting you have admired, only to find that the original is 100 times better than any reproduction could be? I was never a big fan of Monet's work until my wife Cathleen and I went to Paris and I saw a bunch of his original paintings. What a painter! I can't believe how exquisite his transparent under painting looks, and his passages of impasto lights make me feel like I've seen god. But you have to experience the paintings in-person. None of the shimmering color or subtleness of form reproduce well. When I was working traditionally, I always loved to be able to hold the original in my hands after I was done. The tangibility of a painting — the physical "thing" the artist creates — is a wonderful quality, and there is no "thingness" to a piece of digital artwork. You can make prints of the digital art, sign and number them, print them on canvas, have other people or yourself paint on top of them .authenticate its "originality", but when you work digitally you don't get an original that has the same value as an original painting. Anyone who has a real appreciation of art can tell the difference between an oil painting and a Giclée print. By any other name, a print is a print, and no gimmick, no matter how clever, is going to transform it into an original painting. I went to art school with Tom Kinkaide, and knew him a little, so I have been amazed by his success at selling glorified prints to people at fine art prices. Seriously, if you are paying more than 100 bucks for a print, you are being taken.

Not everyone realizes that there is an "original" of a digital painting, but it is in a form that the general public can't appreciate. That is the uncollapsed Photoshop file. If you look at an accomplished digital artist's working file, with all the layers intact, you can learn a lot by going through and turning on and off layers. You can see how the piece was created. Steve Youll, an astonishing artist who has successfully made the transition from paint to pixels, lets me look at his uncollapsed working files. He leaves in all kinds of informative stuff, such as alternate versions of the image, reference pieces, and his transfer layers. You feel like an archaeologist sifting through layer upon layer of a hidden world. Don't ask to see my uncollapsed files — I don't want people discovering my secrets!

The third best thing about working digitally is:
Using your reference directly.

When you work digitally, if you have a perfect piece of reference, like an ideal sky, you can just drop it directly into your composition and avoid the tedium of repainting it. In any composition, there are always a number of things you have to paint. Why waste time recreating something that exists and suits your needs perfectly? Even today, quite a few digital artists consider this using your reference directly "cheating." I think that opinion is impractical — why force yourself to rework an element that nature has already created perfectly? Directly mixing good photo reference with painting is a terrific way to work.

The third worst thing about working digitally is:
Using your reference directly.

(top, detail) **Time patrol**

(right) **Forge of the Titans** *by Steve Whitel, Baen Books 2003 Digital painting using Photoshop*

© MATTINGLY 2002

How many digital compositions have we all seen that are just a bunch of photographs sandwiched together to make a picture, perhaps with a few passes of Photoshop filters over the elements to make them look more "painterly"? One great thing about painting is that the artist must create every element in the composition. When you are working with paint, even with a superb piece of reference, it must be interpreted on the canvas by the artist's hand and brain. Any idiot can drop a photograph into a composition and call it art, but only an artist's hand can really make it so.

Actually, I have a nice compromise between these two positions. One of my favorite digital artists, Bruce Jensen, gave me a piece of advice that changed how I think about composing a picture. A little background information — I assume everyone reading this book knows what I mean by "resolution". If you have a piece of reference that is 400 pixels by 400 pixels, and you drop it into a picture that is 2000 pixels wide and enlarge it, it will look fuzzy and lack detail. When I started working on the computer, I always tried to get high-resolution imagery for every element in a painting, since low-resolution elements look so awful. What Bruce suggested was to drop in whatever reference you have for a composition, not worrying about the resolution, and then paint over it. If your reference is too pristine, and high resolution, you won't want to paint over it, since it already looks so good. If the reference isn't perfect, it will free you up to use it just as reference and rework it with impunity. Plus it gives you a lot more sources to take reference from, since it doesn't have to be high resolution.

Lastly, a few words of advice for anyone struggling to decide whether to make the leap to the computer: Look at your work — are you an artist that takes advantage of what paint can do? When you look at some of the finest painters in the field, like Boris Vallejo, Frank Frazetta, and Donato Giancola, these are guys whose work is all about what paint can do. They glory in what happens when paint blends on the canvas. The decision for me was easy, since my work was never about virtuoso passages of painting, but rather about detail and trying to make the piece look as realistic as possible. If you are an artist that loves the feel of paint on canvas, and your work communicates that, owning a computer will only make your work worse, because every moment you spend fiddling around with the computer is another moment you should have spent painting.

I, on the other hand, have loved being part of the digital revolution. I think I have the same feeling as the artists who lived through the advent of photography — some must have loved it, some must have hated it, but once it happened, picture making was never the same. When photography was invented, it freed artists from the task of just representing things, since you could get a photo of your loved one, or your favorite horse, or whatever, rather than having to hire an artist. That freed the artist to think anew about what picture making was all about and led to a lot of great art, like the impressionists and abstract expressionists. I think the digital revolution will do the same thing. It has removed many of the mundane tasks from the illustrator, even thought it has, sadly, eliminated many markets along the way. Some things have obviously gotten worse from digital imaging — how many of you prefer the illustrated movie posters of 15 years ago to the photomontage pieces that dominate the market now? I miss the time when a month wouldn't go by without a new movie campaign by Drew Struzan instead of the umpteenth digital montage posters we suffer from now. Meanwhile, digital imaging has created new meaningful tasks for artists, like concept art for video games and movies, digital compositing and matte painting, and computer animation. None of these markets existed 15 years ago like they do today.

Living in a time of revolution is never comfortable, but in this revolution there is still work for artists on both side of the lines. Really, who cares how you make a picture — all that matters is "does it work?" or "doesn't it work?". When all is said and done, the artist's only obligation is to make a great picture — who gives a damn how it is done?

(detail) **St. Joan and the Computer** *Personal painting published as cover of* Amazing *magazine, 1991. Acrylic on illustration board, 22" x 16"*

David Burroughs Mattingly has produced over 500 covers for most major publishers of science fiction and fantasy, including 54 covers for K.A. Applegate's Animorphs. and David Webers's Honor Harrington series. He is also a well known matte artist, contributing to the films *The Black Hole, Tron, Dick Tracy,* and most recently *I, Robot.* You can see more of his work in *Alternate Views, Alternate Universes, the Art of David B. Mattingly* (1996) and at www.davidmattingly.com.

"YOU did that on a computer? It looks like a painting!"

Thank you.

Every once in a while someone will mistake one of my digital pieces for an acrylic painting. It's a nice compliment (I say from the archaic bias that painting is a "higher" art form than computer work). Daily I confront the question: Shall my newest creation be digital or painted? Most often these days, I find myself manipulating pixels. Why? Digital technology allows me a more facile handle on different styles. That's important as I try to interpret a writer's deeper meanings effectively in illustrating a book or story.

Over the years, I've worked in both media. When I was an undergrad, I studied acrylics and oils. I quickly abandoned oils, though, because they smell bad and are bad for you. I left art for a few years for grad school to learn to splice DNA (if you do science-fiction art, it's good to know some science). Then I returned to art in 1998 to try to build a professional career, initially working digitally. After I realized that I could sell a painting for ten or fifty times as much as a print, I picked up my paintbrushes again. Now I find myself returning to the computer, because I can achieve a finished look more quickly. (This is also the Dark Side of the Pixel, which I'll address presently.)

Digital techniques helped me capture the mood I wanted for the book cover *Paradise Passed*. The artwork shows our heroes spying on a bonfire lit by dancing aliens (using fire that the humans accidentally taught them to use. Oops.). Inspiration for the illustration came from Rembrandt's paintings of figures in earth tones emerging from shadows, particularly "Man with the Golden Helmet" (which may or may not actually be a Rembrandt) — plus James Bond movies and *Gilligan's Island*. The entire piece was done, essentially, with three Photoshop tools: Digital paintbrush, line tool and smudge. But I didn't use any 3D modeling programs, even for the tiny spaceship at the top. I use real people as models, because I've yet to see a Poser-drawn person with a believable expression or body language. Real faces — especially the eyes — help "sell" the viewer on the surrounding phantasma. For references I also occasionally carve hillocks from Play-Doh or rough out spaceships in cardboard. The spaceship here was initially done the old-fashioned way, with paper and pen and straight edge, using perspective lines. Yes, even when working digitally, I can be a Luddite. I scanned the image and colored it, using the line tool for hardware texture.

Furthermore, I could never achieve the affects I want without my digital tools. The line tool is a total blessing to me. I use it for everything from straight-edged machinery to fur to organically-shaped objects to rocks and sand. How? I set the line width to 1 or 2 points and then draw lines, from 3 to 10 pixels long with the mouse. Then repeat hundreds and hundreds of times. For hardware, the lines are parallel. For curves, each line is at a slightly different angle than the last. For rocks, the lines are random. When the final piece is viewed, the fine lines disappear into texture. Only I know they're there. When I draw lines I also pause after a few dozen to modulate the color. If an object is drawn with a minimum of about 7 shades from light to dark, it will look more realistic, and if the colors I use vary slightly from each other, the piece will be more lively and believable. Another secret weapon is the smudge tool. I can blend bundles of lines, mixing up the pixels that are tell-tale signs of digitality. The smudger simulates the energetic scumbling of canvas painting, allowing me to stir in extra colors.

Now I must let you in on a secret. Something that artists know, but many non-artists do not. Artists never draw people or spaceships. What we do is rearrange blobs of color and light, until the magic happens: the combination we choose is transfigured in the viewer's mind into spaceships and landscapes. The leaves on the trees are simply blobs of colored pixels, drawn with lines then smudged. The spaceship is a dense array of tiny lines. Some are white, which the reader "reads" as windows. Yellows and oranges are chosen to give texture, warmth, directionality of light. A small,

(detail) **Paradise Passed** *Cover for the novel by Jerry Oltion, Wheatland Press, 2004. All digital media.*

THE JOY OF PIXELATION
Frank Wu

hard-edge paintbrush was used on the faces, but a broad, diffused brush on the fire. All these effects, of course, can be achieved with traditional media, but I find them far easier with pixels. Reducing the opacity of the paintbrush tool is easier than preparing an acrylic wash, and I don't worry about splashing water on myself. True, computer artwork can look "pasted together" — like digital Frankensteins — but then, so can paintings, especially airbrushed work. Good digital solutions maintain color unity between objects so as to be consistent in lighting, or work a color or texture throughout.

My magazine illustration for "Losing Memories" (pg. 136) highlights other remarkable effects that can be achieved digitally. To illustrate the tale, involving a female archaeologist studying the runes on the ruins of a far-flung planet, I wanted a foreboding spookiness in the mist. So, I first crafted the runes by hand, using a black marker on white paper. (The runes are inspired by Telegu, Sanskrit, Korean, Mandarin, Urdu and other languages.) These pictograms were scanned into the computer. The white background was selected and erased, leaving the runes on clear digital acetate. Next they were inverted (black to white) and tiled (duplicated) and then distorted so they moved like waves. The glow was added by duplicating the rune layer, then increasing the brightness and blurring it. I'm glad I didn't have to use a *real* paintbrush to do all that! The figure and the rocks were roughed with a wide-tip paintbrush tool, general shapes sketched in black and white, and then various grays added for texture using smaller and smaller "tips." Mist was drawn with a diffuse, wide-tipped "paintbrush," with the edges smudged and the whole thing partially erased (eraser set to 40% or so). As with the fire in the *Paradise Passed* cover, the smudge tool gave a pleasing smoky swirl.

However, earlier drafts of "Losing Memories" looked very different than the final piece. Most drafts had very little sky, with the archeologist perched at the top of compositions mainly illustrating the rock textures, which were overlaid with the runes. *It just didn't work.*

And this illustrates the Dark Side of the Pixel.

A half-complete digital image can look more finished than a half-complete painting. This is because it's easy to add a separate layer of gloss and sparkle early in production (in a painting these have to be added last), but the glow and flash can imply completion while obscuring fundamental flaws. So, even though the runes and rocks looked good, the drafts failed. *The composition was wrong.*

Cloud Dragon *Skies interior for the story by N.K. Jemisin, Strange Horizons, 2005. Mixed media: ink and digital*

Where did the eye go? Did the rocks and overlying runes compete for attention? After trying half a dozen different compositions, I found the answer in my library, in a book on Chinese painting. One of the classic compositions in traditional Chinese landscapes is the "one-corner composition." An example of this would be a painting in which we see a monk on a hillock, under a tree, in a lower corner staring at the moon in an opposite upper corner.

Ah! That was it!

I moved the elements around until the runes no longer overlapped the rocks, and it all clicked together. I have re-arranged objects in acrylic paintings — but this has involved slicing into the canvas with an X-acto knife and then re-gluing elements onto fresh canvas. With pixels, it's easier. The book you hold in your hands may have a 5 x 7 aspect ratio, but the three artworks I discuss here were originally created for different aspect ratios (8.5 x 11 or 6 x 9). Moving elements so they wouldn't be lost when re-cropping the images to 5 x 7 only took about five minutes total, because I could do it *digitally*. In *Paradise Passed*, digital techniques similarly helped resolve problems with the composition. I wanted to show delicious detail on the spaceship, but that would have distracted attention from the flames and faces. The solution? Make the spaceship small on the cover, and put the full-resolution version on the back cover. No re-painting, just cutting and pasting — digitally. Another digital technique I used in "Losing Memories" was the "lasso" tool. To show the runes slowly shifting from white to gray to black, then back to white, I selected parts of the runes with the lasso set to a diffuse edge, and then inverted the selection. Accomplishing this effect may have taken a couple of minutes; it would have taken hours or days to do with a real paintbrush — if it was possible at all. *Voilá*! The piece was done, after only going through 32 drafts.

A final example demonstrating the benefits of working digitally is the artwork I produced for "Cloud Dragon Skies." There, I again ran into the digital deceit of the "unfinished masquerading as finished," but again, the flaws were easily fixed by digitally erasing and re-drawing objects and moving and re-scaling others. However, just as with "Losing Memories" and *Paradise Passed*, the texture and sparkles were achieved with dots and lines. Dozens. Hundreds. Thousands. I estimate four thousand on the face alone. They were applied with a fine-tipped paintbrush or line tool so the individual marks are impossible to perceive unless the image is greatly enlarged. Each dot only took a second or two to apply, but I certainly gained greater appreciation for the artist Virgil Finlay, in that process! His pointillist style involved wiping a pen and dipping it into an ink well — for every single dot. In some cases, digital repetition can be disappointing and deadening. I've seen spaceships digitally rubber-stamped into entire fleets, wherein every ship has identical surface detailing and improbably flies at the same angle as its neighbor. For that reason I think carefully before using such a technique, and understand its purpose. A close-up view of "Cloud Dragon Skies" reveals repeated elements: tiny lines so tiny they are almost imperceptible. Almost. I purposely wanted to leave some repetition obvious, to simulate the rhythmic hammer blows and chisel scars in stone, as if the figure were carved like a Shona sculpture. I wanted the repetition to lend a subtle profundity and quiet solemnity.

The key to success with "pixels" is to know both the potential and the limitations of digital techniques. I can create most — but not all — digital effects with a paintbrush, but the computer makes moving blobs of color around much easier. I'm not about to run around screaming "Pixels rule and paintings drool!" but certainly my bag of visual tricks is bigger with the computer. And, if at the end of the day, my digital pieces are sometimes mistaken for paintings it is because of the thought I put into them, and the hours I spent on the computer working and re-working the surfaces. Computer programs will not teach you heart and soul or symbology, or teach you art history or composition color theory or perspective. Those things you have to learn on your own — traditional media won't teach you them, either. But the computer can certainly accelerate the progress of getting that heart and soul into the form of a finished piece.

Frank Wu has won two Hugo Awards for his art, in addition to the Illustrators of the Future Grand Prize. His work has appeared on various magazine and book covers. His current project is the animated short film, *TheTragical Historie of Guidolon, the Giant Space Chicken*, about a giant space chicken with delusions of grandeur. Learn more at www.frankwu.com

THERE has been considerable debate lately in the world of space art. People have been asking questions such as "Is digital art 'real' art?" or "Is digital art 'cheating'?" Questions that have, naturally enough, led to some heated and prolonged discussions. Chesley Bonestell (1888-1987) was the quintessential space artist, one who is generally conceded to have been the father of modern astronomical art. Classically trained, he worked exclusively in oils (with the rare excursion into watercolors or etching) and throughout his life eschewed such mechanical shortcuts as the airbrush, preferring to achieve the same effects through careful blending or the meticulous use of thinly applied layers of translucent oils. However, while Bonestell's techniques may have been classical, he was not above employing high technology in his work, and he employed this technology in a manner that parallels the way in which many of today's space artists use the computer. For that reason, if Bonestell were alive today, I think he would be among the first to embrace digital techniques for creating art.

The history of art is in part a history of technological advances. Oil paint, geometric perspective, lithography, the *camera lucida*, photography, the airbrush, acrylics and countless other innovations all mark watersheds of one kind or another — -some small and affecting only relatively specialized portions of the artistic community, others diverting the flow of art history like a weir in a fast-flowing river. Some of these innovations were absorbed painlessly and, in many cases, enthusiastically. Before the introduction of geometric perspective, for instance, naturalistic representation was not considered to be the function of art. Instead, the size and position of objects in a picture were determined by their relative importance. Once the rules of perspective were formalized by Filippo Brunelleschi in the early 15th century, however, a turn toward *naturalism* overwhelmed the monopoly once held by symbolism. Some artists, such as Albrecht Durer, even went so far as to construct special mechanical and optical instruments to aid them in constructing mathematically perfect perspective drawings. As for the mediums employed, before the invention of oil paints, media such as encaustics and various forms of tempera dominated the field — although the use of oil as a binder was known as far back as the oldest Mediterranean civilizations. There were so many drawbacks to oil, however, that some authorities went so far as to discourage its use. Once Flemish painter Jan van Eyck perfected oils around 1410, however, the medium quickly became so ubiquitous that virtually all other painting materials were reduced to a secondary status that remains to this day. It was not until the introduction of acrylic paints in middle of the 20th century that oil faced any serious rival, although it is still the preferred media of most gallery artists and many illustrators.

Occasionally, an innovation is not met with such enthusiasm. After the invention of photography in the early 19th century, Paul DeLaroche is supposed to have declared, "From today, painting is dead." A statement that reflected the feelings of many academic painters, whose careers were supported by the creation of highly representational paintings: portraits, landscapes, historical scenes and so forth. The camera could capture such things with fidelity unachievable by even the finest painter. Photography was also relatively cheap and, worse, could be accomplished by anyone. Many artists, though, were quick to exploit the possibilities of photography, looking at it as not a rival but an ally. At about the same time that DeLaroche was wringing his hands, Eugène Delacroix was using photographs of the nude, from which he learned "far more by looking than the inventions of any scribbler could teach me." He also worked from photographs of models when making drawings and paintings. Meanwhile, artists discovered that it was in fact to their advantage to let photography take over the mundane depiction of reality — -thus freeing them to explore hitherto unexpected

Storm on Saturn *Unpublished illustration 2006, originally created for "Scientific American." Digital media, rings produced with StrataPro, the remainder done by hand in Photoshop.*

WHAT WOULD BONESTELL HAVE DONE?
Ron Miller

Panorama of Enceladus *Digital work created for* The Worlds Around Us *(Ellen Jackson; Lerner Publishing Group, 2006), a children's science book. The image combines a digitally rendered landscape, stars and Saturn created with Universe and StrataPro, all finished by hand in Photoshop.*

realms of color, light and composition. It may realistically be argued that the advent of impressionism, expressionism, surrealism and all of the non-representational schools that followed may have been delayed by decades, if not longer, had it not been for the liberating influence of photography.

The parallels to be found between photography and digital art are remarkably similar; much the same panicky statements, followed by biased debate, with many of the same arguments surviving, practically intact. The proliferation — one might well write "flood"— of amateur digital art has had the unfortunate result of tainting the entire genre, in much the same way that "Made In Japan" had once been an indication of cheapness and mediocrity. Perhaps the greatest impediment to the appreciation of computer-generated art as art is the very phrase: "computer-generated art". *There is no such thing.* Computers don't generate art (they may someday, of course, but that's not our concern at the moment). *Artists generate art.* Computers *aid* in the creation of certain art forms. Engineers and architects got it right a long time ago when they developed CAD programs to help them create technical drawings. CAD means "Computer Aided Drawing". No one has ever suggested that a computer has ever taken it upon itself to design a skyscraper or airplane, nor has anyone ever suggested that a building or airplane is any less viable because its architect or engineer employed a CAD program in creating the design. Likewise, a computer left to its own devices all alone in a room isn't going to do anything but hum along until it goes into standby mode. It's not going to suddenly blink with inspiration and start creating things. So perhaps we need to do nothing more complicated than to simply stop using the phrase "computer-generated art" and start calling it by its right name: "computer-aided art". Once we get our minds around that concept, perhaps we'll also get our minds around what is really going on.

Bonestell's reliance on natural media, such as oil paints, epitomize the kind of painting techniques the detractors of digital space art point to when they want a perfect example of "real" art. But … Bonestell used technology to achieve his artistic goals, and in Bonestell's case, this technology was *photography*. Taking things a step further than Delacroix or Thomas Eakins, Bonestell used photos directly in his art. One of his most famous paintings, the iconic *Saturn as seen from Titan* (1944), achieves the nearly photographic reality of its rock formations because the rock formations are in fact a photograph. A master model-maker, Bonestell was adept at creating miniature landscapes from plasticine, rocks and other material. He would then photograph these landscapes, often with a pin-hole camera to obtain the greatest depth of field. A large print would be mounted on an illustration board over which he would then apply his colors, tinting the photo and adding things such as a black, star-filled sky, a planet, spacecraft or whatever else the final painting required. Surviving negatives show that Bonestell experimented with different lighting angles, shooting numerous photos of the same landscape until he achieved the effect he was after. This is precisely what many digital space artists do today. A model landscape or spacecraft can be created in the computer and then viewed from any angle, with light coming from any direction. When happy with the results, the digital artist can then use that model in any number of ways — often in the very same way that Bonestell used his photographs — by adding elements and finishing the artwork by hand (albeit with a graphics tablet and stylus instead of a palette and paint brush). It is, I know, the way in which I work. I create digital landscapes that I can then maneuver until the lighting, shadows, viewing angle and other details are just as I want them … then I use the results as the foundation for hours of work by hand to finish the "painting". I will sometimes follow Bonestell's lead even more closely by incorporating photographs of real rocks or plasticine models directly into the art.

Would Bonestell, had he been born in, say, 1950 instead of 1888, have embraced the computer as readily as he embraced photography? I think so. After all, he never considered himself anything other than a working illustrator. How his artwork appeared in print was the most important consideration and whatever worked best to achieve the greatest effect — in Bonestell's case, this was the effect of photographic realism — was the right thing to do. For this well-known artist, as it is for many artists today, the final image was more important than how it was achieved.

Martian Landscape *for* The Worlds Around Us *(Ellen Jackson; Lerner Publishing Group, 2006). A digital rendering created with the aid of Terragen and finished in Photoshop.*

Ron Miller is an illustrator and author whose space art has appeared on book jackets and interiors, commemorative stamps, and many popular magazines. He has also written and illustrated nearly forty books of his own, including the "Worlds Beyond" series of astronomy books for young adults, the Hugo winning *Art of Chesley Bonestell* (2001), and five books in collaboration with noted astronomer William K. Hartmann. His paintings are in numerous private and public collections, including the Smithsonian Institution and the Pushkin Museum (Moscow). See www.black-cat-studios.com

HE evolution of digital media over the past decade has had a profound and quite unavoidable impact on the visual artist. Regardless of a particular artist's choice of working media, the digital revolution has dramatically changed everything from the marketplace itself — including communication with clients, sales, promotion, printing, delivery of artwork, even simple acquisition of materials — to the tools and modes of expression available to the artist. Digital media have devastated some markets while opening or expanding others, forcing the artist to adapt in one way or another.

As an artist currently working with digital media, I am a strong advocate for the use of digital tools, but I do so with one qualification: digital media, like any tool available to the artist, is used appropriately when it is simply the artist's tool of choice, not a substitute for another tool or a shortcut to meet a deadline.

The impact of digital media on the choices artists make is complicated by the dual capabilities of digital tools: mimicry and creation of the new. The changes in the music industry, brought about by the music synthesizer, provide a useful analogy. The synthesizer's ability to mimic actual instruments, as well as to create new sounds, is a good example of the dual nature of digital media. In the economic sphere, it's much cheaper for a producer to hire one musician with a synthesizer than a whole orchestra, especially if that musician has digital recording capabilities — no need to pay for multiple musicians, rehearsal space and studio time. That's a good outcome for the one musician, but not so good for the orchestra. Sound synthesis, on the other hand, has opened up whole new avenues of expression for the working musician and new forms of digital media have created entirely new sales and delivery venues within the marketplace.

A parallel can be found in the illustration market. Financially pressed publishers looking to cut costs have found a solution in art directors armed with Photoshop and stock image libraries. Although there is a certain amount of entertainment to be derived from watching the art airector's hair turn grey under these circumstances, the impact on illustrators is not so amusing, at least from our perspective as artists. The truly brilliant among us will always have work, the rest of us have to adapt to the new realities of the marketplace. For example, if one chooses to work in traditional media, the ability to convert the final artwork to digital format for submission may be a necessary capability to remain competitive. Digital media can be used in support of traditional media. There are many brilliant painters I know who I would not like to see make the change to digital painting. The quality of paint in their physical paintings that makes their work so extraordinary would be lost. However, were an art director to request changes to a physical painting that would destroy its integrity, a situation familiar to some, an excellent solution may be to scan the painting and make those changes digitally. The requirements of the job are then met and the artistic integrity of the physical painting is maintained.

I have never had much patience with debates over the artistic integrity of certain media or tools an artist chooses to use. When I started out in illustration, there was an ongoing debate over use of an airbrush, which was seen as a form of "cheating" by some. For me, its use was simple: if an artist is looking for an airbrush effect, use an airbrush. If not, don't. This debate was left in the dust with the advent of digital media, with its unparalleled adeptness at mimicry, but I think the same reasoning applies: the artist should use whatever tool the artist deems appropriate to achieve a desired result — and not use a tool as a shortcut to mimic a desired result.

The choice to use digital tools is just that, a choice. For artists who seek to expand their arsenal, digital media provides capabilities that are unavailable in natural media. Having a minor bent toward geekdom, and seeing its potential for helping me realize my artistic visions, I have embraced digital

The Ringworld Throne *Cover for the novel by Larry Niven, Ballantine Books, 1995. Digital image in Strata 3D & Photoshop*

ANOTHER TOOL IN THE ARTIST'S ARSENAL
Barclay Shaw

media since the first IBM PC was introduced. Many years were spent creating totally unsatisfactory digital images with PC Paintbrush and other early paint programs, but with the arrival of the Mac Quadra 950 in 1992, running Adobe Photoshop, the computer became (for me) a truly viable tool. I slowly made the transition from traditional painting to working digitally over a five-year period. During that time, Photoshop matured and lower-end 3D and audio programs were introduced — and the whole learning process became a revelation to me. One of my first book covers created digitally was for *The Ringworld Throne* by Larry Niven (Ballantine Books, 1995). The base image was generated in a 3D program using textures created in Photoshop, and the final image was composited with additional painting in Photoshop. Part of the revelation in the learning process was, since the cover scene existed as a 3D model, it was a simple step to animate the camera in the 3D scene and create an animation from the book cover scene — which is exactly what I did. I then used my synthesizer and an audio program to create a sound track and a movie editing program to assemble a 30-second television commercial which Ballantine Books used to promote the book. In my view, this is an excellent example of how digital media was a perfect choice in this instance among mediums available to me and allowed me to expand my artwork well beyond the limits of traditional media.

Digital media have enabled me to easily create artwork that would be extremely difficult to create using traditional media. *Witches' Brew* (Advanced Rendering Technology, 2000) is a digitally generated image rendered from a 3D model that exhibits a level of detail and realism that I could not have achieved using only traditional painting tools and given the same amount of execution time. Conversely, *Machineries of Joy* (R. Bradbury, Bantam Books 1989) would have been much more difficult to create digitally and would not have had the desired "feel" of an oil on acrylic painting that I was looking for. In each instance, my vision for the realized artwork determined my choice of medium.

Learning to use digital tools is easier than you might expect, provided you initially keep it simple. Begin with an entry-level program, whether it's a digital painting program, photo editing soft-

Witches' Brew *Advanced Rendering Technology, 2000, digitally generated image in 3dsmax & Photoshop*

Machineries of Joy *cover for one in the re-issued Ray Bradbury series "Classic Stories 1" for Bantam Books, 1990. Acrylics on board, 30" x 50"*

ware or whatever you please, plus adequate hardware, then explore the program's depths and add more tools as you see fit. The confusing and disconcerting thing about this digital business is that it is *bottomless*, the depths of complexity are seemingly infinite. I have chosen to pursue a particularly deep level of complexity, using 3d animation, compositing, and audio programs as well as painting and photo editing programs, and the most difficult thing I have to deal with is keeping up with the continual updates to those programs. The good thing is that artists who want to work digitally can choose the level of complexity they are comfortable with and still achieve excellent results.

I tend to regard digital media as a single amorphous entity, rapidly changing but completely interrelated and interdependent. If you understand Photoshop's interface, you have by default a basic understanding of how a lot of other seemingly unrelated programs work. This is not to underrate the difference between programs; that learning curve will always be there. But the more you learn, the easier learning becomes, and the more tools become available to you. Many concepts within a single program turn out to be global across digital media, making it much easier to learn and move between programs. Even artists who abhor digital art can benefit from the use of digital tools, from simply scanning their roughs or paintings for submission to creating their own websites for promotion and/or sales.

3D animation now accounts for the majority of my current work — by choice. I derive enormous satisfaction from working in 3D because it combines my interests in painting, sculpture, animation, sound creation and editing. My current use of digital media is in no way a rejection of traditional media. All the basic principles of good design, composition and lighting apply to any work of art irrespective of the media used to create the art. In sum, having a basic working knowledge of digital media is indispensable in conducting business on a professional level today. Digital media provide tools to the artist that expand the artist's capabilities and in no way limit or replace the artist's existing toolset.

Barclay Shaw has painted over 500 book and magazine cover illustrations, working for virtually every major U.S. publisher. His paintings have received Chesley Awards and several Hugo Award nominations, and is displayed in museums and galleries, as well as SF/F convention art shows. He now provides high-end computer graphics and 3D animation support primarily for government and private sector scientific research and development programs. A collection of his artwork was published 1995, *Electric Dreams: The Art of Barclay Shaw* (Paper Tiger, UK). See www.barclayshaw.com

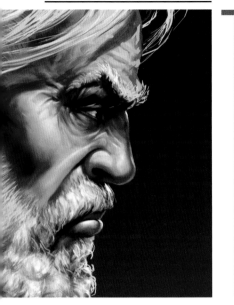

NTERESTING thoughts. Interesting questions. Views will differ. For me, a line is a line, a tool is a tool, and art is mostly a factor of the decisions made by the artist plus his or her skill in manipulating a given media to create a desired image or effect.

Today, for various reasons, I work as an artist creating art for the gaming industry. I am skilled in two dimensional software programs such as Photoshop and Painter, and I have recently (over the past two or three years) expanded my skills to include three-dimensional software such as 3D Studio Max. I have been in this digital field for approximately six years. Prior to that I worked as a traditional artist/illustrator specializing in science fiction and fantasy subject matter. That part of my career spanned eighteen years and began in 1982 when I left legal practice to devote myself full time to art and illustration. I was arrogant enough to think that my lack of skills in painting and drawing could be overcome with many hours of long work, and that a new company called Federal Express would enable me to take on commissions despite the fact that I did not live in New York. Indeed, in due course I was securing work from major publishers. *Tempus fugit*, technology marched on, and I became part of a very fun artistic community. It was a different world back then.

In the 1980's little thought was given to the possibility of using computers to create our paintings. It was simply not practical. For one thing, the watch I wear today has more storage and computing power than the best computer I could have afforded back then, and the software programs were far too basic to offer any real competition to traditional art. I do recall, however, wishing I knew how to work a CAD program so I could create things in 3D. This came about because even though most of my portfolio consisted of fantasy art, I kept getting assignments to paint scenes involving the interiors of spaceships. Do a painting of people against trees and hills and you can just grab your paints and start to work. Most of your time can be devoted to the people, the center of interest. Those darned machined interiors, however, posed problems in perspective that had me spending three of my four available weeks just drafting out the backgrounds and then rushing like mad to get my figures done well enough. What a luxury it would be, I thought, to be able to create my own scene, my own set, then light it, choose the best possible camera angle, take a photograph of that, and then do my painting from that reference shot.

Twenty years later I finally got the chance to learn the skills to do precisely that, when, in 1996 or so, my good friend Bill Fawcett (who owned Catware Software), called and asked me to be art director for a computer game his company was making. Part of the work could be done as traditional media, but other parts, he insisted, would need to be created in Photoshop. The fact that I had no computer and had never opened Photoshop, much less studied it, did not daunt him. This was his big brotherly way of forcing me toward what he saw as the future of science fiction and fantasy illustration. His advance allowed me to buy a decent computer. Then he sent a copy of Photoshop along with an assignment to use it to create a workable in-game user interface in one month. He said I should not let it worry me that failing to meet this milestone might mean the investors would pull all their money from the project. Some five hundred and forty billable hours of work later, I met the milestone, and was well on my way to being a credible Photoshop artist. My lesson? The game industry has never seemed to care whether art was created traditionally or digitally, just so long as it was created on time and was cutting edge cool.

In contrast, in the late 1990s the publishing industry was still pretty much devoted to using traditional media. While technology had finally advanced to the point that it was becoming normal to send in a CD of a high-resolution scan of the art instead of the original painting, they still wanted the art itself to be hand done. If you were unscrupulous and wanted to injure the career of a competitor, all you had to do was let the publishers and art directors in New York know that you

Zeus Game Box cover detail, for Age of Mythology: The Titans © Microsoft 2003. Digital — Photoshop image based in part on scanned painted acrylic artwork

A Line is a Line
David Cherry

(detail) **Daughter of Conflict**
Cover for a Marion Zimmer Bradley novel, DAW 1992. Acrylic on gessoed watercolor board. ©1992 David A. Cherry

had heard that so and so was using Photoshop to touch up his work or, worse yet, that he was doing his paintings entirely in Photoshop. In 1997 I had a call from a publisher offering me two book covers but only on condition that I offer assurances that I would not work digitally. I was amused (someone had obviously been talking), but I could see his point. Photoshop at that stage still did not handle textures very well, and in the hands of someone who was not a very good artist to begin with, the work had this sort of plastic look to it that just screamed, "I was done in Photoshop." I had not intended to do the work digitally, I still worked almost exclusively in traditional media, but it irked me to have this condition imposed upon me. Such a decision should, I felt, be left to the artist. Why should the publisher care whether I did it digitally, traditionally, or with the tail of a cow while standing on my head so long as I turned in good art? Why couldn't book publishing follow the gaming industry's lead? I took the assignment, assured the publisher I would use traditional media and did the work in Photoshop. Since I didn't have to send in the original art, and since I was proficient enough digitally, there was no real way to tell whether I had done it by hand or not. I turned the work in. I needed to prove the point to myself, even if I couldn't share my victory with anyone. The publisher was pleased with it. I pocketed my check and went my merry way.

Importantly, I've discovered that the career choices I've made since then have validated that decision, and support my view that experience with a variety of media is the best way to insure that an artist can remain competitive in an industry that is rapidly changing. In 1999, I was offered an opportunity to work for Ensemble Studios in Dallas, Texas, one of the top game development companies, and I decided to say "yes." There were several motivating factors. For one thing, I had just spent eighteen years freelancing, which meant that I was alone in my house painting for most of that time — and Ensemble would provide the opportunity to work with a team of very gifted artists in a nice environment. Then there was the work I would be doing; for their game *Age of Mythology* I would be spending my time doing portraits of gods and goddesses, and as a Latin and Ancient History major, this was right down my alley. They would need me, at least at first, for my traditional skills. I was to be Senior Concept Artist. And lastly, and of equal importance, most of the artists there were working in 3D, and Ensemble promised me the opportunity to train in that field as well. What I learned enabled me to compete with the best in the world whether I was working traditionally or digitally. And I do that, in fact, every day.

I look around me and hear people arguing. Traditional art, is it dead? Does it have a future? Digital art, is it art? Is it cheating? Does it have value? Does it have validity as art? I am amused. Traditional art is not dead and never will be. It will be replaced by digital art in the field of illustration but not in the field of fine art. Why shouldn't this be the case? For most of us, the act of some person being able to take a white canvas and create an image of a time and place that exists only in his imagination is magic, pure and simple and more elegant than almost anything else mankind has been able to achieve. I can, of course, do the same image on a computer, but I recognize how special it is to do it by hand. There is something about being able to use pencils and paints and brushes to do it by hand that is part of the magic. It is my experience that computer artists who can do it on a computer but not by hand still generally hold the traditional masters in awe for that specialized ability. Further, "commercial value" is and always has been the key to respectability in the world of fine art. To the extent that money can be made from digital art, the world of fine art will shift its opinions to accept it.

Unfortunately for digital art, it has no originals. Prints are about the best it can do, and as much marketing as possible will be done with those, but galleries and museums and the fine art community need originals. They need them to hang, but mostly they need them to sell. Therefore,

totally independent of the magic of its creation and without regard to its value or validity as art, traditional art will continue to be championed by the fine art community because it can be owned, shown, sold, and resold. Digital art will not have the same respect in that community ever, not because it is not tremendous art, and not because it is created in some sly, underhanded way by machines, but because it does not have originals with which the fine art community can play its games. I suppose it is possible that the academic community might look at digital art purely for its value as art and come to the enlightened conclusion that its best examples might honestly merit the label of "fine art". I do not intend to hold my breath until that happens.

On the other hand, virtually all of the illustration we see from here on will be digital. Within the realm of illustration, traditional media will keep a small niche, but that is all. The publishing industry has never fostered it. In 1998 New York publishers were paying less for cover art than they were offering in 1982 when I started, and I assure you that the cost of living had gone up considerably in that time. It takes two weeks to a month, on average, to create a good cover painting using traditional media. On computer a good artist can cut that time in half or more. It is simple economics. An artist who takes a month to do a painting can only create 12 paydays each year. Given what New York pays for covers, not many traditional artists are going to be attracted to the work. This will please the publishers. They always wanted the paintings done faster, and they could care less how they are created so long as the work is good. The current situation should suit them just fine. Moreover, there are things that I can do on a computer that I cannot do by hand. Offset filters come to mind, and I am sure there are other things, like the undo button. How wonderful it is to be able to erase a mistake so easily and completely — but my point here is that the vast majority of the things are simply ways to enable me to do the same things I do traditionally, only more efficiently.

I have said for years that art is making decisions. Other artists will know exactly what I mean. When doing a drawing or painting, every movement we make involves a decision. How long shall this line be? At what angle? How wide will I make it? How dark shall it be? I need a color for this spot. What color shall it be? There are thousands of hues, tints, and shades. Which will I choose? Shall I blend it? Each decision eliminates a million other things I could have done instead. So long as I am exercising my skills in that regard, I am doing my job as an artist and what I am creating is art, worthy of the name. The fact that a new technology offers me a faster, easier means of doing it does not necessarily mean that I am doing something that is a cheat. I train every day to make better decisions and I study every day to broaden my base of knowledge so that I have more options to choose from in any given situation. That is the essence of being an artist. I intend to employ both media in my future. When I have the time to devote to doing my own art, it likely will be traditional and oriented toward fantasy. To the extent that I care to be employed by others, I will be able to work in such a wide variety of media that I will have a far easier time marketing my skills than had I not spent these years learning new media. Of course there are always those who hang a toilet seat on a blank canvas and call themselves artists, but they will burn in hell as liars. All worthy art flows from the decisions and judgment of the artist. Over time, as more and more great works of art are created on computer and impact our lives, and as our culture comes to a better understanding of how little difference there is between working digitally and traditionally, digital art will find a greater acceptance for the true art that it is.

Zeus *Magazine cover, © Microsoft 2002. Digital — Photoshop image based in part on scanned painted acrylic artwork*

David A. Cherry, past president of the Association of Science Fiction and Fantasy Artists, works as a 3D artist for Ensemble Studios helping create computer games such as Age of Mythology and Age of Empires. In the 1980's -1990's he did freelance illustration specializing in science fiction and fantasy. His work was collected in the art book *Imagination: the Art and Technique of David A. Cherry* (Donning, 1987). See www.davidcherryart.com

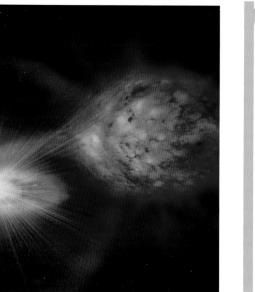

RS Ophiuchi *('RS' is part of the star's name). Commissioned by Particle Physics and Astronomy Research Council (PPARC) UK in April 2006, this digital (all Photoshop) image shows a recurrent nova in the white dwarf component of a binary star, the other component being a red giant. Pure Photoshop. It was NASA's Astronomy Picture of the Day online on July 26, 2006.*

OT all artists working in the genre of astronomical or space art are realists; some produce work that is impressionistic, expressionistic, abstract, symbolic or surreal. While no doubt many of these styles could be adapted to digital methods, in my opinion they are generally more suited to the application of paint to canvas or board. This is not the case for what I and others call "realistic" space art — art that strives to depict, in the most accurate way possible, non-terrestrial objects (animate or inanimate). Analogously, not all artists are content to stay with one technique throughout their lives; some constantly experiment. The fact is, most artists will use whatever tools are necessary to produce the result they want and will keep searching until they find the right tools to achieve their goal. The leading (and indeed, only) organization for space artists, the IAAA (International Association of Astronomical Artists: www.iaaa.org), of which I have the honor to be European Vice President, has members who use every technique imaginable. If accuracy and realism is desired, and adoption of new methods are not an impediment, then digital tools are often better suited to producing astronomical or space art than traditional methods.

I belong to the category of artists we would call experimentalist. This is because, having been required at school to use watercolors, which I found too "wishy-washy", I tried inks, poster colors, gouache, acrylics and oils before settling on the latter two mediums for actual paintings. I also experimented with Xeroxes and then photography, employing "derivative" techniques in the darkroom and using extreme-contrast film and print media, before moving to the computer in the late 1980s, with an Atari ST. Although it was many years before I was able to use my Apple Mac professionally, today almost all of my illustrative work is produced by this method, and generally I paint "traditionally" only when commissioned to do so (although I still enjoy this).

This is because I believe in using whatever tools are needed to do the job. To many people, one of the criteria for being an artist seems to be an ability to draw a straight line, or a perfect circle ("An artist — me? I can't even draw a straight line!" How often does one hear this said?) without mechanical aids. In the 19th century, John Ruskin certainly believed this, as his book *The Elements of Drawing* shows. However, it surely depends upon the type of artist one wishes to be; an abstract painter whose work consists of broad strokes or squiggles of colour is unlikely to be concerned about such matters. On the other hand, as soon as artists began to use linear perspective in order to create the illusion of volume and 3D space within a 2D frame — which dates back to the early Renaissance (Filippo Di Ser Brunellesco, 1377-1446, is usually credited with its first use in art) — various 'aids' began to come into use to assist in finding vanishing points and so on. Artists used rulers, a compass, a set square. Devices like the camera obscura were also used to enable more accurate depictions, and it is known that Vermeer was fascinated by lenses and made use of them in his paintings, as did van Eyck. Of course, it was not until the invention of the telescope, first used astronomically by Galileo Galilei in 1609, that we had any concept of celestial bodies as other worlds, perhaps like the Earth.

This brings us rather neatly to astronomical art and what is familiarly called "space art," which usually encompasses art that includes hardware (spacecraft, bases, rovers and other vehicles) and figures such as astronauts, while "astronomical art" is more likely to depict purely landscapes and/or objects and bodies in space, such as planets, moons, stars, galaxies, nebulae and so forth. For many years there really was only "astronomical illustration," because the only use for a depiction of the surface of another world was to enhance a book, whether factual or fiction. Interestingly, much of this early "space art" seems to have been three- rather then two-dimensional. The first instance of this was in *The Moon*, by Nasmyth and Carpenter, published in 1874. James

PIXELS WERE MADE FOR PLANETS
David A. Hardy

Jetting Galaxy *Illustration showing Jets of radiation emitted from the poles of a black hole at the galaxy's heart. Featured in Futures: 50 Years in Space with Patrick Moore (AAPPL UK/HarperCollins USA, 2004). Digital media: Terragen and Photoshop*

Nasmyth made plaster models of the Moon's surface — mountain peaks and craters — and photographed them against a black, starry background. Around 1920 Scriven Bolton used the same technique for illustrations in *The Illustrated London News*, while in France Lucien Rudaux was producing very realistic if quite painterly pictures, notably for his 1937 book *Sur Les Autres Mondes*. Because he was also an astronomer and often observed the limb, or edge, of the Moon, he knew that the mountains are actually eroded and rounded, virtually predicting the photographs brought back by Apollo astronauts.

The work of the American artist Chesley Bonestell (1888-1986) was not only the first artist to make the public really sit up and take notice of the potential in space exploration, through his series of paintings of Saturn in *Life* and *Colliers* magazines (1944, 1950) but his tight, "photographic" technique influenced many other space and science fiction artists who were inspired to achieve similarly realistic depictions (albeit based on their imagination). Trained as an architect, Bonestell often made models, both of vehicles and of landscapes, to assist his work, and even painted over photographs of these in oils, which no doubt accounts for some of his highly photographic illustrations.

The airbrush, originally intended for photographic retouching and therefore closely following photography, was one more step away from the traditional use of brushes and paints and toward the use of the computer for creating space art. By its very nature, the airbrush lent itself to the very smooth, finished, photographic techniques that are characteristic of science fiction and space art, which found their zenith with hyperrealism — a form of art almost indistinguishable from photographs, although usually produced at a very large size. Although Bonestell never used an airbrush — because his tight oil-painting technique, which involved stippling, made it unnecessary for him — it has become an invaluable tool for most of today's space artists, enabling those who work non-digitally to create smoothly gradated skies and atmosphere, glows around stars, nebulae, and for the subtle hazing of distance. The use of a computer can thus be seen as the logical next step in this process. Digital space art can be, and often is, very photographic.

To return to that straight line, there is no doubt at all that the computer makes it easy to draw one. More important, it makes it easy to draw circles, and therefore ellipses: how much easier it is now to produce an image of Saturn's rings, or the orbits of the Solar System. Imagine having to produce these, exactly symmetrically, of the same width and with no kinks or irregularities; yet this is what many of us had to do before the computer! The latest version of Photoshop (CS2) even has the ability to scale objects in perspective. The kind of training that Bonestell undertook seems hardly necessary today. An artist can still "draw and paint" in Photoshop — it's just a matter of pushing pixels around instead of paint — and other programs (e.g. Artmatic and ArtMaster) can also make it easy for almost anyone, even those with little or absolutely no artistic ability, to convert photographs or use other methods to produce what looks, to the untrained eye, like a piece of space art.

The term "computer generated" (hated by most artists) suggests that an image can be produced by the click of a button, but in my opinion the quality of what is produced depends upon the degree of input by the person using the computer. Space artists trace back their roots to the Hudson River School of artists of the 1880s, founded by Thomas Moran and Albert Bierstadt. They accompanied scientific expeditions to wild areas such as Yellowstone and Yosemite. These artists were even instrumental in the creation of national parks, because their often huge canvases enabled an awed public to see wonders that had previously seemed to exist only in fanciful stories. To them, it may as well have been another world.

Here may we find a parallel with today's artists who also seek new frontiers; in order to depict scenes of this type, whether on this or another world, it is necessary to do so with a fair degree of realism and accuracy. Space artists, and often science fiction artists, need to work out, for instance, how big a planet will look from one of its moons, e.g. Jupiter from Europa, and computer astronomy programs like *Starry Night* definitely make this easier. Later, artists will want to interpret these in their own, individual ways, and perhaps to introduce more philosophical or spiritual elements; but one cannot deny that in its original or "pure" form, there is an element of education in astronomical art.

The trend of the act of creation being taken over by a computer program is taken even further by 3D programs, which have essentially replaced the need to make physical models and use photography, such as Bonestell did. There are many of these, some (such as Strata 3D, Maya and ElectricImage) making it possible to "model" any object, such as a spaceship or vehicle, and rotate it in any desired direction, giving it realistic textures, reflections, and lighting. Digital techniques are ideal for producing realistic, even photographic, yet fantastic images of other worlds (and naturally this extends to animation and movies). It does of course take skill to learn and use 3D programs, but the best results will always be produced by those who have a solid background in traditional artistic (and even photographic) techniques, and do not merely let the computer do all the work

(next page) **Exploring Mars**
Illustration featured in Futures: 50 Years in Space *with Patrick Moore (AAPPL UK/HarperCollins USA, 2004). Digital media: Terragen, Poser and Photoshop*

for them. Other 3D programs concentrate on landscapes (for instance Bryce, Terragen, vue d'Esprit, MojoWorld), and again, these can allow even a novice to produce a scene quickly, be it on the Earth or another world, which looks very realistic and even spectacular; yet in other hands these can be valuable tools for producing substantive artistic works that are clearly departures from the applications that made them possible.

A controversy is running amongst artists and art "experts": can the output of a computer really be considered to be "fine art," or is it limited to illustration? If it is difficult for the lay public to know, simply by looking at a piece, how much is the work of the artist and how much was the result of a series of zeros and ones, should that matter? The old adage of "I don't know much about Art, but I know what I like" still holds good today, and the message carries equal significance for the creator, for whom there exists a wide range of artistic media to choose from. Today the Artist's repertoire of tools has today expanded from hand-held aids and photography, or models and airbrushes, to encompass the computer. For artists concerned with realistic portrayals of fictional or non-fictional non-terrestrial objects and landscapes, where the accuracy in their depictions are of paramount importance, the benefits and advantages of using digital tools cannot be disputed, nor should they be ignored, because it is surely the end-product, not the means of its production, which forms a work of art.

David A. Hardy, European Vice President of the International Association of Astronomical Artists (IAAA), and recipient of its Lucien Rudaux Award, may be the longest-established space artist, having illustrated his first book (for Patrick Moore) in 1954 at the age of 18. As well as painting, he now works digitally on a Mac, and has written and illustrated seven of his own books (and a novel) as well as working for TV, video and movies. His art book *Hardyware: The Art of David A. Hardy* was published 2001. See www.astroart.org.

still paint. What's more I'm a better painter now than I used to be — and I think I can go on improving. I owe this in part to new freedoms suggested by engagement with "the digital." I sell my paintings, and I occasionally produce a painting for a publisher client. Some of my paintings are pretty damn good, I think, and some are forgettable. I also create illustrations for publishers entirely on the Mac. Some of these I'm extremely pleased with and some less so. The world of illustration I inhabit seems to me to be a far more interesting and diverse place than it was when I left art college back in 1972. It's also a more challenging and frustrating place and nothing is easy any more.

For one thing, an artist has to be far more proactive than ever before under this dynamic new digital régime. I have tried to take the wide, all-embracing view, not always easy, as opposed to the narrow regard of the "all-is-now-changed" digital brigade and the "if-it's-virtual-it's-not-art" brigade. It strikes me as absurd to believe that because a damn clever new bunch of kit has arrived then illustrators are going to stop using paint. It simply does not follow — I cite myself as a case in point — an illustrator who invested in the gear required to "go digital" almost 10 years ago, who uses that gear on a daily basis but at the same time paints in acrylics. As far as my own experience has proved, the two approaches can sit in perfectly happy union with each other, the one feeding helpfully into the other and back again. At the same time, the big difference it has made is that the artist, illustrator — come to that the composer, musician, film maker — each now has a very powerful additional creative tool to add to the arsenal. And why stop there?… the bank manager, the military man, draughtsman, architect, doctor — is there any occupation left that has not felt the impact of this new technology at some level? And found that pressure to adapt (and adopt) practically impossible to ignore? It is not a matter of "if," it is merely a matter of "when." So Jim Burns bought the kit, he thought ahead … but as far his *modus operandi* is concerned, all the computer represents in Jim Burns' studio is a fantastically capable tool — sometimes a means to an end, sometimes an end in itself.

Can anyone deny that it is a fantastically capable tool? For the creative person and perhaps in particular the artist/illustrator, the fruits of digital technology are not only transparently "visible," but beguiling. Digitization is everywhere now, in the printed form, television, film — and despite my just referring to its visibility, as the technology becomes ever more powerful, it paradoxically becomes increasingly less visible as it becomes more convincing. To identify a piece of work as a CGI (computer-generated image) is becoming more an intellectual process than one of clear visual identification. Viewers think "That simply cannot be … therefore it must be CGI." The natural media software now available can muddy the field still further. It's simply not obvious any more that something is an oil painting or a watercolor — except perhaps to the most highly discriminating eye. For an imaginative, creative person such a tool is seductive in the extreme — except perhaps to the most diehard conservatives — although I would argue from my own experience that to deny oneself the tool is to shortchange oneself with regards to the possibility of developing one's "traditional" painting skills. Why deliberately strive to narrow one's options simply out of a dislike for technology — which many artists feel has no place in their studio?

Yet, there is historical precedence for rejecting whatever is new and unfamiliar. I suspect that something not dissimilar happened in the 19th century with the invention of photography. When those early, blurry images of the likes of Nièpce and Fox Talbot were first magicked into existence around the 1840s — I imagine that one whole bunch of artists saw huge opportunity, whilst another bunch saw nothing but the devil's tool. It was ever thus with change and so it is with all things digital. Knowing that, is it not a rather silly and pointless exercise to take a stand against these changes — or even to simply "have nothing to do with them"? Shortsighted in the extreme.

The Nano Flower *Cover for the novel by Peter F. Hamilton for Pan/ Macmillan (UK), 1998. Digital (Photoshop)*

THE ART OF FENCE-SITTING

Jim Burns

When photography came along — did that mean the death of art? Or even the death of those styles of art that photography was particularly well-placed to usurp, such as the portrait? Most emphatically not. But it did mean that artists had to take note and the whole direction art took was inevitably changed forever. It's intriguing to try and speculate on the direction art might have taken had photography not emerged into the world. It perhaps displaced a huge part of a whole tradition of a certain kind of figurative expression but I would argue that consequently the actual materials that painters used were suddenly seen to have whole new potential and vitality and I rather doubt that the history of late 19th century and certainly 20th century art would have followed the same hyperbolic series of quirky, manic, schizophrenic, angry, eccentric or political manifestations that it did, had photography not entered into the dialogue of artistic expression.

There are those who will disagree with this assessment, believing the Impressionists to be the first phase of the Death of Art. I can't go along with this at all. Nothing was killed off by photography other than stale tradition, and neither will CGI mean the death of anything other than that which, perhaps, is analogously stale, today. Don't imagine that illustrators and artists are going to deny themselves the real, old-as-humanity, hands-on, tactile, direct, olfactory experience of creating "non-virtual art." But do accept that the seductive Mac — just like the essential Nikon before it and alongside it — can sit in perfectly accommodating harmony with the traditional gear, the brushes, pencils, paper and canvas (and the airbrush, come to that, around which for a little while back in the 70s and 80s another little bit of anti-progressive posturing revolved).

Proactively adapting to change can also affect an artist's reputation — another factor that interferes with the goal of keeping my options open. A couple of times now I've been flatteringly labeled "a legend" in certain articles. This is rather humbling and depressing, at the same time! I suspect I'm regarded by some as being one of those practitioners solely of the painted form, but while the truth is that I ventured enthusiastically into the Brave New World of digital art with a particular, somewhat half-baked agenda as to what to do with this new tool, that doesn't mean I want to be defined by my medium. It seemed to me, back then, that the advent of digital methods spelt a quantum change in my field of endeavor and that it would be singularly ostrich-like to ignore it. I quite like nifty gadgets and had had some engagement with computers — mostly through the work I did with the pioneering Sir Clive Sinclair, helping to promote his early ZX81 and Spectrum home computers. I found myself free to play with some very early incarnations of those limited little machines, and soon came the quantum leap into the world of the Amiga, bought for my kids really . . . but suggestive to me of the leaps and bounds this technology was obviously taking. What I do not find myself free to do, however, is to define myself based on that flexibility. After learning I could digitally emulate my own painted style of work (ultimately to streamline the whole process of producing illustrations for my clutch of clients out there in the world of publishing), I find I cannot re-position myself publicly as an artist "with choices." Audiences want to believe that despite the incorporation of new skills, I am the same old painter. For a while I did that — and sometimes people were fooled into imagining that something totally digitally created was in fact a painting., but deception like that is totally dissatisfying, and a dead end for me, creatively speaking.

Recently I received an email from a fellow artist, someone who's been working in this field almost as many years as I have, who has never really taken to the idea of the computer as a fabulously useful tool. He was a little outraged by the fact that some magazine article had suggested that a painted piece of work of mine was described as digitally-created. He maintains his belief in the importance of the media associated with any painting being accurately defined, and that as artists we have a vested interest in ensuring that the provenance of our work is correctly recorded.

Well, of course he's right about that as far as the historical record is concerned — but it gives me a little *frisson* of amusement that these minor confusions appear — given my original agenda of trying to emulate digitally what I was previously creating in paint! There was a tone to his email, however, which seemed to suggest that he felt that an illustration can only be "good," is somehow only "valid," as art if it's a traditional painting, which, in my opinion, is not the case.

What I perhaps hadn't anticipated was the way in which the computer, and Photoshop in particular, was to change my whole way of working — and still does to this day. My own digital skills are limited and I rarely step outside the world of Photoshop. I have no 3D skills at all and I've never tried natural media programs like Painter. However, the process of creating large acrylic paintings has totally changed and the evolution of these pieces of work is now a far more interesting process than it used to be. Composing digitally has enabled me to ward off the onset of staleness or, perhaps boredom with the genre with which I'm most connected — namely science fiction. The best way I can sum up the feeling I get from being able to go from canvas to Mac and back again on a particular commission is that it gives me a sense of new freedom and powerfully expanded potential.

What presents the greatest challenge, however, is that digitally created art has made it more difficult to discern the good art from the bad, and as a result, changed the relationship between freelance commercial artists and their clients. Judging whether a piece of work is of high-quality or simply mediocre, I would argue, was once the province of Art Directors, whose job it was (among other things) to decide what was good art, on a client's behalf. This determination has

(left) **Bios** *Cover for the novel by Charles Wilson, for Tor Books (1st ed) 1999. Acrylics, 20" x 24".*

been made immensely difficult by shifting the responsibility of deciding to consumers, and by the sheer cleverness of the software. With minimal artistic skills it's possible for almost anyone to produce a very passable, superficially effective piece of work for, say a bookjacket. And why not? The way the image is regarded by the client, whether it's in paint or pixel, has everything to do with how well that image works to sell the client's product — that alone qualifies the art as "good" — and almost nothing to do with an Art Director's tastes. The bottom line for publishers is their budget; good art is art that sells the product. Young, creative, hungry, energetic folk come out of art college, where traditional drawing and painting skills are effectively sidelined by "sexy" media-savvy CGI training, and they're looking for jobs. They're coming armed with a whole bunch of scarily competent digital skills, skills often superior to those who are hiring them. Publishers interested in the bottom line put them on a salary, sit them in front of some neat kit, show them the stock art libraries and royalty-free art and say "give me an image that will sell…." I have absolutely no gripe with this. I understand the way this works. It was inevitable the moment digitally created art stepped beyond a certain threshold of sophistication and competence.

Changing criteria and responsibility for assessing quality have affected artists' judgments and attitudes, as well. I rather dislike the idea of the artist as *prima donna*, so it's troubling that so many artists working freelance in the field of publishing as commercial artists or illustrators have attitudes toward their own art not so very different from those of high-end, so-called fine artists. Many find it wearisome when I trot out the adage "He who pays the piper calls the tune" but it's the philosophy I've always maintained in my relationship with Art Directors, and on the whole it's served me well. I refuse to adopt an overly high-falutin' attitude to my own place in the artistic scheme-of-things, but many old pros seem to have been outraged by the way that they have been given, in effect, the old heave-ho by long-standing clients. Something must be to blame, they think, and the computer makes a fine villain. This kind of thinking is defeatist and dreary. Do we imagine that commercial artists are alone in this, in the face of a rapidly changing world? *Time to get real.*

At the end of the day I'm very happy to remain perched on the fence I've built. It's not easy to straddle, when one side of the fence, at one time or another, seems to be so much more definitely green than the other (depending on your mood, or who is the "piper"). The use of digital tools is indisputably valuable and exciting but that does not mean that I abandon paint. As a fence-sitter I know I risk a bumful of splinters — the dismay of collectors, the derision of fellow painters, the frustration of those who would prefer to label me as painter or pixel-manipulator. But the view from both sides of the fence is intriguing, and as people take up opposing philosophies. I find it impossible to see the advent of digital tools as either a wholly good thing or a bad thing. It's simply a new thing and it's a question of whether an artist wants to employ the *new* thing or not.

(top) **Threlxelpia's Little Sister**
Cover for Heavy Metal *magazine,*
2003. Acrylics, 36" x 24"

Jim Burns graduated from London's St Martin's School of Art in 1972 and has been working as a professional science fiction and fantasy illustrator ever since. Most of his output has been for the publishing industry, but he has also produced pre-production work for film. He has won a number of awards including the prestigious Hugo Award — three times. His third art book, *Imago*, was published 2006. He lives in Wiltshire in the U.K.

Flaubert asserts that an artist's only possible camaraderie can be with other artists, writing "Mankind hates us: we serve none of its purposes; and we hate it because it injures us. So let us love one another in Art, as mystics love one another in God."

My Case for Retributive Action
cover for Weird Tales #324, 2001 illustrating the lead story by Thomas Ligotti. - 90% traditional watercolor and 10% digital

THAT darling of fate, the artist, is thus tempted to suppose that his aesthetical formulations are definitive. At the drop of a hat he will pontificate about methodology. As far as he is concerned only the worthy — fellow artists — will comprehend these doctrines. The corrupt and the unenlightened will be stupefied. More than anything else these assumptions explain why the "digital versus non-digital" controversy continues on its wobbly way. By peeking behind the polemical capework it becomes clear that this dispute has nothing to do with technology or morality or art. Rather, it has everything to do with the politics of a created image and how digital apologists clash with anti-digitalists, thus creating a quibble of Brobdingnagian proportions.

Some might disagree, but I feel that artwork is not legitimatized through use of paint or pencil or other traditional graphic arts materials. Comparisons of methods are instructive but are not a yardstick of merit. As for computer technology … well, digital devices are routinely utilized by artisans and ordinary mortals. It is only a technology, after all. What reasonable person rants about the legitimacy of, say, a car engine? The automotive engine is only a contraption, a feat of engineering equipped with pistons and a crankshaft and valves. Engines are blameless. And yet as the Automotive Age dawned, blacksmiths and horse-and-buggy manufacturers condemned this apparatus because it represented a *mechanical alternative to the Power of the Horse*!

Progress equals displacement. The grumbling of blacksmiths and ostlers; vaudevillians griping about nickelodeons; academic painters grumping about the onslaught of photographers — and now the groaning of anti-digitalist daubers. It all amounts to the same thing: a foghorn moan always emanates from those who will be displaced. There is no point in blaming the gadgetry, and there is no point in blaming the *Modern Age* because every era is modern, at least temporarily.

A few years ago I became embroiled in this vibrant if ill-considered controversy. It started with a long-distance phone call from a friend — a sunny utopian fellow — who invited me to join the online illustrators group he had founded. Out of respect I acceded, but I had misgivings. Most of the 25 participants were unknown to me. Only a few knew or cared about my work. Too, I doubted that *collegial politesse* could weather the storms and amperages generated by a coalition of artistic temperaments. As far as I was concerned a flashpoint was inevitable; I felt that an online forum of 25 practitioners could not do otherwise than degenerate into a *mêlée*.

My chief disinclination. however, was that I was not prepared to come out of the digital closet. I was unwilling to declare that my technical orientations were not entirely traditional. This reluctance was not shame-based. Simply put, I am not a controversialist. This is largely due to my idiosyncratic relationship to illustration. Assignments tend to paralyze me, at least initially. Like the professor in Lampedusa's story "The Professor and The Mermaid," I'm obliged to wait — "tense and alert" — for the approach of my dæmonion, whose muse-like promptings I follow. Furthermore, my "artistic point of view" (if that's what it is) is nothing more than a wordless flux of visual impressions. In short, I had no formulated theories that I could present. Hence, my wish to sidestep this controversy.

Then, by mischance, someone in the forum posed a question about scanning resolutions. My unguarded, supportive response included hints about my digital experiments ("… my watercolors, with about 10% digital enhancement, constitute about 90% of my dust jackets."). Swiftly, an *anti-digitalist* sniper had me in his sights. I was a pro-digitalist target because my perfidious methods violated his lockstep doctrines. I quote from the sniper's very public denouncement:

" … you have made GREAT pains to *emphasize your 'digital-ness' in your illustration work*

THE DIGITAL MOMENT: DIGITAL POLITICS
Jason Hollander

… you should read what Arkham House says about your DRAGONFLY cover painting. It leads me to suspect that more than 10 percent was digital manipulation of the watercolor base…. "

This demolished my stance as a non-controversialist. In the eyes of the sniper and a few others, I was an apostate, one who renounced hand-wrought artwork, a turncoat who disavowed craftsmanship and draftsmanship. Another friend in the group, a devout pen-and-inker, took exception to the assault on my digital prerogative. He meant well, but the digital stake was driven more deeply into my torso when he presented his defense:

> " … I have an artist friend, whom we all know and love, who produces great work with the computer. In fact, the *computer* has been a Godsend to him … now with his *computer skills* he has taken his talents to new levels …."

In a single paragraph my beef-witted advocate went on to invoke the word "computer" twelve times — an incantatory feat. Linked thusly, I felt myself morphing into a poster-boy for the handless and the fingerless and all whose reliance on computers are deemed prosthetic. One or two representatives from the pro-digitalist faction courted me. At the same time, I continued to be vilified by anti-digitalists. Collegial politesse evaporated from this forum … this so-called "online community" … this *squalid digital tenement* where my tattered reputation flapped wildly and dirtily in the wind generated by defenders and detractors.

"The politics of a created image got me into this mess," I heard myself mutter. To reverse the anathematic tide, a spirited defense was essential. Accordingly, I formulated a jargon-laden response. This response, I felt, would confound my detractors and stupefy the unenlightened. In the manner of *Oz the Magnificent* I proclaimed:

> " … for interior illustrations I mostly use computers to digitally optimize line-artwork (pen-and-ink or stipple). With digital enhancement, the interstices of cross-hatching are more likely to be preserved; and heavily stippled areas are less likely to fuse. This process is the line-art equivalent of extending dynamic range in a grayscale image (i.e., details in dark and shadow areas)."

For good measure I included a sop to the anti-digitalists:

> " … the [Photoshop] software has an assortment of digital brushes. To operate these tools you flex your fingers and wrist; you manually adjust the virtual brush and the pressure and the flow, except that a mouse is used. The brush tools are virtual, but the manipulations are physical. To this extent, the 'brushwork' — no other terminology is appropriate — is similar (though not the same) to any Winsor-Newtonically paint-laden stroke wielded by our non-digital *confreres*. Best of all: no brushes to clean!"

No one caught up in this imbroglio dared to disagree with my pronouncements. To show my nobility of spirit I concluded with a Paean to Art:

> " … it behooves some of us to understand that there are no borders and no border patrols on the pathways to the imagination. Artists crave imaginative release. They

(right) **Attack of the Jazz Giants**
Cover for the novel by Gregory Frost,
Published by Golden Gryphon Press,
2005 - all digital

need to soar. The aethers of faery billow more easily for those who can reconcile the (perceived) polarities of technical liberation and technical constraint. At the end of the day all that matters is beauty…."

eauty. Every era has a particular concept of what this means. Beauty is a very fluid, very abstract notion — but the *competitive instinct* is neither abstract nor fluid. The *competitive instinct* is common to all cultures and eras, and marks every arena in the arts.

The commercial art continuum is no exception. Before Wozniak, Jobs and Gates refined the technologies that rocked the graphic arts world, commercial artists (and other artists) routinely utilized Letraset, opaque projectors and other labor-saving tools of the trade. At the tail-end of this bygone era I vied for and won a position as graphic designer for a company whose products included driveway coatings and burial vault sealant. Properly suited, freshly coiffed and newly hired, I remember installing my trusty Artograph DB300 opaque projector in the tiny unventilated office assigned to me. A co-worker, whose nephew made an unsuccessful bid for this same job, wandered in. In a nostrily way he complained that the projector gave me an "unfair advantage" and in a way this was true. It was unfair that I had made myself more hireable by having better samples in my portfolio. It was unfair that my career focus was beadier and that my production strategies included an Artograph. And it is supremely unfair that some artists — including myself — have conceptual or imaginative limitations, while other artists soar in these aery spheres; but what can any of us do about this kind of inequality?

Yes, it is at least partially true that mediocre technique can be camouflaged by digital methods, but digital devices can't redeem an uninspired concept. So methods and technologies are not the point. First and foremost a *developed sensibility* is what matters. A *heightened sensibility* is the most crucial tool-of-the-trade. It is also the *mechanism* that is most frequently overlooked, and possibly the least valued. Ultimately, it is with this kind of "mechanism" that I am chiefly concerned. Like a nimbus, sensibility hovers over the heads of people in the arts. And woe to those who do not seek to fit their head to this lustrous crown.

Conversely, our yearning for beauty will not be satisfied by the outpourings of a blunted mercantile sensibility. In a commercialized market, where the work of many genre illustrators merge into one huge and unaffecting tapestry, it becomes apparent that the most compelling illustrations are not necessarily created by the kind of traditional artist whose renderings are icily precise. Polished technique is well and good, but a perfectly rendered image — digital or nondigital — is very nearly an affront to the human spirit. This is because perfection, at some level, carries a veiled criticism of human limitation. For this reason photographically-based illustrations and computer-generated illustrations are tinctured with troubling associations.

No one feels this more acutely than the kind of traditional artist whose insecurities take the form of competitive reckonings, who disallows current technologies, preferring technologies that are merely less current. The sovereign impetus is aggression, to punish trespassers on the open range of art, which is a delimited frontier. More than anything else this might account for the resentments engendered by the digital moment.

What is the ultimate measure of artistic validity? Levels of skill? Sensibility? Methodology? Art will not be defined by the doctrines of our particular moment. The doctrines of today only point to competitive bohemias where artwork is ratified by nosecount. A broader reckoning takes into consideration the private nature of Art, the singularity of the artist, which is perhaps suggested by the old Gallic expression, *la patte*, meaning the artist's touch, his personal style, his "paw" … like the paw-print of an animal. This seems to refer to a characteristic style of paint application, but it also hints at flaws or technical infelicities that proclaim the fallible humanity — and the mortal actuality — of the artist, who abides in his creations.

It is instructive to take a backwards glance, from the perspective of eras unencumbered by doctrines and critical vocabularies. In the western edges of the Massif Central and the northern slopes of the Pyrenees there are more than a hundred limestone caves, the most renowned of which is Lascaux. Within these caves are animal and anthropomorphic representations that were created over 15,000 years ago. These images all but vibrate with life, with the exuberant spirit of the dauber. The brushwork is expressive, imprecise, antic. The artwork is imbued with powerful sacramental magicks that were deeply felt, whose essence continues to resonate through the procession of centuries. Through the Crystal of Time we glimpse the pageantry of a vanished world, and in the glint of its facets we detect our own vanishing moment, the dearness of all that is frail and perishable. *Sunt lacrimae rerum; et mentem mortalia tangunt.* "There are tears in things, and all things doomed to die touch the heart."

Divinations of the Deep
*Dustjacket illustration for the book
by Matt Cardin, for Ash-Tree Press,
2003. All digital*

In seventh grade **Jason Van Hollander** painted a watercolor of dead flowers and flunked art class. Undaunted, he followed his misshapen muse and eventually won the International Horror Guild Award and two World Fantasy Awards. Though known primarily for illustration, Jason's book of story collaborations with Darrell Schweitzer was nominated for a World Fantasy Award. See www.jasonvanhollander.com

Mr. Hands *Cover for* Cemetery Dance *magazine, Issue #32. Digital media, 1999*

WHILE it is true that a computer is merely a heartless contraption containing nothing but ones and zeros, an artist will find within it a means to spontaneity and wonder. Webster's dictionary defines the word *pixilated* as "eccentric or mentally disordered, whimsical or prankish." This meaning comes from a time when it was thought that people who suffered from such inconvenient behavior were beset by pixies. A *pixel* is the smallest element of an image as seen on-screen. The word *pixelated* means an image in which the pixels are large enough to be seen clearly by the naked eye. What is a pixie but a fairy, a mote in a beam of light, a source of inspiration for the imagination? So, the pixel, too, is a bit of light with a lot of possibility. Although the computer was brought into existence to relieve us of the task of processing the least inspirational of data, we may now employ it to help us create magic, wonder and, yes, even art.

Among artists today there are those who feel that the computer is a lifeless mechanism and no more. They believe that working exclusively in a digital medium is an exercise in futility and that the soul of an artist could never be revealed by such effort. I have heard it argued that without the physical act of painting, there is too little feeling involved in the production of art for the work to be of value — but isn't an idle brush lifeless as well? It is the artist who brings the brush (and the computer) to life. In a world that is more fully documented and explained by science every day, the human imagination still knows no bounds.

However, there are also those working with digital media who excel at presenting their ideas with distinctive style and compelling originality. I believe the difference is whether the artist took the path of least resistance — computers provide a lot of these — or went the extra mile to make the work his or her own. I agree that much digitally produced art looks mechanical and provides me with little sense of the creators. Since many digital artists use the same tools, I often have difficulty distinguishing one artist's work from another's. But then, there are amateurs in all creative pursuits.

My opinion results from being largely a traditional painter, one who works with paint and brushes. I have been a freelance illustrator for over twenty years, primarily creating book cover illustrations for genre publications: science fiction, fantasy and horror. I know what goes into the development of distinctive style and compelling originality in traditional painting. I know that the experience of working with paint and brushes is a very tactile one and that over time there is much emotion surrounding the discovery involved in learning to work with a medium like paint. I also know that, inevitably, the limitations of the medium and tools — mostly brushes — used to push it around, the patience of the artist using them, as well as his or her emotional make-up, affects the development of an artist's technique.

The artist makes decisions, perhaps subconsciously much of the time, that affect the look of his or her individual works and ultimately helps to provide a style that can be seen in the overall body of the artist's work. The artist makes discoveries in this process as well. Mistakes, experiments, and exploration of new methods and media create opportunity for these discoveries. What an artist embraces or rejects sets the pace of his or her artistic innovation.

Moreover, the importance of discovery in art is not limited to the years an artist spends learning and developing technique. Throughout a career in art, an artist travels a path of self-discovery, one that is revealing to his or her audience. This level of communication often transcends the subject matter of a given piece and provides a glimpse of the artist's psyche. This is one of the most valu-

PIXELATED OR PIXILATED
Alan M. Clark

able aspects of visual art. The process of mastering the craft of painting is so highly charged with emotion that it becomes a part of and is expressed by the artwork itself.

"Humanity," the artwork shouts, and we listen. Sometimes we are comforted and realize we are not alone in our experiences. At other times our assumptions about the world around us and our place in it are challenged. This is a singular and unbounded form of communication about the human experience. But each artist must find his or her own voice for expressing this *humanity* if his or her work is going to communicate on this level.

For me, discovery is the key. Work that is contrived — that is, work that contains no accidents and in no way surprised the artist in its making — will always come off as a device. To explain something of my artistic process, here's a revised excerpt from my art book, *The Paint in My Blood*:

> *I discover a portion of nearly everything I paint while producing it. I pack the process of developing an image with as much opportunity for discovery as I can. While working up an idea, I distract myself to promote free association and automatism. I scribble when sketching and explore any line that suggests a new and interesting direction. In painting I use what I call "controlled accidents" and "forced hallucination."*

> *"Controlled accidents" is my term for spontaneous image generating techniques I use to help me discover subject matter. They involve pushing paint around on my painting surface — usually a smooth primed hardboard — with all kinds of odd things such as rags, plastic sheeting, tin foil, stiff acetate, rollers and stiff boards — I even blow the paint around on a surface with my vacuum cleaner hose on exhaust. The results are suggestions of texture, shapes and contrasts — at times almost photographic in their range of values.*

> *Artists have explored "found imagery" throughout history. Da Vinci referred to the discovery of pictures in a stained surface. Toward this goal, the surrealists developed such techniques as* parsemage, *which used ground pastels or charcoal and water to stain a surface,* sfumage, *a candle flame used to apply carbon to paper in suggestive ghostly shapes, and* decalcomania, *the bending and warping of images in wet paint as they are transferred from one surface to another. Rorschach ink blots are a well known decalcomania technique.*

> *"Forced hallucination" is my term for finding potential subject matter within the intriguing, but often nondescript images generated by these unorthodox painting methods. Just as one might see faces in wood grain or animal shapes in clouds and rock formations, I find images in the paint. I think of it as something like an archeological dig: There are vague outlines of structures covered in jungle or buried just beneath desert sands, waiting to be unearthed. It is exciting.*

> *Using highlights and shadows, and adding color where needed, I bring what I see to life on my painting surface. First I see it, then I capitalize on it, and finally homogenize it into a composition. The parts of the controlled accident that do not work are replaced with contrived material. This is where the "found imagery," which is essentially meaningless on its own, is given context. The forced hallucination is often so elaborate that I must be accomplished enough with the use of my imagination and my brush techniques to match its rich detail.*

> *There are times when an entire painting is generated using these techniques. Other times I might start with a sketch, but large parts of the whole are undeveloped. I have some idea what controlled accident techniques to use to complete the composition in those areas, but I do not know in advance just exactly what the results will be.*

Whether I am using these techniques to help develop a focal point or create middle or background subject matter for my painting, the process brings into my work the element of chance, an aspect that I would be hard pressed to achieve by careful planning. The unpredictable element of chance in the world, in life, is what keeps me fascinated. The excitement of discovery in this painting process spurs me to experiment again and again and to continually produce new work.

Helltracks *Cover art for the novel by William F. Nolan published by Cemetary Dance Publications 2006 Digital media*

(detail) **Stickmen** *Appeared as an illustration for* The Devils of Tuckahoe Gorge *by Stephen Mark Rainey in* Dark Discoveries *magazine, Summer 2006, Issue Number 8. Digital image (Photoshop) based on scanned natural image.*

It can be seen from this except that my process is eccentric. Some might consider it mentally disordered, whimsical or prankish. Perhaps *pixilated* is a good term to describe it. Whatever the case, my process did not immediately mix well with the disciplines necessary to learn how to employ the computer. Part of the reason for this was that the computers I had access to were slow to process information, and the means for storage of that information was limited. Files had to be small, so the images I was able to create were rather pixelated. At the same time, I was too pixilated (beset by pixies?) to see the possibilities digital painting offered at the time and so did not reconsider working with the computer for many years.

However, as computer technology grew, so did my ability to see and exploit its potential. First, I learned to document my work using the computer and to store the images and prepare them effectively for commercial printers. Since I am an illustrator producing work for printed products, this was invaluable. My use of the computer to prepare my work for publication was a boon to my business. Still, I was not *painting* in the computer. If I wanted to work with controlled accidents in the computer, I had to use the "textures" provided in the various art and image programs available (other people's accidents — accidents preprogrammed and therefore not accidents at all) or scan and import my own. If I was going to do the latter, however, why not just develop those accidents with paint since I had much better facility with a brush than a mouse or digital tablet and stylus? I found I could scan *objects*, essentially making a digital photograph with my scanner. In the textures of these natural objects I found something akin to my controlled accidents, something I could manipulate much the way I did the images I found in the paint. I could discover images, then alter, cut and paste them with photographs of landscapes and interiors to create startling compositions.

An example of the process is the piece titled *Stickmen*. I did not set out to create this work, but found myself working on it until it reached its present completed state. A friend sent me a worm-eaten stick through the mail that looked quite a bit like a headless human form. I decided to scan the stick and make a head for it and send the image to my friend so he could see it. I opened the scan of the stick in Adobe Photoshop, borrowed texture from the body of the stick, an area that contained two holes like eyes, and built that into a head, adding highlights and shadows to create a nose and mouth, then placed it on the body where it belonged. Then I realized that if I turned the stick over, I could scan it again and have another stickman body. I used the same borrowed texture I used to create the first face to create another head, but this time, I flipped it over and built a different nose and mouth. Using smaller versions of the stick image as hands, I completed the two figures. Now I had stickman companions and decided I should cut them out (digitally) and place them in an appropriate environment. I found a picture I had taken in the forest at the Oregon coast and placed the figures in it as if they were walking through the trees. I changed the color balance on the cutout stick figures to make them appear to be illuminated by the same ambient light as the trees in the photo. Since the forest scene was backlit, I limned the figures with new highlights to give them the most natural appearance.

Using the technique that is akin to "controlled accidents" I have been able to find a route to discovery, to spontaneity and wonder within a digital medium. The element of chance I so valued to help inform and provide voice for my artwork was there all along. I had but to think less rigidly about the computer and suddenly the pixel was pixie. Does this mean that I will only work in the computer now? No — I love working with paint and brushes. There are aspects of my traditional painting that cannot be achieved without working in the physical world, but that does not diminish in any way what the computer can do for me.

Today I remain pixilated as well as pixelated.

Alan M. Clark is most known for his illustrations for fiction, non-fiction, textbooks, young adult and children's books. His awards include the World Fantasy Award and four Chesley Awards. As a writer, he has had his short fiction, his nonfiction and three novels published. Also see www.alanmclark.com

(detail) **Temeraire** *Digital media. Book cover for* His Majesty's Dragon, *by Naomi Novik, Science Fiction Book Club Edition 2006.*

I am often asked if digital art can rightly be called Art. Many people expect Art — and, specifically illustration art — to be a tangible thing, a singular object that can be collected and held, traded like a commodity, sold or resold, or simply hung and enjoyed. Regardless of what form the image takes on the book or the product, which is a function of marketing objectives, the original artwork is assumed to be the single best version of that image, superior to the printed cover or art book reproduction. I say they are confusing Art with the material object itself, the definition of which has been made difficult by the intrusion of computers into what was previously one of the last bastions of old-style craftsmanship.

Each of the Arts has, since the time of electricity, been associated with a medium, or type of media, which enables an audience to appreciate the work — as a "work of art" — without being present at its inception. With music, it was a record — an electronic recording on a circular vinyl disk. With dance, plays — the performing arts — there was film, then tape, and now CDs and DVDs. With visual arts there was a painting in oil or watercolor, pastels or acrylic, and so on. A sculptor chooses his stone or block of wood, and the final work is documented in a photograph or a reproduction on paper. The point is that, according to the *Merriam Webster* dictionary, *media* is something in a middle position — a go-between, an intermediary step. It is a means of effecting or conveying something; a channel or system of communication, information or entertainment; a mode of artistic expression or communication that enables viewing of an object at a distance … whether in time or space.

What separates Art from non-Art is not the original medium, but whether or not the media chosen for communicating the artist's vision does that successfully, and in a way that enables their audience to appreciate the work. Good art gives you a glimpse into the inner workings of the artist's mind and elicits a response from the audience, regardless of the media chosen. The art reveals things you might not have seen or thought on your own. It conveys an idea or evokes an emotion. It tells a story or expresses an opinion. Painting and drawing, sculpture, dance, theater, movie-making, and literature are not "great art" because of their medium, but rather are great art because the ideas they express have achieved a level of aesthetic quality, and demonstrate a level of expertise sufficient to encourage, inspire, and influence those few who may strive to emulate it. At the same time the art manage to bring pleasure to everyone else. This is a big idea. The dancer, the musician, the artist … becomes an Artist (capital A) when their work inspires others to follow, when it draws the viewers or listeners in and encourages them to return to the work again and again.

Without some visceral, emotional, psychological affect, no print of a great painting, no recording of a brilliant symphony, no televised play, nor almost any copy of any kind of movie is going to be valued very highly. Photos of Rembrandt's *Night Watch* impress because of the power of the image. Photos of Frank Lloyd Wright's *Falling Water* move you because it is stunning architecture. Again, what makes any work of art outstanding is not the board it was painted on or the type of paint that was used, or even the fact that it was ON a board at all, and made of paint. What is important is the message it gets across, and if there is no meaning for the viewer, then the work has "failed" as art.

The future may well hold aesthetic pleasures derived from digital media impossible for us to describe. Historically, we have revered original oil paintings because (among other reasons) in such works it is possible to see the hand of the creator. You can peer closely and analyze the layers, see the brush strokes, step back and admire the whole, then lean in again for another detailed discovery. For that reason, we've come to value an original painting for providing levels of enjoyment that no print of it can approach. In the same way, we've come to appreciate that scale also affects the viewers' responses; large paintings can have an impact that few printouts or small-scale works can hope to achieve. However, even if all these things are true, they do not eliminate the possibility that physical pleasures unknown to us today are yet to come from digital media. Movies

Is It Art?
Todd Lockwood

are arguably the signature art form of the last century. Who, 150 years ago, could have foreseen the impact they would have on audiences? Digital media may make it possible for millions of people to experience visual imagery that would otherwise never have been accessible. The cross-cultural benefits alone make such efforts worthwhile.

A digital painting program provides a medium for expression, no more and no less. If people respond to the art that is created with it, then of course *it is art*. It seems it is the lack of a singular original that causes critics to deride digital art, but this is a rather shortsighted view. Some art forms are more ephemeral than others; a ballet production or a jazz performance can happen only once. When the performance is over, the "original" is gone forever. Yet we have not rejected recordings of rock concerts, or films documenting famous stage performances. To be sure, over-reliance on prepared computer models can diminish artists' ability to communicate their vision, just as many artists who rely heavily on traced photos cannot draw out of their heads; but neither contradict the truth that "works of art" reside not in the way those works are communicated, but in the very fact of the communication.

Mirror Prince *Digital media.*
Cover for the novel by Violette Malan, DAW 2006.

Todd Lockwood entered the SF field in 1994 with a staff position at TSR™, illustrating the popular fantasy role-playing game Dungeons & Dragons™. His work appears in *Spectrum: The Best of Contemporary Fantastic Art.* and the *Communication Arts Illustration Annual*, and he has won twelve Chesleys, two World Fantasy Art Show awards, and numerous industry awards. His art is collected in *Transitions: The Art of Todd Lockwood* (2003). See www.toddlockwood.com

LTHOUGH I have completed several commissions for a few small publishers and have been recommended for a British Fantasy Society award, I know I am a beginner here . . . just starting out in the field of book illustration. I consider myself a novice compared to those who have worked in it all of their lives. Yet I have managed to form a few opinions as to how to go about making an effective book cover design and also about what techniques and methods work best for me. One of these is that computers are pretty much indispensable and that there are far more right than wrong reasons for using them.

The job of a book illustrator is to grab the attention of those looking at the cover in such a way as to intrigue them enough to want to find out what lies behind the cover image. The techniques and method used to achieve this are secondary. One of the main reasons I have chosen to be a commercial artist, and think the digital art produced as an outcome of my ideas are suited to SF and Fantasy illustration is that, in this field, imagination and image have always been more important than style or technique. The artist may at times look on the process of creating an image as an intellectual or spiritual exercise but the goal, regardless, is the same: to elicit an emotional response from the viewer sufficient to result in a purchase.

In addition, the commercial illustration world — and therefore what is appealing to people — is moved by what is marketable, fashionable and popular, and computers and digital art have certain traits and qualities that lately have made them very popular and fashionable. While, as with any new idea, there are those who mistrust computer-based art, those who completely embrace it, and those who stand somewhere in the middle who are in the majority. I myself have been using a computer to help me create images for the last few years and although I often hear people say that it makes the artist more lazy and that a certain elusive element of the creative process is lost, there are so many good reasons and advantages to computers that they far outweigh any so called disadvantages.

First, I think that computers in general and the digital art programs in particular have unleashed a tidal wave of creativity and ideas. It may be that a large number of people creating art today wouldn't be doing so if it wasn't for these various art programs that are now available. There are large communities of artists online devoted to digital art, which means that there is a lot more support for people trying to break into this world of being an artist. Any kind of atmospheric or stylistic effect can be easily created and if you have an idea for an image that you are unsure how to realize using a computer then I'm sure that a quick search on the internet would provide several sites devoted to explaining with a step by step tutorial just how to achieve this effect, style or technique. This makes it far easier to create an image than painting it in oils by hand and it also therefore increases the number of artists and the amount of art being produced because of the simplicity and support behind it. This does, however, mean that there is a lot more rubbish being produced but also that there are a lot more excellent artists around who may not have taken the plunge if it wasn't for programs such as Photoshop or Painter. There is no need to spend years in isolation at the easel trying to perfect a technique that can be produced on a computer with very little effort

Second, there is less need to spend so much time and energy in careful planning, preparation of materials and rough sketches. Computers allow you to just jump into an idea for an image, and let it fluidly and organically develop as you work on it without worrying about ruining hours of careful work by being a bit too bold or crazy with a particular idea that could lead to days of reworking if you were producing a traditional painting. There is obviously also no need for under painting at the

The Death Posture *2004, mixed media (photography and Photoshop) used on the cover of Estronomicon, online ezine, 2006.*

A DIGITAL ARTIST FOR THE RIGHT REASONS
Ben Baldwin

beginning of the process, or waiting for various layers of paint to dry (which has always frustrated me with traditional painting) before continuing with the picture. I have often found with some of my oil paintings that having to wait a few days for various bits to dry makes me loose all momentum and inspiration for the idea and in the case of professional illustration this really isn't an option. Computers allow me to work much quicker and with hardly any worries about making errors.

Moreover, in some important ways, creating art digitally and creating it in traditional media is the same. There will always be the start of a sheet of blank paper or an empty computer screen waiting to be filled. All the usual ideas about art still have to come from the artist — computers don't yet make the choices of light and shade or composition for you. Just using a few Photoshop filters on a photo isn't really digital art, and the actual involvement of the artist at the primary stage of creating a new image remains the same as it always has. What computers do (which makes the illustrator's job much simpler) is to allow mistakes to be corrected, or alterations to be made, with ease. Clients can often change their minds or request several minor changes in the artwork produced. If it is a traditionally created piece of artwork, then this can be very frustrating and time consuming, but with digital artwork any changes or corrections usually don't cause too much bother to the artist. Something that could take days to correct or modify in an oil painting can be done in a matter of minutes on a computer.

Another important reason for choosing to create art digitally is the flexibility and convenience of the media. When I first started using a computer I initially used hand drawn images and paintings as a basis for the picture, but now all the digital art I create at the moment is nearly all to do with photo manipulation and photomontages. I've never been that interested in using the computer to replicate what can be done with traditional materials. Using a computer in this way strikes me as just plain laziness unless there is a lack of space or traditional materials, in which case using a computer becomes incredibly useful. I have recently been traveling around Ireland and found the portability of my laptop allowed me to continue to create highly finished pieces of work without the need to carry around lots of supplies such as paint, easel, canvas, etc. I also like the idea of having a small rectangular box in which I can easily carry around all my ideas and pictures, which would be impossible if I was creating as many paintings on canvas as I do pictures on the computer.

I sometimes think that it is the fact that a piece of digital art can be reproduced exactly the same as the original image an unlimited number of times that makes it loved by some and disliked by others. For illustrative purposes and book publishing, however, this is obviously a massive advantage for digital over traditional art. Computers are just far too useful and even if I do sometimes think of them as slightly inferior to traditional techniques (in terms of personal creativity) that doesn't really matter in the field of illustration. No artist who is today planning a successful career in the field of illustration can ignore computers. It would just put them at such a disadvantage to those who are using them in terms of speed of production, quality of product and versatility of design.

For example, computers allow the artist to make several different versions of an image easily using different ideas/colors, etc. without having to go through the time consuming process of drawing each idea for a picture by hand. For my computer work I often have 4 or 5 different versions of the picture I'm working on and gradually discard those ones that I feel aren't working as I progress with the idea. Also, effects and images can be created with digital manipulation programs that are virtually impossible to create with traditional paint or photographic tools. Computer programs such as Photoshop are also vital in the production of small-scale print-on-demand books by independent publishers or for artists wanting to publish their own work.

It is true that by using equipment that filters the artists' intention through other people's ideas (i.e. a computer program not created by the artist using it) and allowing intense art experiences to be instantly replicated by various media, something vital from artistic process and experience may be lost. This, I suppose, is my only concern and problem I have with using a computer for my art. I personally still enjoy creating traditional paintings from time to time, and get more satisfaction and a bigger buzz from creating a traditional painting than I do from creating an image using a computer, partly because using a computer and the various programs on it is not as immediate as just using an actual pencil or brush. But all experience is mediated to some degree and some experiences are more mediated than others so that, for example, watching TV is more mediated and requires less imagination than reading a book or telling a story. Yet we don't give up watching TV, because we are compensated in other ways. I have fairly recently got a Wacom tablet and I think that this is one of the most important tools today. Because the tablet allows images to be made on the screen by the traditional method of drawing directly on a flat pad, the tool bridges the gap between digital and traditional art. And it is probable that computer art would be much more accepted as being "true" art if the various artists producing it could all write and use their own

An Occupation Of Angels *book cover, author Lavie Tidhar mixed media (photography and Photoshop), Pendragon Press, 2005.*

unique computer programs to create their images.

These, however, are just a few of my personal thoughts about the actual process of creating an image digitally, and in the case of any book covers I produce I don't imagine the publishers being that interested in my thoughts on the creative process involved. What they are looking for is an original striking image that will grab people's attention, and what they care about is that it's in a format that allows it to be easily reproduced etc. It is the audience's reaction to the image that counts, not mine (I'm not being paid to please myself) and for me I don't think there will ever be any doubt that with any illustration work that I do computers will be involved somewhere. But whether or not the purpose for it is commercial, I believe that true art must come straight from the soul of the artist and speak directly to the soul of the viewer. Whether I've been able to achieve that yet I'm not sure. That is my aim, however, and I intend to use whatever tools are at my disposal to achieve it.

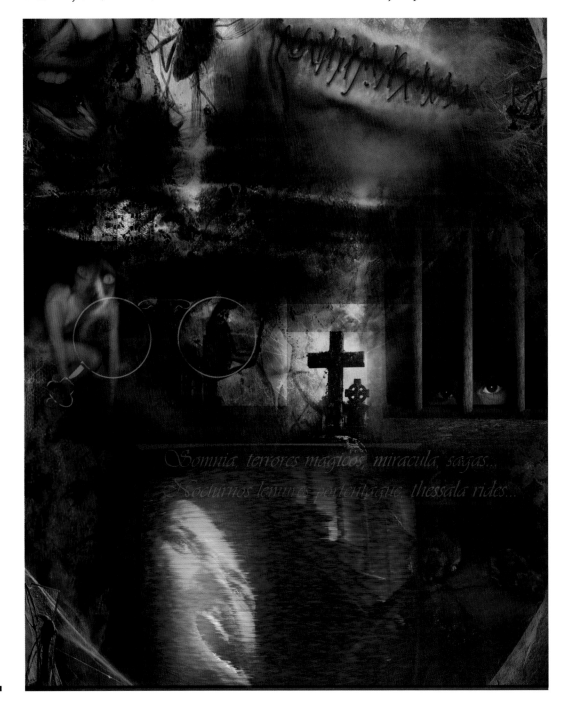

Dark Corners *book cover for an anthology of short stories by Stephen Volk, mixed media (photography, pencil and Photoshop), Gray Friar Press, 2006.*

Ben Baldwin is a self taught 27 year-old artist who works with a range of media. In the last few years he has taught himself how to use Photoshop and this is the medium he uses most at the moment. He has created art for night clubs, private individuals, magazines, book publishers and was nominated for a British Fantasy Society award for Best Artist 2006. See more at www.benbaldwin.co.uk/

IN the mid-nineties, after having spent over two decades as a professional illustrator working mainly in acrylics, I gradually became aware of a new phenomenon. I had seen computer graphics before, of course, and looked at the machines necessary to generate them. Huge, slow, lumbering beasts that at best were capable of generating poor quality pictures at very slow speed. The novelty here was simply that it was possible to create an image using a machine at all. Shortly after that systems like the Quantel Paintbox and Silicon graphic machines made appearances, systems costing tens of thousands of pounds and requiring a technical expertise bordering on genius to maintain. The average illustrator had nothing to worry about; computer graphics were to remain a niche item beyond the means or ability of the average person. And after all, there were so many other ways to create an image, why go to all that trouble and expense? Anyway, could an image created by a machine ever have any kind of value?

Now, I say "by a machine" because that was how I felt at the time, but what I should have said was "with a machine." I was exhibiting the kind of ignorance that has dogged the digital artist in some quarters ever since. When I first was exposed to computers, I knew nothing about them, and, because my mathematical abilities border on the dyslexic, I assumed there was no chance I was ever going to go down that route. At the same time, although I had worked successfully for over twenty years, I had never settled upon an ideal method. Nearly every image I created involved some kind of experiment in technique. You may think this a good thing but actually I found it endlessly frustrating. I seemed to spend far too much time battling with intransigent media. It seemed to me that there must be a better way than spending two whole days working up one square inch of canvas to the finish I wanted, and I searched for it continuously. Later I discovered that using the computer to solve technical problems was more like a game than a capitulation to a dictatorial machine that would be producing art for me.

Fear of change, reinforced by lack of preparation for it, is another major factor in artists' resistance to the digital revolution. I remember the day vividly when a change I should have seen coming was rudely thrust upon me. I had been working flat out for over ten years, always with about ten jobs booked ahead neatly stacked on a desk behind me. I was so busy, so involved in trying to bend that damn acrylic media to my will that I didn't really register that there had come a time when the pile stopped being replenished. Then one day, like running at full speed over the edge of a cliff, there were no more jobs. *I was stunned*. Then, someone showed me a magazine article about new software called Bryce. "Have you seen this," they said "you won't need to be an artist soon!" That sentiment, born out of ignorance, again. The product wasn't even in the shops at that time, but here I was, seeing the kind of imagery my contemporaries and I were striving to create, produced by a machine! This article appeared about the time the publishing and illustration industry was in a state of flux, going through changes that have since affected everyone working in the field. I looked around, and saw that the landscape had changed considerably. The Apple Macintosh had come of age with the power PC. A desktop machine, still expensive, but now within the grasp of the average person. With powerful, user-friendly software that seemed to be able to accomplish .... well, anything. I had been left behind, it seemed, so involved with painting that I had missed the boat and a new generation of techno artists were about to steal my livelihood.

What was I to do? I felt I had to get on this particular boat, like it or not. In fact I felt like the boat had already left port and I'd better swim fast to catch up. With only the vaguest notion of how one went about creating such images with a computer, I resolved to dive in. Fortunately it was all very new and there being not much to choose from, which made it somewhat easier. The computer had to be an Apple Mac, all my graphic design friends who had made the plunge assured me

Change of Command *Digital media, Cover for the novel by Elizabeth Moon, for Little Brown, 2000.*

THE LURE OF THE PIXEL
Fred Gambino

of that and I had to have Bryce because it was the catalyst that had set me off on this new journey. Bryce is 3D software, unlike Photoshop, which is 2D. Bryce specialized in landscapes, although I still needed Photoshop to paint in this new world and if I were to go down the 3D route properly I would need another 3D software that was more generalized, an application called Alias Sketch. That and a scanner, printer and monitor came to a tidy sum. I had to cash in an endowment to fund it. I decided I would generate my images from scratch, within the machine, where others would bring external material, photos or sketches into the digital environment for further manipulation. This led me down a slightly different path than some of my contemporaries but I chose it because it was in part related to the way I had always worked.

Luckily for me, in a very short time I found that not only was I comfortable with this new way of working but that I really enjoyed it. At last I seemed to have found my perfect medium and it echoed my traditional way of working. I found I loved this process, as much as an oil painter might like the feel of oil on canvas. The problem solving was like a game; how do I get this software to

Remnant Population *Digital media, Cover for the novel by Elizabeth Moon, for Little Brown, 2002.*

create the shape I want. In a way it was similar to battling with paint but I found this way of working much more rewarding and less frustrating

Unfortunately, the rest of the publishing world had yet to come to the same conclusion; art directors and editors still expected to see a piece of artwork, and they just couldn't make the connection to a disc in the same way. Their jaundiced view was not helped as results from the printers, also scrabbling to catch up, were varied to say the least. The art directors would pounce with glee at anything that looked like it may have originated from a photograph. "Aha", they would say, "that looks like a scanned piece of photography". There is a true irony to this, as now the publishers can't seem to get enough scanned photos. But as I was pushing 3D at the time, I got a lot of work. I gave publishers a new look (photographic but didn't look like a photograph), got an American agent and had work published in Dick Judes' book, *Masters of Fantasy Art*, which helped me find my way into Hollywood. All this was a direct result of my making the decision to buy the computer at the time that I did.

At the same time, with many more illustrators chasing fewer jobs, things started to get tough for those working in publishing and advertising. The new technology was only to blame indirectly, however, by giving easy means to art directors to change the way they wanted to package their products. I know there are some illustrators who still blame the technology for the fall off in work, but it's a simplistic view. When they want illustrations on covers they still need to commission artists to do it. Even with computers they can't do it themselves, despite that earlier misconception still held by some. And so, amidst these massive changes and the angst and self-doubt, the old school split into entrenched camps. Did you in fact need to be an artist anymore? Does an image produced digitally have as much worth as one painted traditionally?

If we are talking about illustration, we are talking about an image produced commercially for a specific purpose: To package a product in the case of a book or to add seasoning to a product in the case of film. In both cases the illustrator is only being commissioned because his work might help sell someone else's. Why would anyone want to do that the hard way? But, it doesn't mean you no longer need to be an artist. All the same rules still apply, it's just the tools that differ. And contrary to the belief of some, the "paint me a great picture" filter in Photoshop has yet to be realized. I suspect a bit of envy in those who complain the loudest that their once elitist position has been breached. Yes, the tools are much more powerful and yes, it enables a lot more people to stand up and be counted but those with the artistic talent will shine, they will always take the tools they are given and do something extraordinary. And, it doesn't matter to the art buyer how the marks are made, as long as they perform the function for which they were commissioned. It doesn't matter to me as artist or viewer as long as the image communicates something.

I recently upset a fellow artist by stating that I didn't think what I did had any other worth than it was a pleasant way for me to pay the bills. Plainly he placed a higher value on his imagery, as this observation didn't sit well. This same individual took it upon himself to berate my use of 3D software. " When I look at your work, all I see is 3D," he said, to which I replied, "When I look at your work all I see is Photoshop," at which point he went ballistic. He seemed to think that his technique was somehow invisible in a way that mine wasn't. He was kidding himself but from my perspective, why should he worry that his technique was obvious? I didn't mean it as a criticism and I didn't mind one whit if he saw through my technique — I wasn't trying to hide it. When I look at a Jim Burns or a Chris Moore, I can see it's an airbrush illustration but that doesn't detract from my enjoyment of the content of the image. In fact it adds to it as I happen to like that aesthetic.

So, can an image produced using a machine ever have the same value as one produced traditionally? For me the answer is a resounding yes. It doesn't matter how the image is produced, oils, acrylic, watercolour, digital. It's the end result that counts, and really for me it boils down to this: I enjoy the process of working digitally and using 3D in particular. I'm very glad to be standing where I am now, producing conceptual and design work for films; it has led me to some very exciting work, to parts of the world I never thought I would get to visit. It has also enabled me to sidestep my old hunting ground in publishing, to get into the movie industry, which really is it's natural successor. Recently I finally packed my airbrush and compressor away. I never intend to pick up an airbrush again. That doesn't mean I will never paint again, just that should I ever get back to painting, I will find myself exactly where I started, which is probably a good place to end.

BattleSpace *Digital media, Cover for the book by Ian Douglas, Eos Books 2006*

Fred Gambino has been working in the science fiction genre for more than twenty-five years, with thirty covers for the Mech Warrior series alone (Penguin, U.S). In recent years he's moved into concept and production art for the film and TV industry, with projects such as *Jimmy Neutron, Boy Genius* and *The Ant Bully*. His work was collected in the artbook *Ground Zero: The Art of Fred Gambino* and an illustrated book *Life Size Dragons* was published 2006. See www.alisoneldred.com

N art, as in war, new technology brings irrevocable change. Although there is no singular startling event we can point to —no Hiroshima or 9/11 to serve as a powerful symbol marking our passage — it is clear in retrospect that we have crossed the digital Rubicon. What is not so clear, is how we're doing in terms of climbing the banks on the other side. The arrival of the digital age has been slow and stealthy, more akin to a creeping glacier than a fiery nuclear blast. Yet the landscape of commercial art has been utterly transformed by its inexorable advance. Many artists have had great difficulty making a "paradigm shift," and finding their balance within a world rapidly transitioning to a new medium. Some have despaired at the gradual, alarming erosion of time honored traditional wisdom and knowledge. Others have experienced a sense of dislocation and loss, even as they sense the great potential and new possibilities offered by the new technological media. Those unsure of their footing during this period of fundamental change may mistakenly believe that a compromise of sorts is the answer. But digital art will not fully develop so long as artists, designers and software developers stay focused on replicating traditional media using digital tools. The simulation of traditional painting, photographic realism in 3D graphics, and the manipulation of stock photographic images that are prevalent today are impeding the evolution of a fundamentally new art medium.

Artists' preoccupation with simulating the comfortable, familiar look of traditional media largely ignores the promise digital technology represents, and has served to delay the exploration of an uncharted and potentially vast new realm of creative expression. People like the way oil paintings, watercolors, pencil sketches —just to name a few easily recognized mediums — look. This simple fact is not going to change, but that is not grounds for closing the door on the possibility of developing a new aesthetic. Indeed, it is difficult to envision the form pure digital art might take, because we really haven't seen very much of it. It is interesting to read speculative descriptions of future art works contained in science fiction novels, and inevitably I find myself thinking "wouldn't it be fantastic if someone actually did that?" After all, the ideas are out there, but it won't happen as long as artists continue to focus their efforts on matching the texture of paint or chalk on a flat screen monitor.

A second obstacle to innovation in the digital arts is the emphasis on simulation as an expression of artistic "tradition." This emphasis is grossly misplaced; it locks artists into a descending spiral of endlessly reiterating the great works the past, and fails to acknowledge or build upon the innovative spirit of past masters. Actually, I am very suspicious when I hear the word "tradition". To me, it often seems like another way of saying "formula." The great artists of the past are remembered not because they plodded dutifully down the well-worn path, but rather because they chose to diverge from it, and in so doing expanded the definition of what art and illustration could be. These artists used the techniques and materials available to them to express their creative vision. It seems very doubtful that a lot of time was spent trying — for example — to simulate a charcoal drawing using oil paint, but that is more or less analogous to what many artists today strive to achieve with digital media. It is goal that is all too readily reached with applications specifically touted for their capability to replicate known painting and drawing effects. A traditional medium such as oil paint has intrinsic physical properties that evolved over time to reflect artists' desire for ever better materials. If digital tools are ever to push into uncharted territory, we are going to have to relinquish the simulation of physical art materials as the primary goal.

Moreover, digital art education at present aims to produce "operators" trained in the use of specific software, while failing to instill the fundamental skills and processes of art and design. In recent years, many institutions have sprung up to capitalize on people's hopes for a magic shortcut to a

Sighting *Personal work ©2006 featured in "Concept Design II" Design Studio Press, 2006. Lightwave 3D 7.5, Adobe Photoshop 7.0*

Stalled on the Banks of the Digital Rubicon

Stephen Burg

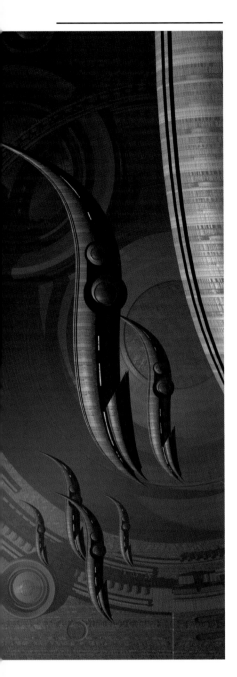

career in commercial art or entertainment. While some classes are led by working professionals, more often than not the instructors are qualified mainly by a superficial knowledge of "where the buttons are." Knowledge of anatomy, perspective, composition, form and light, color and design are not optional skills of marginal value in the new digital age because, without a working knowledge of these essential skills, any art career will be very short lived. Technology is always changing, and it is not wise to stake one's value to a potential employer on the use of a particular method or gimmick. The only way to survive, in fact, is to understand what it really takes to succeed as a digital artist — and the answer does not rest on "computer skills."

I entered the film industry in the pre-digital era, working with such antique devices as optical printers, motion control cameras and animation stands. This entire technology vanished in the space of about two or three years, as did those poor unfortunates who gambled their career on those "traditional" methods of creating motion picture special effects. This dramatic example of the impermanence of technology deeply affected me. "If the tools we struggle to master are so easily disposed of," I wondered, "what then is our core value as artists?" The answer is of course that we must — above all else — become *problem solvers*. Technologies come, technologies go, but the central problems that need solving remain very much the same. Knowledge of a specific mechanical process is not Art, it is "manufacturing." Any art education should focus on the discipline of solving visual problems with a full arsenal of knowledge placed at the artist's disposal, not two or three computer programs that in all likelihood will be long gone five or ten years down the road.

The longer we allow ourselves to focus in digital art on replicating the look of traditional art media, or in the case of motion picture visual effects, on simulating a photographic reality, the more we slow our progress towards new modes of expression without any discernable benefit to traditional painters. As digital art, once rare and exotic, becomes commonplace and the mastery of traditional art media becomes a much rarer skill, the perceived benefits of exploring an entirely new mode of expression will become clear. The shadows are swiftly lengthening on the age of traditional painted illustration, and I do not foresee the reprieve of a second dawn. It is bittersweet, to be sure. The rich history and tradition of illustration remains to inspire future generations of visual artists. It is our heritage, but to equate the art itself with the mechanical method by which it was produced would be a fatal error.

The central issues of art, design and illustration are eternal, and they transcend technique. The driving force is the communication of an idea, or an emotion. Since it has never been the purpose of mass media to produce a body of collectible art works (that has always been ancillary to the process of manufacturing and selling the product), there's nothing to prevent continual change but our own reluctance to pursue it. Indeed, it is likely that pixels will be superseded by something better as digital technology continues to evolve. Will we see a return to traditional art materials as the preferred method of producing illustration for the mass media? Barring unforeseen cultural forces, this seems highly unlikely given the current rate of acceptance of new technologies. There is no going back, of that I am sure. Isn't it time we began moving forward? The ultimate potential of digital imaging technology will remain unrealized until artists are able to let go of the past and embark on a path of exploration and true innovation. What will we find on such a journey? Truthfully, I do not know — but that journey is the whole point of artistic creativity. Up ahead, across the river, the future beckons — there is a dark riverbank with uncertain terrain that first must be climbed, but in the distance, a field bright with promise. It is a blank canvas (or should I say monitor?) and it awaits the artist's hand.

(detail) **Threshold** *Personal work ©2003 featured in* Concept Design I *Design Studio Press, 2003. Digital media, Lightwave 3D 7.0, Adobe After Effects 5.5*

Steve Burg began his career in cinematic visual effects, became well established as a versatile designer/illustrator with extensive credits in entertainment design and now works for a major publisher of console and video games. Largely self taught in traditional media, Burg embraced digital media in the late 1990s, working as concept artist on SF films, among them: *The Abyss, Terminator 2, Total Recall, Starship Troopers, Waterworld, Contact* and *The Chronicles of Riddick.* His digital works are collected in *Concept Design Vol 1, 2* (Design Studio Press, 2003, 2006).

3

*If there were
dreams to sell /
What would
you buy?*
Thomas Lovell Beddoes

WITNESSES TO CHANGE

P EOPLE perhaps wondered, when the first press-printed books began to appear, would the hand written and wonderfully hand painted manuscripts that had dominated European and Eastern intellectual scholarship become a thing of the past? Did that new idea for setting type and printing multiple copies of a work represent, or devalue, hand made books? Was the cruder (and mechanical) method more representative of the values and ideas expressed by an author, or — as another example - was the content of the Holy Bible devalued by mass printings? Did people fret, when the piano replaced the harpsichord, thinking that the newer instrument brought no better understanding or depth of musical feeling to works that previously had sounded "real" and correct when played on their original instrument? Societies and civilizations rise and fall, and each new idea challenges us with the same sorts of questions. Will the moving picture replace live staged dramas and plays? Will television render movie theaters obsolete? Will gas-driven cars completely replace railroad trains? Will recorded music on circular disks cause the end of "live" performances of classical music? Will the "mall" destroy downtown business districts in larger cities? Will radio force newspapers out of business? Will the comic book spell the end of comic strips in newspapers? And now, will the Internet replace all new media formats? With each step we take toward acceptance of unfamiliar technologies, and the changes they make in our daily lives, there are those who reject change and question whether change is constant and unavoidable, and always for the good. Aren't at least *some* changes, perhaps, for the worse?

Artists today must confront tremendous ethical and philosophical questions brought by new technologies, with regard to crafting original works that retain their meaning and humanity. For some, it is akin to walking a tightrope between two worlds, and creating works of art in both of them. Changes are unavoidable. The standards of traditional illustration were changed forever in the early 20th century when photography, almost overnight, relegated the etched plate illustration to antiquity. Later, just as "modern" art was finding its ground with the abstract ideas of Cubism, Surrealism, and other plastic forms, a new art form of completely non-referential painting developed in America — where artists such as Jackson Pollock and Franz Kline and Mark Rothko questioned the fundamental ideas about classical painting altogether. Then right after the abstract expressionist movement came the revolution inspired by Marcel Duchamp, and the artists Jasper Johns and Robert Rauschenburg questioned what an art object itself was. The methods used by Robert Rauschenburg, especially, bring illumination to the subject of this collection of essays. Can the machine, or the modern computer render traditional forms of artistic expression obsolete? If history is any predictor of the future, the answer is "yes."

Obsolescence, however, is not the sole determiner of worth; obsolescence does not obviate appreciation of beauty. A critical factor in assessing worthiness is whether — and how well — the methods, techniques, formats for presenting art enable artists to manifest their artistic visions in such ways as to elicit what we in the science fiction field call "sense of wonder."

To make the point, let me use as an example the question I raised earlier: Does anyone feel that the chords struck on a harpsichord (where the musician is playing, let's

CROSSING THE LINE BETWEEN ART AND MACHINE
Jerry Weist

Jael: **The Dream Lives** *(detail) personal work 1986 done in memory of the Challenger disaster, used as frontis for Perceptualistics: Art by Jael (Paper Tiger, 2002) one of several publications of the work acrylics, c. 24" x 18"*

say, just the right J.S.Bach piece) feel or sound the same as those on the piano? Wouldn't you rather sometimes hear a live harpsichord, while another time choose to listen to Beethoven's Waldstein Sonata played on a piano? Can't you wonder and thrill to the original 1927 film *Metropolis* — in black and white, with all its now "dated" science fiction images — in almost the same way as you look at the 1950's version of H. G. Well's *The War of the Worlds* and find that "sense of wonder"? Can't you also pore over pages of original 1890's etched illustrations for Jules Verne stories, and derive as much satisfaction as you would with the very best Virgil Finlay black and white *Weird Tales* stories? Isn't viewing the original *Star Wars*, or *BladeRunner* in a movie house on a large screen better than watching it at home on a wide-screen high definition television set (even with surround sound)? Can't you still enjoy the "real" difference between listening to a great (and mint) Bill Evans or Miles Davis 33 1/3 vinyl recording and then hearing the same "re-mastered" performances on a CD? In other words, are not all these DIFFERENT formats for presenting art, and music, and ideas wonderful in each of its different manifestations?

From my past experience as an artist, and as a current collector of science fiction artwork, author of two price guides about artwork and other books connected to science fiction illustration, I know the answer to all these questions is "yes." If the artist uses any new machine (camera, computer, spray-gun, video camera, etc.) with the same dedication as any previous artistic tool (paint brush, charcoal pencil) then the result can be a serious new creative work of art. No creative "line" gets crossed by current science fiction artists when they use the computer to advance their ideas. Choice of tools does not validate a work of art.

I was as stunned as any other human being would be when last year I asked the artist Rick Berry if I could buy one of the paintings from his incredible partnership with Harlan Ellison for *Repent Harlequin! Said the Ticktockman* (Underwood Books, 1997) and he answered, "Jerry, there are NO original paintings, I handed that book's illustrations in on a disk." He then told me I could commission a painting from one of my favorite pages in the book if I wished to have something to hang on my wall.

But, folks get a grip! For gods sake, or ghu's sake (whatever your disposition), we live in the age of discovery — and are all supposed to be interested in this idea called science fiction and wondering what the future will be like. Can't we adapt to changes in our forms of artwork? It's now been nine years since Rick's ground-breaking illustrations appeared, and still they are not accepted by many people! I know that Harlan would love the very idea of this confusion, as folks struggle with whether Berry's illustrations are "artwork" or not. Of course they are! Must we forever cling to Pre-Raphaelite forms of figurative art and methods of painting — and declare everything else that does not hew to that model to be false? Believe me when I tell you that science fiction fans in general are the most conservative group of visual judgment-makers on the North American continent. Many science fiction fans cannot tell you why Marcel Duchamp changed American (and Western Art) forever, and that's OK, most Americans can't either — but hey, aren't we SF folks supposed to be intellectually curious, and be at least a little familiar with the *avant garde* ideas of our age? Shame. Here we are, still questioning whether or not in the hands of a committed creative artist any new tool (even Adobe Photoshop) can't be the NEW paint brush! But then society always plays catch up with truly creative minds anyway — right?

So where's the problem with change? The problem appears to be related to the possibility that we lose something when we, or artists, rely entirely upon a machine-driven image. The probability is that we also will gain something from a changing world, even if it is appreciation for what was lost. Meanwhile, the central question for the arts remains the same: what are the aspirations, beliefs, dreams and challenges for each generation? *Human.* As Ray Bradbury and a number of other important science fiction authors (especially Philip K. Dick!) are there to remind us, the central question is how humanity incorporates new technology, and makes it part of its experience and social framework. If framed that way, the question becomes "how to create art with human meaning and purpose?" not "how to create machines that will replace our humanity?" If we keep our hearts and minds focused that way, we can avoid serious pitfalls that computers may spring on us.

Only a short while ago we were wondering if children's illustrated books were dead — indeed we were thinking that children were never going to read anything again: a childhood filled with nothing but *Teletubbies, Barney, Sesame Street, Power Rangers,* animated *Barbie* "movies" followed by *Nintendo* and video games! Then along comes a lad named Harry Potter, and with his arrival, an entirely new generation of children's illustrated books . . . and artists. Yes, current books can look boring and more abstract, and then along come "retro" covers — where an author as popular and current as Maureen Dowd (*Are Men Necessary? When Sexes Collide*) uses a painting by artist Owen Smith, known for his work in *The New Yorker* magazine, that looks like it's smack dab off a PULP cover from the 1940s — and *voila'* we are back to live, pulsating, archetypical redheads/brush on canvas book covers! Do you really think all of those incredibly expensive Stephen King limited edition books by Don Grant books sell for hundreds (and some thousands) of dollars because they have limited numbered editions? Or (maybe) it's the incredible paintings of Michael Whelan, Phil Hale, Berni Wrightson, and a host of others that might be drawing the collectors' eyes? There's room, folks, for it all! We can have ozone-splitting mind-bending works brought forth with pixels right alongside hand-painted-oils-on-canvas. Each will have its own merits and each its own creative energy and thrilling "sense of wonder." We are in the great age of discovery, as Arthur C. Clarke has said many times, and if our beloved "Good Professor" Isaac Asimov can conceive of artwork made out of pure light (*The Naked Sun,* written in 1955!) then cannot we now accept that current masterpieces pouring out of computers can be as worthy as beautiful traditional glazed and layered paintings? Indeed, can't they exist side by side? SENSE OF WONDER, that is what science ciction was always meant to be about, and we don't have to be afraid of crossing the lines.

Steve Burg: **The Fliers** *(detail) Personal work ©2003 featured in "Concept Design I" Design Studio Press, 2003. Digital media, Lightwave 3D 7.0, Adobe Photoshop 6.0*

Jerry Weist's varied interests and careers include that of former retail bookseller with both The Million Year Picnic (1974) and The Science Fantasy Book Store (1975) in Cambridge, Massachusetts. He has authored two *Comic Art Price Guides, The 100 Greatest Comic Books,* and *Bradbury: An Illustrated Life* (Hugo nomimated, 2002), as well as over a dozen catalogues for Sotheby's in New York as their science fiction and comic consultant. Currently he is working on a book about Frank R. Paul, and a large color volume on sf fanzines.

George Hagenauer portrait
©2006 by Mary Ellen Hagenauer

FOR over 25 years, I've done the background research for Max Allan Collins' historical mysteries including the *Nate Heller, Road to Perdition* and *Disaster* mystery series. As a person who collects illustration art, I've always wanted to own a cover painting from one of the novels I helped research, but collecting illustrations from specific authors you enjoy is not as easy as it sounds. Above and beyond the cost, which runs hundreds or even thousands of dollars per illustration, is the problem of scarcity. In comic books and animation, hundreds or even thousands of original drawings or cels exist for any specific character, cartoon, series or artist. However, the opposite is the case in book illustration. A prolific writer may produce at most one or two novels per year. Those novels may only have one edition per decade at best. Indeed, the 25 years I have worked on 25 novels with Max represent less than 40 different covers. Some of those covers are photos. Many are pieces that frankly I wouldn't want on my wall. For instance one of my favorite novels, *Stolen Away* — which was about the Lindbergh kidnapping — has a monochrome cover that consists of a ladder leaning against the wall. While a powerful image for selling the book, it is not a piece I would expend a lot of energy or money to own.

So I was very pleased a year ago when a collection of his short stories came out with a really nice *noir* detective cover painting. I immediately emailed the publisher asking for contact information for the artist. I got the reply that every collector dreads.

"Sorry there is no painting as the image was created on the computer."

This is increasingly a problem in the illustration and comic art fields. The original of the image you want to own doesn't exist, at least not in a physical form. Or the image only exists in a preliminary or partially completed state, i.e., the rough drawings that were scanned into the computer. You can have a print made of the image, signed by the artist, but if you collect original drawings and paintings, a print is not what you want. A print doesn't have the brush strokes, stray pencil lines and other things that make original art so fascinating. A print also is not one of a kind. It is a nicer larger copy of the cover that you already have on the book.

Collectors who collect original drawings and paintings (as opposed to those who collect prints and posters) tend to want the "real" thing, the actual original work, not a reproduction (even when the original can only exist as a printed out reproduction). That's why the extensive use of computers in illustration, comics and animation has created a new problem for collectors and for artists who enjoyed the extra income generated when the art was sold after publication.

In addition, the collecting field tends to be quite conservative. The current use of computers follows a series of technical innovations in ways artists create illustrations for various publications. Many of these innovations have resulted in better quality reproduction of the artist's images as well as images that often cannot be created through traditional means. Yet, for the most part the collector market has debated the extent to which these creations are original art, instead of embracing them as innovative ways to create art, *in spite of the fact* that innovations prior to the recent use of computer generated art have resulted in physical as opposed to electronic creations. Reviewing some of these prior innovations, therefore, and their effect on the market, might provide some insight as to the current dilemmas faced by artists who choose to work using computers (versus brush

COMPUTER ART AND THE COLLECTOR'S MARKET
George Hagenauer

and pen) and collectors, who prefer to collect what they (conservatively) define as "original."

First, let's consider "bluelines" and other innovations which have impacted collectors of comic art. Comic books and some illustrations, while published in color, have traditionally been drawn in black and white ink and then later colored as part of the printing process. The original artist or a later colorist in the production department would create coloring guides for the printer to use to add the color. These guides were usually hand colored photocopies or photostats. Many original art collectors view these as similar to pages that have been clipped from coloring books and colored (and I remember one colorist who would color huge pages from the Berni Wrightson and Will Eisner coloring books and sell them as hand-colored one-of-a-kind prints). While I think that attitude undervalues the talents and contributions of the colorist (the printed books were only representations of the original coloring), nonetheless coloring guides tend to sell low — usually under $50 and often as little as a few dollars each. (There are exceptions like Marie Severin's coloring guides for 1950's EC comic book covers which have fetched over $500 each though still far less than the thousands and tens of thousands for the actual EC cover pen and ink art.) Indeed, "coloring guides" are often classified by collectors (along with production stats and other printed material) as "ephemera" rather than "original art."

A new technique developed in the early 1980's, however, provided the colorist a wider range of effects … and also changed collector's attitudes toward this step in the process of creating comic art. In the new process the original line art was copied first onto a clear sheet of plastic and then in non-reproducible blue ink onto a standard piece of illustration board. Since the black lines were printed in non-reproducible blue ink the colorist was able to color in the other parts of the art. Christened "bluelines", these new guides allowed the colors to be shot directly off the board as opposed to the color photostats which were just used as guides for the printers. As a result the colorists were able to create a wider range of more painterly effects. Equally important, the end results of the process were small tonal paintings (albeit with the lines on overlays), which not only greatly improved the coloring in these comics of the pre-computer age but also enabled colorists to pitch them as *paintings*.

Collectors, by nature conservative, were dubious. The painted area was missing the line art, which itself was just a print; only when the line art was atop the tonal painting was there a complete image. Separate the two and there remained abstract blobs of color in the painted area. Many collectors avoided them, arguing that painted bluelines were still ephemera since much of the image was printed. Yet, bluelines garnered higher prices than normal coloring guides (though still a lot less than traditional paintings), at $20-50 for a nice cover — sometimes a lot more for an exceptional image or key cover. Those higher values signaled a willingness among collectors to make comparative evaluations of innovative techniques, but they are not necessarily indicators of acceptance, because defining *what* the product is, exactly, is tricky. Without clear definition as to what constitutes original art, new artistic approaches will remain controversial, and collecting markets will balk.

Another innovation used especially in paperback cover illustration was the melding of photography and art to create interesting photo-realistic effects. I own the cover to Andrew Vachss' thriller *Strega*. It is as large as any painting in my collection. However, very little of it is painted. The artist took a photo of a man's face with sunglasses on. He then worked with it, adding various coloring accents to make the photo more like a realistic painting. Finally, he printed a large version of it, mounted it on board, and painted the images of the woman on the sunglasses. In the world of fine art this would be considered a multimedia work. Illustration collectors however don't know what to make of it. Is it like the paste-ups for paperbacks with totally photographic covers that are considered "ephemera"? Many judge the piece by the amount of paint on it, a small fraction of the actual surface of the art. The end result is a nice image that was the cover for a major novel but devalued in the marketplace because it did not fit the definition of so-called *normal* original cover art.

Then came drawing on Mylar. Ron Villani is a Chicago illustrator heavily influenced by the comics he read as a child. Many of his freelance jobs, especially during the first 25 years of his career, were done for clients who wanted a comic book feel to their art. When *Playboy* was doing a feature on Flash Gordon or Buck Rogers, Ron was usually the artist who drew the illustrations. Most of them were drawn on Mylar laid above an illustration board where the color was painted in or done with Pantene color film (like zipatone only in bright colors). This gave a striking and bright but very defined comic art style coloring effect to the finished art. Although it is a logical media for inking over existing pencils, and the originals can be fantastic and beautifully detailed, the biggest hurdle to many collectors turned out to be the idea that the pieces are on Mylar. Some people think they are prints like the printed line work on Mylar that is part of a normal blueline. Others mistake them for cels (which today more often than not are also printed lines on clear plastic).

The flexibility of publishers also adds to the confusion in collecting markets. Charlton, one of the lowest paying comic book publishers, was also the most flexible in terms of art formats. In the early 1970's Charlton shifted to using painted covers on their comics. The shift itself was strange because Charlton had the worst printing presses in the business and almost all the paintings reproduced fuzzily at best. It resulted however in some very interesting originals by a wide range of artists. One artist who took great advantage of Charlton's flexibility was Tom Sutton, who painted in a wide variety of media: acrylics or oils, done in pen and ink colored with watercolors, and pastels (including one on velvet, just like those Elvis portraits from Mexico), plus a series of paintings on Mylar. These, which I dubbed the "Stained Glass" covers, were painted with oils or acrylics on plastic Mylar sheets and then dry mounted on boards. When the dry mount has loosened, the painting can be removed from the backing board, resulting in a clear painted piece that can be lit from behind like a stained glass window! Until they loosen, however, they often are indistinguishable from his regular paintings since the paint fully covers the Mylar. For that reason, there are many collectors who own one without realizing it, but — and to the point — from my experi

ence the Mylar paintings go for about half what his regular color pieces bring, done on board. The ink, pencil and paint on Mylar pieces are all pure original art, but because they were done on non-traditional media they are not as attractive to collectors unfamiliar with innovative media.

When better graphic programs appeared in the 1990's, a number of artists began using computers for various aspects of creating art. As part of a trade deal I once got a nice full color pinup of *Tarzan* by Mark Wheatley. In creating it, Mark drew a number of prelims that he scanned into a computer. He refined the piece in the computer, then printed it out onto a full size 11" by 17" plastic-backed sheet. He then inked portions of the drawing, and colored it, including painting sections of it in either gouache or acrylics. Unlike

Mitch O'Connell's *Badger* cover, there were sections that definitely were printed but most of the piece was painted, colored or inked. It was also the only piece ever produced of that image. There were no finished completely inked drawings floating around.

I kept that piece a number of years and then sold it. The selling however took some time, as it was very difficult to describe. Was it a hand-colored computer print out? - or a mixed media piece? Does it count as original art or is it some form of production ephemera? Mark saw it as the final original art for that page as did ultimately a buyer, but the question still remains: how much of a piece needs to be actual hand-drawn art to be considered an original piece? This is a similar problem with originals that include large stats or pasteups. I own a beautiful *On Stage* daily but to save time one panel is mainly a stat from the Sunday page of the day before. The inclusion of that panel, which is not all original art, dropped the cost of the original by over 60% although it includes one of the nicest portrait shots of the heroine Mary Perkins that I have ever seen.

Given that many collectors have devalued art that is partially original and partially print, it is not surprising that the original art market for comics and illustration art has not greatly embraced the end product of computer art. In some ways this has been offset for some artists by the ability to create better quality prints. Painters especially have the ability now through improved printing technology to create *Giclées* (fine art print from a digital source using ink-jet printing). A painter who before created a single piece of cover art that might sell for $4000 after publication, today can offer a limited edition of 20-50 *giclées* of the same image for often several hundred dollars each providing he was savvy enough to retain those rights. The result is an expansion of a higher-end print market for those collectors who enjoy prints. The downside is that the technology is still new and the life span of a *giclée* is not yet known. A print that looks like a painting but fades over time is no replacement for high quality oil on canvas with a lifetime of centuries.

For collectors who only want original art, the market has followed the lead of the animation market. Animation began extensively using computer-generated images in the late 1980's. While this created incredibly complex effects and better movies, it posed a problem for the then burgeoning market of collectors of cels and background paintings. Rather than lose that market, the Disney company commissioned a series of recreated cel and background paintings for key scenes that were sold at auction to collectors. At the time, similar activity was occurring in the comic book art market. Much of the art for key series from the 1940s — especially by DC and Marvel — was destroyed shortly after publication and were almost impossible to find. The Collector's Bookstore in Los Angeles began tracking down many of the Golden Age cover artists and had them recreate their original covers for auction. Usually these were done in color to differentiate the copy from the original line-drawn cover in case it should still exist. Some were line-by-line copies of the original image, while others were reinterpretations by the original artist. These proved popular to many collectors and some (like the painted recreation of classic scenes from Disney comics by Carl Barks) have appreciated greatly in value; other lesser known artists have not fared as well, but the recreations did fill a desire for collectors to own images that probably no longer exist in their first incarnation.

What began as a means to recreate art that was lost has in recent years become a cottage industry for many comic book artists. As prices rose, especially for comic book cover art, artists from the 1960s, 70s and 80s began recreating their classic covers for collectors who could not afford — or obtain — the actual original drawing or painting. This phenomenon is not limited to the comic art field; many paperback artists, especially in the science fiction and fantasy field, also supplement their commercial art with commissions or recreations. Since in most cases the original cover art still exists, the recreations can cause confusion in the marketplace — especially if they are close to exact copies. While there still are collectors who won't touch recreations, the existence of the recreation and private commission market argues that the solution to the problem caused by computer-generated art is that the artist can just recreate the piece later at usually a far higher price. This of course is predicated on the artist being able to paint with a brush as well as a mouse, but for the artist skilled in traditional media, the option always exists to recreate electronic art in other media.

At this point it is still too early to tell how computer art will affect the art market for collectors. After all, the use of illustrations extensively in books and magazines is barely 125 years old, comic strips 100 years, and comic books about 65 years. Fantasy and science fiction really only became an accepted major genre in popular culture within my 56-year life. The art markets for illustration, comic art and animation are young markets. We don't know if the paintings many of us covet from the early days of the pulps will be equally cherished by the next generation or — like dime novels — fade into obscurity. My preference for paint over pixels may be gone in the generation who today are growing up with computers from birth, communicating with their grandparents over the Internet as opposed to the backyard fence. These are children whose fondest memories may not be sitting in a lap being read to from a book but rather sitting in front of a screen. As adults they may have picture frames with hundreds of their favorite images that can change from day to day with a flick of a switch.

On the other hand, as fewer paintings and drawings are made the ones from the past that do exist will become scarcer and possibly even more valuable. Meanwhile, those of us who love paint and ink and canvas and paper will need to get used to having our hunt end in vain … or accepting fleeting electronic ephemera instead of art that we will enjoy on our walls.

Romas Kukalis: **Children of Amarid** *cover for the novel by David B. Coe for Tor Books, 1997 in acrylics 20" x 30"*

George Hagenauer has collected genre illustration and comic art for over 40 years. He writes about collecting original art for www.comicartfans.com and the *Comics Buyer's Guide* magazine. His latest book is *Mickey Cohen Gangster* out in 2007 from Altitude Press, He can be reached at yellowkd@merr.com

F OR many art collectors, the advent of digital art has been something akin to the blowing of the sixth trumpet — it's not the end of the world, but the end is on the horizon. Are they correct? As a science fiction art collector — twenty years from now — will I be forced to jump ship, clinging desperately to the tangible, obsolete original art I've collected as younger collectors gleefully hoard limited edition prints of digital works and the few available "real" paintings are traded between millionaires? Or, worse yet, when the time comes for me to pass my collection along to the next generation, will there be no one who cares?

Fortunately, much as the image of my being an aged, wild-eyed eccentric surrounded by mountains of forgotten art appeals to me, I don't think this scenario will play out in reality. This doesn't mean that the emergence of digital art won't affect the collecting market — far from it — but its effect will be more along the lines of accelerating and accentuating natural changes in the market, such as a variance in demand for certain artists or periods and increasing prices among contemporary illustrators. Now, some may see these changes as the end of the world, but that's hardly digital illustration's fault, now is it?

For starters, let's consider the natural progression of the market apart from the influence of digital art. The SF art market, like any collectible field that is at least partially nostalgia driven, rises and falls with the shift of generations. At the present time, there is a tremendous demand for the illustrators of the 1940s and 1950s — Virgil Finlay, Hannes Bok, Kelly Freas, and others. Not surprisingly, the generation of SF fans that grew up with these works is now at the height of their earning powers — and they have been very happy to spend those earnings, in greater and greater amounts, over the past 30 years. The top-notch Finlay purchased for $50 in the early 70s is now selling for several thousand dollars — when one can be located on the market. The reality is, though, that most top examples of these artists are tied up in permanent collections from which they are dislodged only with great difficulty. In fact, it is this lack of supply within the market that has contributed significantly to the rise in price. If the only way to get a prime Bok away from its owner is with an exorbitantly large check, then so be it ….

However, this "rarity" is a transient one. There is, in fact, no shortage of works by these artists; the vast majority of their voluminous output remains extant. The rarity within the marketplace is reflective only of an unwillingness of current owners to sell. Although many collectors have uttered the words "I'll be buried with this piece," it seems likely that few will actually choose to follow through with that sentiment. Thus, the current bottleneck in supply will ease in the future as existing collections are broken up upon the death, retirement, or transmigration of their owners.

"Ah," you may say, "but this will be the time when hordes of younger collectors will finally be able to acquire these works, and the overall rarity will remain constant as the market absorbs the works that appear." This is a common perception — an assumption that as long as the collector base grows or remains constant, the demand for any given set of works will grow or remain constant as well. It is a common perception — but it is a shortsighted one. This belief requires another constant — collector taste — that, over time, is anything but constant.

This is the way the world ends This is the way the world ends This is the way the world ends Not with a bang but with a pixel.

THE FUTURE OF COLLECTING
Pat Wilshire

Yes, many top collectors these days are focused on the works of the 1940s, 1950s, and early 1960s. (For simplicity's sake, let's refer to these works as pre-Frazetta.) As this generation of collectors passes the baton, their places will be taken by the collectors of Generation X — who are every bit as rabid as their predecessors. However, just as the Boomer generation has an affinity for the works of their youth, so to do the Gen X'ers. For Generation X, the focus is post-Frazetta — the works of the 1970s and beyond. These collectors choose Whelan over Freas, Sanjulian over Bok, and nearly anyone over Valigursky.

When considered carefully, this shouldn't come as a surprise. The decision to divide the SF art world into pre- and post-Frazetta is not a purely arbitrary one. Pre-Frazetta works have a distinctly different feel and sensibility. So the fact that younger collectors who grew up in the post-Frazetta era should prefer these works to the earlier ones is only logical.

As a result, the assumption that these collectors will absorb the same amount of pre-Frazetta works as the current generation is suspect, at best. Certainly, there will be those rogue collectors who are more inclined towards the earlier works, just as there will no doubt be those lucky few who have the wherewithal to collect everything over the entire history of the genre. (Although, as we will see shortly, that latter group is on the edge of becoming a great deal smaller…) If current indications hold, this new generation of collectors, on the whole, will be far less interested in pre-Frazetta works than their collecting forefathers. Indeed — among the 50 or so collectors I know, there is not a single person under the age of 50 who is seriously involved in collecting pre-Frazetta works. (Note that when discussing pre-Frazetta works in this context I am referring to the post-pulp era. SF art from before 1940 is genuinely rare in absolute terms — there are little more than a dozen Margaret Brundage *Weird Tales* covers known to exist, for example — and there will always be enough collectors to absorb these minute amounts of art.)

As this shift occurs, pre-Frazetta works will have yet another strike against them — motivated sellers. Today, most of this artwork is in the hands of collectors who have lovingly (some may say manically) collected them for decades. However, when these collectors are gone, who will be selling the artwork? Family? Friends? Bob the Estate Auctioneer? In any case, these sellers are likely to be far more interested in money than in the art. As a result, they are unlikely to be interested in sitting on a painting for months or years waiting to get top dollar. Art will be sold for what the market bears at a given moment and, given increasing supply and decreasing collector interest, those prices will not keep pace with the current market.

Someone out there is no doubt stomping his feet in impatience at this point, bursting at the seams to cry out "False! What about comic books? There has been no drop in demand or pricing for Golden Age books, even as demand has increased for comics from the Bronze Age."

This is certainly true, as even a casual reviewer of auction results will realize. However, comics have a connective tissue that SF art, as a rule, does not — continuity of character. Younger collectors are still interested in Superman because he continues to be a viable, current, and popular character. The same is true for Batman, Spider-Man, and all the other icons of heroedom. Take a look, however, at auction results on secondary characters that are no longer popular. Key books in the history of comics featuring these characters retain their desirability but the "average" book shows a much less impressive price curve.

In addition, comic collectors tend to be completists — a Batman collector would like to have every Batman comic, old and new, and the non-unique nature of these items makes that an accessible goal with enough time and money. On the other hand, an art collector desiring to possess every Virgil Finlay (or even every Edgar Rice Burroughs cover painting) will have better luck grabbing Sisyphus' apples.

So, to recap — we will see demand and pricing on pre-Frazetta works decrease as demand for post-Frazetta works increases. This is the inevitable ebb and flow of the market, and has nothing to do with the rise of digital art. That does not mean digital art has no impact on this ebb and flow, however. Let's move back to the present now and examine the direct impact of digitally-created artwork on the contemporary market.

I once heard a seasoned collector say of a digital piece, "It's certainly art, but it ain't a painting." This is where digital art differs from historical shifts within the art field — a painting is still a painting whether done with tempera or oils. Some have likened the digital revolution to the development of photography and its impact on portraiture and landscape painting. This comparison feels valid, but it overlooks an important point — portrait painters did not stop painting en masse to switch to photography. The existence of the photographic medium simply gave rise to a new breed of artists and gave fans of portraits or landscapes a choice — paint or photo.

The current trend in illustration is very different. The risk of the digital revolution in illustration is not that fans will choose the new media over the old, as doomsayers feared with the rise of the camera. The risk is that the old media will be abandoned by its practitioners, so that for collectors of illustration art *there will be no choice*.

A worst-case scenario is not necessary to precipitate major changes in the collecting field, of course. The current situation — some digital, some analog — is more than enough to trigger significant changes. These changes, I believe, will be in two directions: an additional increase in demand for earlier post-Frazetta works (beyond that predicted by normal market generational change), and an across-the-board increase in prices for all post-Frazetta paintings.

If you assume that the collecting field even remains stagnant in terms of number of collectors, then a significant reduction in the number of available new paintings will necessarily translate to an increased demand for earlier paintings. Remember, as I said earlier, the new generation of collectors will prefer post Frazetta works to pre-Frazetta works. Thus, demand for these works will increase dramatically. In cases where there is crossover with the comic art collecting community (Jeff Jones, Berni Wrightson, Michael Kaluta, and the Warren Publications' artists) this has already occurred. The comic art community is roughly a decade ahead of the SF art collecting community in terms of expansion (and, sadly, speculation). An average *Frankenstein* illustration by Bernie Wrightson recently sold at auction for almost $30,000. Ten years ago, this illustration would have been fortunate indeed to make one-third of that amount.

Obviously, increased demand without increased supply leads to higher prices, but there is another pricing force at work that will push prices for late 20th century works higher yet — the price of contemporary (21st century) paintings. As artists produce fewer and fewer analog paintings, the prices they ask for those paintings are rising rapidly. The speed of digital production has led publishers to lower their rates for cover paintings, assuming that artists will work digitally and be able to do more paintings. As a result, an artist who insists on working traditionally (read *slowly*) has to recoup his money somewhere. Often, that "somewhere" is the original art market. (Of course, this is still an improvement over the other option: turning to the movies — a great maelstrom into which brilliant illustrators like Iain McCaig have disappeared, never to resurface.)

Ten years ago, $1000 would buy a nice painting from a wide array of contemporary illustrators. Today, $1000 *might* buy a nice painting by an unknown artist just starting out, but starting prices in the $2500 and up range for young contemporary illustrators is not uncommon — and some ask for much more. (Remember that inflation would suggest that roughly $1400 should buy the same art as $1000 ten years ago.) The trend is not likely to be reversed; artists are putting increasingly higher prices on their works, yet continue to find buyers — often new to the field and, as such, less resistant to the higher prices because they don't remember "the good old days" of the late 90s.

So what does this mean for the field as a whole?

In the short term, we will see a dramatic increase in the prices of 20th century post Frazetta works. These artists tend to have a higher perceived value than young contemporary illustrators — they have stood the test of time. As the average price of new works increases, the prices of earlier works will seem a bargain — and will then, in turn, quickly escalate to reflect their perceived status vis-à-vis contemporary pieces. The result of this escalation will be that the bar to entry for collecting SF illustration art will creep ever higher — not due to speculators or critical art world acceptance, but simply due to synergistic market forces. The days of middle-class collectors building world class collections are numbered.

So where does this leave those ancient pre-Frazetta works? Unfortunately, higher costs mean most collectors will be able to buy fewer paintings, which guarantees they will focus even more on the works to which they are most drawn — the works of the post Frazetta era. Eventually, reduced demand will leave the prices of pre-Frazetta works well below those of the later works — and then, finally, they will begin to appear on collectors' walls with some frequency. Interestingly enough, this "rediscovery" of the art of the 1940s, 1950s and 1960s will eventually lead to price and demand increases — but not anywhere near the relative levels of the current market.

The astute reader will no doubt have noticed that, with all of the "pre-Frazettas" and "post-Frazettas" riddling this essay, there has been no mention whatsoever of Frank Frazetta himself. The Frazetta scenario is interesting enough to deserve its own consideration.

Currently, Frazetta stands alone atop the SF art pricing structure. Contemporary, vintage, not yet born — Frazetta is at the top. The current record for a Frazetta painting is $360,000 in cash and trade, or roughly triple the record price for any other artist in the genre.

The reasons for this are many, but simple. First, Frazetta is widely acknowledged as one of the most influential illustrators in the history of the genre. Second, because of his earlier career in comics, Frazetta is as revered by the comic art collector as he is by the SF art collector. Like the earlier-discussed Wrightson, the attention of the comic art market on Frazetta's work means far more eyes and many very deep wallets want to acquire his work. Third, Frazetta is one of the very few SF artists deemed "collectible" by mainstream illustration collectors. It is not unheard of to see a Frazetta hanging alongside a Nielsen or a Rackham. Finally, and most importantly, the Frazetta family has maintained an iron grip on the market by withholding the vast majority of Frazetta's work from public sale, and subsequently asking record-breaking prices when they agree to sell works.

It is this last and final reason that provides for future instability in the Frazetta market. In absolute terms, published Frazetta paintings are not rare. No catalogue *raisonné* exists, but the number is somewhere in the vicinity of 150 — almost all of which are extant. Even at an average price of "just" $100,000, the market would need to have $15 million ready and waiting to be poured into Frazettas in order to absorb these works — an unlikely prospect. Thus, the pricing structure is absolutely predicated on a permanent artificial shortage of works on the market.

At present, the family is far more interested in pushing Frazetta further atop the pricing tree than they are in selling large numbers of paintings. Will this remain true over the coming years? Eventually, the family's holdings will not be in the hands of Frank and his wife Ellie, and what will happen then is open to conjecture. If the Frazetta children determine to follow in their parents' footsteps, then the pricing will hold — and escalate — for another generation. If not, however, and the children decide to release any significant number of works on to the market — and want them to sell — then pricing will rapidly decrease to a figure that is much more in step with the remainder of the field. Frazetta will still sell for more than any other contemporary SF illustrator — but not for multiples of his peers.

So, yes, in exploring the natural progression of the market — pre- and post-Frazetta, as well as the Frazetta factor itself — it's evident: there is a sea change coming in the SF art collecting world, but digital illustration is only one of many forces that will make a lasting impression on the market. To collectors, digital illustration is definitely a shadow; however, it's not the black hole that will inevitably engulf SF art collecting as we know it.

Are there other possibilities, other predictions I could make? Of course there are. In the future, new generations of collectors may come to take pleasure in limited edition prints, much as the "fine art" market operates today. Speculators may enter the marketplace and set the whole field afire until the inevitable spectacular crash that follows. We may find that we are not alone in the universe and discover that our intergalactic neighbors don't particularly appreciate the way they have been depicted over the decades — leading to the relegation of SF art to the back of the storage bin with the Uncle Remus books. If science fiction and its art teach us anything, it's that anything is possible.

We sage prognosticators must ever deal in probabilities, not possibilities. The rise to prominence (and lofty pricing) of late 20th century works, the rapidly increasing price of contemporary illustration, and the drop in demand for pre-Frazetta art are the most probable outcomes of the convergence of trends — digital and otherwise — that will drive the SF art market over the next 25 years.

Patrick Wilshire is an avid purchaser of art and an occasional purchaser of groceries. He has supported his habit over the years by designing illustrators' websites and eventually creating his own, *The Illustration Exchange*, to bring artists and collectors together. He lives in central Pennsylvania with his wife, Jeannie, and his dog, Brom.

I am on vacation in Nevis in the West Indies. As I sit writing this essay, I am watching a new home being built. It is a 4,000 square-foot luxury home with a vast "great room", covered by a thirty foot vaulted ceiling. Peering through a wall of windows, the open eaves are fully visible, as stucco walls rise up from handcrafted, 16-inch floor tiles. Built into nearly every wall are numerous niches, trimmed to mirror the appurtenances of a central trellis that encompasses the kitchen. The furniture and fixtures are handmade, nearly all from African straight-grained mahogany. The sinuous trusses are hand-hewn, no two alike as they meander toward a ridge in the center. The actual roof is thatched with a 12 inch layer of water reed over bamboo laths. There are ten such homes, eight already built and two under construction. They all have multi-million dollar price tags. They are inefficient residences to say the least; difficult to build, costly to maintain, more labor intensive and expensive than modern alternatives, and yet there they are, hand hewn crooked beams, custom-made furniture, marble, hand-made tile, thatch, cabinets crafted from all natural material. Why are these less-than-practical elements central to the design of this contemporary home? We must conclude that artifacts created by hand are one of a kind, unique and hence … more desirable.

It is indisputable that consumers today want choices. Henry Ford was famous for telling car buyers "you can choose any color you like so long as it is black." This worked nicely when his were the only cars in town, and demand greatly exceeded supply. Soon, competitors entered the market, Buick offered color choices, then General Motors was born. The drive to differentiate us from our neighbors is strong, imbuing a sense of pride of ownership. Choices make that kind of differentiation possible. Modern homes sell for less than "traditional homes" because by definition, the moment they are built they are no longer "modern." Yet, while we wax nostalgic over older homes with "character" and "charm" the truth is that those terms have cost homeowners incalculable amounts of dollars and aspirins. As contractors like to say, "they do not make them like they used to… thank goodness." Yet consumers are willing to pay the price so long as their choice sets them apart.

Why do we appreciate craftsmanship and gravitate toward it? We admire those who play musical instruments, we attend live concerts, the "classics" have been performed repeatedly, yet we feel that each rendition has a unique interpretation — so we want to experience it. The same is true of live theatre as opposed to movie or television productions. The same cannot be said of objects that are the product of modern technologies: we never hear anyone speak of the craftsmanship of a computer or a modern jet. Yet, the fine Italian marble counter tops, the imported mahogany cabinets and other furniture, often camouflage imposing stainless steel refrigerators, stoves, dishwashers, audio gear, televisions and other "modern conveniences". It seems that functionality comes at a price, because those who require choice are convinced that "older is better," and crave the distinction that uniqueness bestows.

Further, there is great variance in "personal preferences" or "taste" and our tastes are always changing. From art to fashion to music, to all aspects of one's life, preferences or tastes in all societies are in constant flux, a state of affairs that demonstrates our attraction to what is novel, new, different … unique. Repetition and familiar patterns may comfort us but it is the new hemline, the new car model, and the new song that we want

IT JUST MAKES $ENSE FOR ORIGINAL ILLUSTRATION TO CONTINUE
Joe Mannarino

to be seen in, drive, and whistle. Research into our behavior, and explaining the attention-getting appeal of novelty, is the basis for the sciences of sociology and psychology. I am neither a sociologist nor a psychologist, so I cannot — nor will I pretend to be — either. However, twenty-five years of working in marketing and management, and participating in strategic planning sessions (in particular designing training programs for the graphic arts industry), I believe qualifies me to volunteer some possible answers to the above questions, based on observation and experience, and relate them to illustration art. As in the case of any issue this complex, there is no single answer.

Humans are very adaptive, yet also they continually strive for individuation. Explaining how these polar opposite drives can be influenced by learning, and that learning influences how we "see" the world, have consumed psychologists since the inception of the science. Yet despite decades of research we still do not have a definitive answer. From Pavlov to Gagne to Behaviorism to Cognitivism and beyond, there seem to be as many methods and theories as there are people. Each person learns in a different way and at a different pace. There are commonalities, we all retain a percentage of what we read, a percentage of what we hear and a percentage of what we see. Interactivity combined with reinforcement (positive or negative) does affect behavior. Effective training should be made up of all these factors. If this was not the case teachers would simply assign reading to a "student" and issue a test. Instead we have "students" attend a class where we can apply all of the above educational pedagogies and require them to read a chapter a week, and test them to monitor progress. If we used just one method we would either fail to reach all the students, in ways they learn best, or run the risk of our "pupils" tiring, and losing interest out of sheer boredom. The same is true for peoples' predilections. Input from a single source, or in a single form quickly loses effectiveness.

In his seminal work, *Ways of Seeing*, a highly influential book based on a BBC television series aired by the UK in 1972, John Berger forensically examines the topic by comparing the differing ways in which we view an "oil painting" and "publicity art" (illustration art). He concludes that a classic oil "painting" (fine art) represents a possession of what is beautiful and desirable in the world. "Seeing" alone provides a pleasurable reaction, requiring nothing more of us than being a viewer. Possessing art appeals to us because it is a unique item that can be bought, owned and displayed — in effect providing what Berger called "a celebration of a pleasure-in-itself." On the other hand, "Publicity art," Berger claimed, succeeds when it produces anxiety in the viewer by creating a desire for "happiness" — which is achieved by acquiring something more, i.e., what is being depicted. The great illustrators bridge this gap, taking the opportunity presented in illustration to express themselves. Mediocre artists or illustrators cater to the requests of clients (or patrons), in effect selling their soul while selling books for publishers.

So where does this leave us?

For nearly a century, publications and illustrations in all types of formats and categories featured cover images and interior illustrations that complemented the text. As technology improved so did the color, detail and production. Sales followed. Pulp magazines and comic books were ubiquitous. In their golden age, individual comic book titles, by a myriad of publishers, "were routinely selling over 1,000,000 copies," report Beerbohm and Olsen in their article chronicling the history of the American comic book.[1] They also write: "By early 1946, circulation soon hit its all-time highs with well over 1.3 billion periodical issues sold a year," so that "By the early 1950s one in three periodicals sold in the USA was a comic book … 90% of all children admitted they read and enjoyed comics." Yet, by the mid-fifties they were all but gone. Movies had been around since the turn of the century; radio then came along, soon followed by the greatest threat of all to these mediums, *television*. At various points, revenues in each of these mediums dipped dramatically. Just as the eulogies were being prepared, however, the subject resurrected, eventually surpassing previous performances. Which model will book illustration follow? Film, radio, television, or magazines?

Some forty years ago, illustrations on paperbacks had become boring, repetitious, common, pasteurized and ineffective in marketing the "product." Then a man named Frazetta came along. Vibrant, emotional, striking, exciting and sensual images assaulted viewers, changing the landscape for decades. Sales of paperbacks skyrocketed. Interestingly, the landscape of publications seems to have come full circle. A survey of books and publications today reveal little "illustration" beyond simple inanimate objects or static images. It appears that publishers feel that a foil embossed title on high gloss, varnished paper does more to promote sales than a beautifully rendered work of art. However, a survey of "high tech" products reveals a sharp contrast. Music CDs, video DVDs and especially video game packaging features inventive accomplished art! This seems to suggest that when we experience a futuristic event we do not want to leave the safety of the conventional. However, when we partake of "traditional" visual experiences we are more persuaded by images offering a semblance of the future, perhaps to convince ourselves that we are not standing still or falling back.

All of these observations, experiences and facts point to one conclusion: If the art is good, if it satisfies a person's desire to be different, if it spurs an emotion, moves the viewer and most importantly — if it translates into sales — then painted illustration art will continue. An outstanding artist may need to reconcile opposing forces; many of today's illustrators were inspired by generations of artists whose chosen field was illustration, achieved through painting. In addition, not every artist is able or willing to endure the poverty that the traditional path of "fine art" engenders. The field of graphic design provides the artist the environment to create, while maintaining a standard of living. Yet artists recognize that owning the original work provides the opportunity to alter the illustration and create fine art, or even present it that way, if they so choose (and the market agrees). Is there any question that a talented artist will come along and lead us back to the Promised Land? If Frazetta provides any example, it is to demonstrate the probability of that happening. Is there any question that someone will seize that opportunity to market a product? Of course: because it just makes $*ense*.

1 The American Comic book: 1929 — Present by Robert Lee Beerbohm & Richard D. Olsen, PhD ©2006 as published in the Official Overstreet Comic Price guide by Robert Overstreet 36th Edition.

Joseph Mannarino has an extensive background in the Graphic Arts Industry and is a recognized expert, collector and professional in the field of comic and cartoon art collectibles — the co-owner of http://www.allstarauctions.net. He is a long-time member of the American Institute for Conservation of Historic and Artistic Works, President of Comic Art Appraisals LLC, agent for several prestigious artists, and special advisor and contributor to *The Overstreet Comic Book Price Guide*. He is Charter and founding member of the American Association of Comic Book Collectors Committee for Authenticity Certification and Grading.

I N writing an essay concerning digital art's impact on the field of illustration art, it only seems appropriate to paraphrase one of illustration art's greatest creations, the immortal Pogo: "I have seen the enemy, and it is digital art." Speaking as a collector of original illustration art — chiefly science fiction — it's the greatest threat the field has ever faced.

Having said that, it's an enemy for which, on one level, I have some appreciation. This, of course, just makes it that much more insidious. It's tough to be on your guard against something you admire and enjoy looking at. I'm not entirely an "old-fashioned art" snob; I can and do respect good digital illustration art and the craftsmanship that goes into it. There are some very good artists turning out top-notch work in that medium. While some digital artists are perfectly capable of wielding a brush, others lack that facility and, in that respect, digital art can be seen as a boon to the illustration art field. Several digital artists who could never have earned a living by painting have given us the benefit of their imaginations, and they've created some fascinating works. There are several I could name where I'd love to have the original in my collection, but aye, *there's* the rub — regardless of how skillfully executed or beautiful, you just can't collect the *original*, since there is no original to collect.

Don't talk to me about limited edition prints of the work, no matter the quality or whether they're signed; a great deal of the allure of collecting original art is the thrill of collecting the unique, of knowing you have the only *one* of this painting in existence — not that you have *one* of a series where more can be produced by simply pushing a button. It's what makes each painting in our collection one-of-a-kind. Even a collector of limited means can acquire a piece that more well-heeled collectors would love to add to their collection, but can't. After all, there's only one. Digital prints lack the cachet and soul of an original painting. When I was in my teens, I bought my first science fiction magazine off the stands, an act prompted solely by the tremendous cover painting. Thirty years later, I finally was lucky enough to buy the original painting. The artist isn't terribly well collected today, and his work is relatively inexpensive, but I have an emotional connection to that painting, which is reinforced every day when I see it hanging on the wall. Owning a print of it might be nice, but couldn't possibly deliver the same sense of immense satisfaction.

If the shift to digital art continues, it will have a significant impact on the collecting field. Similarities in the behaviors of collectors across collecting fields, in combination with economic and cultural factors known to have influenced the market life-cycles of other rare or unique collectible objects, suggest that the effects will be felt short term and long term, and a majority of them will be negative.

In the short term, a shift will likely drive prices up. It's the old story of supply and demand. At the moment, there is a group of collectors of illustration art and the size of this group has led to the demand for original illustration art being at a certain level. It's a fairly closed system. However, each digital illustration used as a cover to a book or magazine means one less traditional painting created. As more digital art is produced, not only will there be this one-for-one effect, but some traditional artists will undoubtedly leave the field, driven out by competition from their digital peers, as they will no longer have enough assignments to make a living. This will further reduce the pool of new art available to collectors. As a recent ebay auction noted, it was a rare opportunity to collect an original piece by the artist in question, since most of his work was being produced digitally. For a collect-

THE DEATH OF ILLUSTRATION ART COLLECTING
Doug Ellis

ing field that is already witnessing a steady decrease in the amount of new material being produced each year, due to a decrease in the number and type of markets that use illustration art, the move to digital art is yet another sign of the economic pressures affecting the industry, and another — possibly the final — nail in the coffin. If the number of paintings being produced dwindles significantly, collectors will compete for an ever smaller market of new material, leading to an increase in prices. Initially, longtime collectors may view this as a positive development, as the value of their collections increases to reflect the growing scarcity of original art, and those that sell art during this time will reap the benefits. However, these benefits are likely to be ephemeral, and those that hold on to their collections will find that the increased value of their holdings is not sustained.

That's because another, less immediate but equally important, impact of the shift to digital art will be a decrease in the number of people collecting original art. A significant reduction in the amount of new illustration art available and the resultant increase in prices will eventually drive the beginning collector and the collector on a more limited budget, as well as the casual collector, out of the market. Where once this field may have filled a vital niche, by making it possible for emerging and/or middle-class collectors to become part of that group who take pleasure in owning originals, such purchases will simply be too expensive for them to enter or indulge in the hobby. As a result, a number of people who would otherwise collect original art and contribute to a robust collecting market will either leave the field or never enter it in the first place.

Every collecting group needs an infusion of new blood from time to time to remain healthy. Let's face it — the market for collecting original illustration art has never been a large one. With fewer new collectors entering the field, attrition will eventually reduce the size of the collecting group; as collectors are priced out, they will not be replaced. To remain viable, the market needs to grow, not stagnate or contract. Eventually, our numbers will be too few to sustain prices, and the market will collapse. It's happened before in other areas of popular culture where new material isn't produced — just ask all those dime novel collectors out there, if you can find one. On the other hand, collectible markets for items such as comics and sports cards are still going strong.

A further negative impact of the shift to digital art stems from the relationship of illustration art to the so-called fine art establishment. For years illustration art has been looked down upon by the art-collecting community at large. The prevailing attitude seems to have been that if it was created for a commercial purpose, it can't have any artistic merit and isn't worthy of being collected. It's only a fairly recent development that illustration art has been accorded some respect, as more people have come to recognize that even though they were painting to eat, great illustrators were also great artists. Ironic that this recognition has come as the field is facing its greatest challenge.

There's already a bias against illustration art in most art circles. A Tom Lovell or Nick Eggenhofer pulp cover doesn't command nearly the price of one of their "fine art" paintings. A shift to digital art — where the illustrator may have no art training whatsoever, or any facility with brush and paint — will only exacerbate art establishments' scorn and erode what little recognition and respect illustrators have achieved. It seems unlikely that, with the exception of some artists whom the larger art community will view as avant-garde and cutting edge, digital art will be viewed as "real" art. As a result, collectors who are slowly moving into the illustration art arena, as its merits are being discovered, but who are sensitive to socio-cultural pressures, will once more disdain to enter it, further shrinking the field.

Finally, and perhaps hardest for collectors to bear, digital art brings none of the same satisfying social and psychological pay-offs that accrue from collecting original illustration art. For collectors, there's always been the "thrill of the hunt" in tracking down original art and enjoyment in sharing your tales of success (or even failure) with fellow collectors who can relate to the experience. The thrill is gone if the artist can just print out another one anytime he or she chooses. The thrill is also diminished if you're the only one hunting. Collecting is a social activity; as our numbers dwindle, the sense of camaraderie will slowly vanish as well, muting the pleasure of collecting. Yet if the trend towards digital art in illustration continues to grow, this too may be added to the butcher's bill.

It seems a combination of factors, both cultural and economic, are conspiring to do away with the notion of collecting unique works of art, created by hand, that coincidentally function to sell products like magazines, games and books. It's a shame, because for collectors used to, and wanting, originals, digitally created art is no replacement for the joy of owning something "one of a kind," that can't ever be recreated identically. It's all very good to quote (or paraphrase) Pogo, or to be a fan of Walt Kelly's art, but if Pogo was a creation of the digital age, you just wouldn't be able to collect the originals. Even if you could afford them.

Frank Wu's **Losing Memories**
interior illustration for the story by
K. Bird Lincoln, published in
Darkling Plain *magazine, Fall 2001.*
Mixed media: ink and digital

Doug Ellis, a collector of original SF art and pulps for 20 years, is co-organizer of the annual Windy City Pulp & Paperback Convention, which has become a leading venue for the sale and display of vintage SF art. He's the author of a book devoted to pulp art, *Uncovered* (Adventure House, 2003)

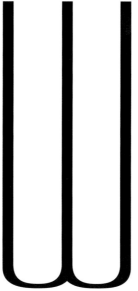

WHAT was almost exclusively the domain of scientific endeavors, software, has become an everyday and indispensable tool for extending human thought, from blogs to creating works of art. At the same time, organizations have grown increasingly dependent upon software applications, and the artifacts they produce, for creating and maintaining official records. On one hand, this has proven a boon for a variety of industries, particularly those which are arts related. Digitally created art has been embraced throughout the arts community from painting, photography, and film production to web-based multi-media and installation art, and can even be found as elements of sculpture. In particular, the field of illustration arts has experienced tremendous growth of digital art production in recent years, due largely to the publishing world's recognition of the economic benefits involved: improved production processes and lower costs. University art departments have formalized digital media programs, and museums and private collectors have begun to show interest by acquiring digital works of art for permanent collections. On the other hand, however, while we expect art to be preserved as long as possible, to record our cultural and intellectual activities, a proliferation in digital records and digitally created artworks is occurring at a time when the ability to preserve digital artifacts for the long term is in serious question. Our ability to access and retain records is being lost due to obsolescence of both the hardware and the software used to create them. Digital art, sadly, will be one of the losers in the endeavor to preserve digital information, and — given the disdain accorded advertising and commercial art — the illustrative arts will fare least well of them all.

Museums and private collectors that acquire works of art with the goal of preserving them for posterity are being faced with technological issues they are unprepared to resolve and that have no clear solution. Typically, such collectors are only interested in acquiring the original works of art — with digital art this means collecting the data files used by applications to create the images that comprise the work. Because image files such as JPEGs do not provide insight into the tools used by an artist or how an artist worked with his tools, they can only be considered "prints" of the original and, as such, of little interest to collectors. Maintaining and accessing the original data files, therefore, is the crux of the problem with regard to preserving digital art for future generations. In the last ten years, preservation of digital artifacts has developed into a critically important area of research among museums, libraries, and governmental agencies throughout the developed world. Out of this research, several approaches to preservation have emerged; all of them useful to some degree, and all of them deficient in some capacity deemed necessary by the preservation community. In addition to these actual preservation approaches, techniques are being explored to understand better what information is needed by those involved with the preservation of digital artifacts, and what processes are needed to derive and maintain that information. These data are collectively referred to as preservation metadata. The complex nature of digital preservation, however, combined with users' lack of knowledge, is retarding development of fully satisfying solutions.

DIGITAL ART, A.K.A. VAPOR ART
David Leucht

At the heart of the digital preservation problem is the technology that is used to produce and store the artifacts. The physical lifetimes of storage devices is relatively short, so that maintaining a digital file "long term" requires periodical copying of the file to new storage media, to protect against device malfunction and media decay. While such routine copying of the files is rather benign, it rests on the underlying assumption that files can always be accessed when needed … an incorrect assumption, given the nature of the digital artifacts. All digital artifacts exist in an encoded form that is only decipherable by specific software applications. While the digital artifacts remain static after creation, the software used to read them and decipher the encoding is not static. Software applications are continually evolving, and at some point become entirely obsolete. To complicate the situation further, the hardware platforms needed to run the applications also experience change, and eventually even they become obsolete. In 1995 the American National Research Council issued the following statement: "The fact that most electronic hardware is expected to function for no more than 10 to 20 years raises very serious problems for long-term (more than 20 years) archival preservation. Even if the operating systems and documentation problems are somehow dealt with, what is the archivist to do when the machine manufacturer declares the hardware obsolete or simply goes out of business? Will there be an IBM or Sony in the year 2200? If they still exist, with they maintain a 1980-1990 vintage machine? Moreover, it must be realized that no archival organization can hope realistically to maintain such hardware by itself. Integrated circuits, thin film heads, and laser diodes can not be repaired today, nor can they be readily fabricated, except in multimillion-dollar factories." Today it is only possible to find an Atari computer in museums or computer swap meets, despite the Atari being considered an advanced graphics development tool in its time. Recently, Silicon Graphics entered bankruptcy and Apple Computers announced they are shifting to the Intel architecture for their computers. As we can see, the hardware platforms are far from stable.

Another obstacle to preserving digital files is lack of agreement as to what information must be maintained in order for future users to access and understand our contemporary digital artifacts. Preservation metadata refers to data collected about a work, and maintained in association with that work of art. Among the data needed to be collected are those descriptive in nature, such as name, artist, date, content description, exhibition history, and contemporaneous works. Digital preservationists, however, are also concerned with administrative data such as rights management information, provenance information establishing authenticity, and change history information. Additionally, they must also maintain structural information, such as which digital files are necessary to reconstruct the work, which operating system, hardware platform, display devices, encryption or compression data and even color bars to assure display integrity. But is this enough? Research is ongoing to determine what information is necessary to capture. The greatest challenge is the uncertainty of knowing whether every critical datum is being collected. Meanwhile, a tremendous amount of digital art is being created today, disseminated and displayed with little or no information being collected by anyone except the few museums who have chosen to acquire digital art. Having an artifact and not knowing what it is or how to access it is like not having it at all.

The simplest and least costly approach to digital preservation, "refreshing," actually does not protect at all against the obsolescence of the hardware and software needed to access the digital art. "Refreshing" involves the serial copying of digital files from one storage location to another and attempts to keep a digital art artifact intact in its original form and preserve it as long as possible. Because of the fragile nature of digital storage media, "refreshes" must be performed periodically to assure an artifact is not corrupted or lost due to media failure. Refreshing assures data integrity and can preserve authentication with the parent copy if conducted in a manner approved by preservation organizations. While true that files can be copied from one medium to another, it is not necessarily true that tomorrow's media devices will be able to communicate with the software needed to display the digital artwork. Refreshing can only be considered a stopgap method of ensuring a copy of the digital artifact exists for later preservation activities and is not itself a solution to the long-term preservation and access problems. Having possession of an artifact but not having the ability to read or interpret the artifact is not a solution.

The simplest approach to working around the obsolescence problem involves upgrading the digital artifact so it will function on the latest hardware or software platform. This approach, referred to as "migration," does not ensure the integrity of the work — it only produces a functionally identical copy of the parent artifact (at least, this is the intent). The integrity of the data may, and most likely will be changed; the child copy will no longer be identical to the parent from which it was derived. Furthermore, it may not be possible to revert the child back to a copy of the parent due to data loss or change during the migration process. "Migration" is now routinely practiced by anyone who uses a computer for any length of time. In its simplest form, it involves moving a file of a data from one version of a software application to another version of the same application. The process is usually trouble-free because software vendors strive to ensure forward migration without loss of content, although they typically will not guarantee lack of change. More troublesome is migrating a digital file from one software application to a competitor's application. Although vendors will often provide tools to import a competitor's data files, the tools are rarely complete and trouble-free. Thus, when a user moves to a new vendor's application, existing data files often appear to misbehave or fail to function in some critical manner under the new application. For digital art, the consequences can be disastrous, if some aspect of the artwork is changed or lost. If the alteration is only a slight color change, or a slightly different appearance on-screen, and IF the creator is available for consultation and correction, this may be correctable. With the artist's death, that option disappears, whether the changes are mild or extreme. Entire works of art may be corrupted and pass unnoticed, in that state, into the future. Serial migration only aggravates and magnifies the difficulties and problems related to data format changes and corruption. Authentication of the migrated copy also is suspect since it cannot be demonstrated that the migrated artifact is identical to the parent. For museums and other collectors, the artifacts need to remain intact, unchanged, and accessible in order to retain their historical and cultural significance. Clearly, the "migration" approach is also not a good solution.

To avoid problems inherent to the "migration" approach, "standardization" has been proposed as a means of ensuring that all digital artifacts will be fully operable by any given software application now and in the future. With this approach researchers are attempting to anticipate what will be useful or needed by future users. Standardization involves determining which file formats, application features and hardware features are needed to achieve the goal of preserving a digital work in a manner that supports migration without its inherent loss or corruption of data. The difficulties related to standardization involve determining which formats and features to use. Standards themselves evolve over time and are not always forward compatible, so it is unlikely the standardization approach will be a preservation strategy superior to application migration. Freezing today's standards is unlikely to result in preservation also because of technology obsolescence over time. Further, it is unlikely that all digital art will convert to the selected standard format precisely because an artist chose to use some proprietary feature of software in order to render the work. Artists thrive on implementing innovative tools, and successful software and hardware vendors achieve and maintain success by being innovative — and innovation is rarely rewarded unless the innovation can be kept proprietary. Thus there is little incentive for artists to hew to standard formats, nor incentive for vendors to reveal to competitors or a standards committee how their innovations work. Only those artists who avoid use of proprietary software features are likely to see their works survive under a standard format. Restricting artists to a set of standards cannot be considered a solution when it stifles creativity and expression.

If we can't count on applications or hardware to remain static in design through the centuries, and we need to be able to access digital artifacts created under obsolete environments, the only solution is to keep the artifacts and applications intact and emulate the hardware platforms used to run the creator applications. "Emulation" is accomplished by developing software applications to mimic the behavior and functionality of the entire hardware platform. Thus the attraction of emulation to digital preservationists — it promises to display a digital work in its original environment without requiring the original hardware platform. What is significantly different about this approach is the magnitude of scope; it requires the original software application to run the digital artifact as well as the original operating system and any ancillary software applications (e.g. plug-ins) required by the digital work. Although promising in its scope and flexibility, emulation is years away from a reality in any capacity other than proof of concept, and the maintenance model for such an approach is very troublesome. As each generation of hardware obsolesces, it must also be emulated. Over time, the amount of retest both for the artifacts and preceding emulations becomes more and more burdensome. Eventually, the effort required to maintain the emulation approach will overwhelm the resources of preserving organizations and hard choices will have to be made in terms of which artifacts to retain and which to prune from the collections. Achieving sustained maintenance of the emulation approach from now until eternity (or a complete paradigm shift in computing, whichever comes first) is a monumental effort and will require coordinated efforts and commitments of governments, commercial firms and preserving organizations. Further, the costs associated with emulation may prove prohibitive for all but the most necessary artifacts unless some breakthrough technology is discovered to ease artifact verification costs.

One of the leading researchers of digital preservation, Jeff Rothenberg, observed in 1997, "Digital documents last forever—or five years, which ever comes first." It is now almost ten years since making the observation and the world remains without a long-term strategy to ensure existing digital artifacts will be available in the future. Because of the short periods between machine and software improvements, digital art created as recently as fifteen to twenty years ago is now challenged in access and exhibition. The problem will only worsen in the years to come. The hardware and software continue to evolve, making it more and more difficult to exhibit older works of digital art. We don't really know what information must be collected to assure preservation of digital art for future generations. Refreshing and migration, the only techniques currently available for preservation, are known to be inadequate and worse, destructive over time. Any attempt at standardization imposed by the preservation community will be detrimental to the arts community. Finally, emulation, the only promising approach to preservation, is years away from practice and will ultimately be so costly that our descendants may have to choose what to preserve from their past. Museums and arts organizations are not equipped to address the problems that preservation of digital works pose to them. The effort and costs associated with dealing with repeated upgrades and access activities will quickly consume whatever meager resources they can bring to bear on preserving access to their digital collections. Organizations currently practicing refresh while awaiting a permanent solution will be forced to migrate their collections soon, if they have not already begun the practice. Serially migrating digital works of art every ten years while awaiting the emulation solution, will only assure that change occurs in the art works and many will be lost forever for lack of a migration path. What does this mean for those of us interested in illustration art? Museums and the general arts community typically are not inclined to pay attention to the interests of the illustrative arts; indeed, they usually refer to illustration art with disdain if they bother to address it at all. With very few professional organizations devoted to illustration arts, the resources that can be brought to bear on the problem of preserving digital illustration art will be very meager indeed. In the end, we are going to lose the majority of the digital art created during the blossoming of the information age.

Firestorm ©1982 Janny Wurts. *Later published by Renaissance Greeting Cards and by* Science Fiction Chronicle *as a magazine cover, Sept. 1988*

David Leucht has more than 20 years experience in the engineering and development of spacecraft software and computers and currently finds satisfaction in managing software development efforts. Despite suffering education in Chemistry, Microbiology and Computer Science, he has managed, since childhood, to retain a deep affection for science fiction and is a passionate collector of science fiction art.

D ON'T *touch the art!* I've only been tempted to break that rule once. In The Cloisters' inner courtyards, low, thin columns whose capitals bear distorted faces separate the covered walkways from the herb gardens. The sculpture isn't particularly fine. What's more, it's unpolished, roughened by at least a thousand years of weather before it was hauled from Europe to New York City. What tempted me to reach out and touch was the chisel marks on those grotesque faces. They are the sign that, more than a thousand years ago, a craftsman laid hand to tools and created the work I see. That sign connects me to the long-dead artisan and the tradition of which he forms a part.

I never meant to collect science fiction and fantasy art. I grew up not just with art but with the Old Masters as models. My uncle and aunt were both WPS artists whose works hang in the Metropolitan Museum of Fine Art, the Vatican, the Whitney, and many private collections. While other children colored within the lines, I was given crayons, pastels, huge sheets of paper, and the encouragement to enjoy myself. From the books I received for my birthday stared Velásquez's solemn royal children, Botticelli's ethereal figures, and the distorted, eerie saints of El Greco. My uncle would sit me on his lap and explain how you looked at the light in a Rembrandt, why the flesh tones in a Rubens were so remarkable, and that if Picasso drew clowns, you had to call them saltimbanques and the color he used was rose, not pink. Yes, he said, their arms and legs were elongated, but Picasso could distort the human form because "once you learn anatomy and can draw figures correctly, then you get to do what you like."

At age six, I was sent to the Butler Museum of American Art in Ohio, where I learned charcoals, pastels, the fiendishly difficult medium of watercolors, and finally, in my teens, oils. To this day, when I smell the sharpness of turpentine, I remember being part of a bunch of kids covered in multi-colored smudges. We drank nickel Cokes, got dizzy peering up three floors at coffered ceilings, and had to be chased away from beneath the piano near the John Singer Sargents whenever the Junior Leaguers held their teas. We always hoped they would share. They never did.

We had better luck descending all the way into the basement, giggling and darting past the immense boiler and into the art shop. There we goggled at the prices of the paintbrushes and hypnotized ourselves on pigment names: alizarin, ultramarine, viridian.

I began reading science fiction at about the same time. If I thought about the covers of the books I read, it was as something to hide from my teachers, who had decided opinions on what was suitable reading for an honors student. I do remember some images from my teens: Jack Gaughan's stunning purple-and-orange, elongated figures on the cover of Marion Zimmer Bradley's *The Bloody Sun*; the Dillons' cryptic, shadowed cover for Ursula K. Le Guin's *The Left Hand of Darkness*; Pauline Baynes' sketches for the Narnia books; and the iconic Ballantine paperback covers for *The Lord of the Rings*, which I often saw embroidered on rich-hippie jeans.

In the late 1970s, I became more intelligently aware of science fiction art as I began selling fiction and going to conventions. My first purchase was a "rough" by Janny Wurts, one of the cover sketches for *White Wing*, which Shariann Lewitt and I wrote for Tor under the pseudonym Gordon Kendall. That was swiftly followed by Nancy Weisenfeld's batiks for *Silk Roads and Shadows*.

I began to see more and more of what I liked. Still, I held somewhat aloof. After all, much of the art was in acrylics, and they had not been in good odor in the training I'd had. Two-dimensional, not subtle, my family sniffed. Then I saw the textures that Frank

*And time
for all
the works
and days
of hands...*

"The Love Song of J.
Alfred Prufrock,"
by T.S. Eliot

CONFESSIONS OF AN INVOLUNTARY ART COLLECTOR
Susan Shwartz

Lurz and Bob Eggleton could achieve with them, and my horizons widened — fast.

It was the sketches that really won me over. My fine-arts background pricked up its snobby ears and told me: pay attention. These people can really draw. My first major purchase (for me) was a David Cherry sketch of Guinevere, swiftly followed by a Dawn Wilson lithograph of Morgaine that I still think turned out far better than the final rendering in tempera.

At the huge World Science Fiction Art Shows, I noticed that the work by leading, Hugo-winning artists was taking on what I could only call a Royal Academy feel: very painterly, with increased use of oil and oil washes, superb drawing and increasing subtlety of color and composition. I began to talk to the artists. More to the point, I began to listen to them. And I began to meet the dealers.

Doom was near at hand.

The final blow fell at Boskone, the venerable science fiction convention held by the New England Science Fiction Association (NESFA) and noted for its art shows. A number of Jack Gaughan roughs were up for sale, including one of a highly masculine, elongated, and brightly colored warrior-scientist terrorizing some wizards with highly weird electronics. Just as the Wall, the group of volunteers who walk through a convention art show to signify that it was ending, passed by, I turned to the man beside me and asked, "Do you mind if I outbid you for that one? I need it for my collec — oh God, I'm so doomed."

I had finally admitted I was a collector.

At another Boskone, Rick Berry was Art Guest of Honor. His work showed me something I hadn't noticed before: digital art, either hyper-realistic or abstract, computer-generated and printed on archival-quality paper. For me, computer-generated work was, and still is, too much like posters or reproductions. I admire it; it's technically perfect; some of it is eerily beautiful; and the one digital cover I had (Stefan Martiniere's prize-winning work for *Hostile Takeover*) was fantastic. What I want most in the art I collect is, essentially, the laying on of hands: the flow of talent from the artist through his or her medium onto the canvas. What intrigued me about Rick Berry's work was that he'd taken a portrait of a woman in a white dress, and painted on it in oil so it reminded me of Whistler's Woman in White. But it was far out of my reach. So I bought a sketch of Medea, dancing. Rick Berry can really *draw*!

That was the Boskone at which I saw Dave Seeley's work. It, too, was digitized and painted. I could see in his composition that he'd trained as an architect, and he had a flair for high-tech. So, I dragged my editor over. We agreed it was just what we wanted for *Second Chances*. The finished work was computer-generated, but Dave added depth and humanity by overpainting with oils. The composition was pure Caravaggio, a wickedly intricate circle of struggling figures. Two years later, I bought it. Two years after that, Dave was Guest of Honor at a Balticon (in Baltimore's Inner Harbor). "I've got to show you!" he told me and brought out his portfolio. We both knelt on the floor, turning over the pages until I saw a *Star Wars* painting he'd done for Lucasfilms. Based on a suggestion I'd made once, it was a Pieta, with a dead Imperial Storm Trooper draped across a painted figure's lap. It gave me shivers.

Officially, I suppose I've been collecting for at least ten years now. The most eclectic things appeal to me. Shang jades, T'ang statuettes, hand-blown paperweights, netsuke, and Wedgwood in all colors jostle each other on bookshelves and tables. Sketches from *Star Trek* designs for Romulan ships and scanners hang across the hall from a Bonestell nautical oil painting. A graceful, decadent Omar Rayyan geisha reclines by a pool of koi. Below it is a pencil and tempera sketch by my uncle, Jack Levine, of a Japanese waitress from *Facing East*, his portfolio collaboration with James Michener. It's unfinished. I can see the brushstrokes, the pencil marks.

Orbiting Bob Eggleton's Io, with its brilliant volcanoes, like a thousand Pompeiis, are Donato Giancola's sketches. Sepia with white highlights, his Gimli, Legolas, Aragorn, and Gandalf remind me of the da Vinci sketches I saw at Windsor Castle. Then there's Alan Pollack's *A Long-Forgotten Gohei*. While I suspect a "gohei" is some sort of message used in a Japanese-based game, I bought the painting for the way Pollack built textures with layers of oils, then slashed them with a palette knife and the grisaille, the interplay of gray and white, light and shadow glistening off signal, rock walls, and a dim sky.

At a World Fantasy Convention in Washington, D.C., I happened by, accidentally on purpose, as Jane Frank was setting up. As she lifted from its packing a Richard Bober portrait of a Renaissance lady whose cloak and flowers draped over a painted gilt interior frame in exquisite *trompe l'oeil*, I succumbed, then spent the weekend countering people's laments of "it's NFS (not for sale), but the woman looks just like you!" with "I already bought it, and I've never met him!"

My passion for art has brought me closer to the artists. I've discussed with Randy Asplund how he grinds his own pigment for his illuminations, then switched, as Donato Giancola came up, into an enthusiastic hand-waving conversation about heraldry and the Battle of Agincourt. I've leaned against the wall beside Randy Lagana at a master class, just as artists, collectors, and art-lovers have always assembled to watch, whether in New York, on the Left Bank of Paris, in Renaissance Florence, or Golden Age Athens — perhaps even in the ancient caves of Lascaux.

I've fallen in love with a large, delicate watercolor, painted with the most astonishing tenderness by Gary Lippincott, who looks as if he could shoe a horse with one hand while painting with the other. I think I'm as enchanted by the contrast of the painting and its creator as I am with the work itself.

The May 4, 1970, killings at Kent State University have always had terrible meaning for me. I remember when my late aunt Ruth Gikow created a series of charcoal sketches and an immense oil painting as part of a memorial presented to the University in 1971. In 2005, while researching her work, I found one of the sketches up for sale. I called the dealer, burst into tears, and went out to the art colony in Brooklyn to buy it. Although most of my pictures are framed elaborately, that one is not. As I told the dealer, who suggested I reframe it, "No. Jewish coffins are plain wood."

I find that what I collect are fragments of the works and days of artists' hands. From the moment I come home, they surround me. Each time I look around, everywhere I look, I see things differently: a trick of the light, a shift in my mood, pieces juxtaposed so I can see what a Gikow lithograph of Queen Esther looks like near a Richard Powers unicorn. My walls are crowded with a silent, eloquent, never-ending dialogue.

Sometimes I hold my breath and move until my nose is almost against the canvas — Because, except to hang my art, I don't touch it. The artists' hands brought these works to life. Now, it's they who touch me. That is all I want and more than I ever thought to have.

Susan Shwartz has published 30 books and over 70 pieces of short fiction and non-fiction in nine languages. A career Wall Street businesswoman, Susan earned her MA and PhD from Harvard University and her BA in English from Mount Holyoke College. She lives in Forest Hills, New York.

The portrait is an 8"x11" watercolor by Everett Raymond Kinstler from the JVJ Publishing hardcover edition of Everett Raymond Kinstler: The Artist's Journey Through Popular Culture, 1942-1962, *2005.*

LL physical art, when you get right down to it, is but the artist's best attempt to make manifest the artistic vision she sees in her head. It is only when the commercial aspects of art are brought into play that arguments such as "Paint or Pixel?" arise.

It can be argued that "Artistic Vision" is the genesis of all art. I define "Artistic Vision" as that original concept that the artist calls into existence from nothing. Of course, there is generally a stimulus. Claude Monet watched the light change on Rouen Cathedral and felt compelled to capture it in paint. James McNeil Whistler saw symphonies of shades and explored them in his nocturnes. Robert Crumb faced his inner demons and exorcised them in ink. This new concept may be stimulated by inner passion, by hunger or by an art director's or patron's assignment, but its prime characteristic is that it is unique to the artist. It is capital "A" Art and it demands to manifest itself in the physical world. Therein lies bliss, confusion, depression and money.

Ask an artist sometime just how precisely his "art" matches the Vision that was in his head. The happiest ones are satisfied with their efforts and will tell you that they came pretty close. There are those, of course, who will say that it is a precise manifestation. For some very talented few, that will be true, but I would suspect most such claimants of falling prey to the conceit that since they can hold it in their hands, it must be Art and therefore must have been what they intended. The most unhappy practitioners are those who have failed to satisfy themselves — no matter what the critical or popular views of their accomplishments. In all cases, the expectation or receipt of monetary rewards can accentuate or alleviate the emotional impact.

Most artists would prefer to make a living from their talent and skill. To do so, their vision has to be shared. A patron, appreciator, art director or gallery owner has to see what the Artist has envisioned before it can be printed, sold, reproduced, or otherwise translated into money. It is the transition from the "Artistic Vision" to a physical rendition of same which leads to the confusion of what Art is. Is Art the imagination and insight which preceded the execution of the image, or is it the image itself?

An industry has arisen founded on the notion that Art is something you can hold and buy. It is the status of "original" that conveys value. There is only ONE "original" and, as such, it is unique and therefore rare. The painting is the Art, not the image on the canvas, although it is the image that determines how much the canvas is *worth*. This dichotomy has led the art industry to perform some odd mental gymnastics with regard to some artistic media.

Because artists want to share their "Artistic Vision" with as many people as possible and because the public actively searches for artists whose vision resonates with them, artists were always experimenting with reproduction techniques.

In the early sixteenth century, Albrecht Dürer found that the technique of copper engraving combined a manifestation of his vision with a means of disseminating it. His engravings are NOT his "originals." That honor would have to belong to the copper plate onto which he engraved his vision, and despite its lack of "uniqueness" the art industry will be happy to sell you one of his prints as an "original" Dürer. At the turn of the twentieth century, Alphonse Mucha used lithography to share his vision with the world. The lithographic stone, by its very nature, eliminates the possibility of an "original" in the commercial sense of the word. The images are drawn directly onto the stone and the

IT'S THE VISION, NOT THE MEDIUM
Jim Vadeboncoeur, Jr.

same stone is then ground flat again to prepare it for the next Artist. Nothing remains except the lithographic prints which, despite their multiplicity, are sold as "original" Muchas. Norman Lindsay was a master of the etching art. Given the complexity of his images, it is surprising that he produced 375 etchings. For Lindsay, it was only the plate that mattered. Bringing the image from his mind to the metal was his artistic challenge. When he had completed work on an etching, it was incumbent upon his wife, Rose, to actually pull some prints from the plate. Norman couldn't be bothered.

The lithographic stone is also the medium of choice of Michael Parkes, a modern-day Artist. To manifest his vision, Parkes creates 12- to 15-color lithographs in edition sizes of between 100 and 300. Recently he has turned to the computer to create *Giclées*, not because they better represent his Art, but simply because his stone lithographer is retiring and he can no longer execute the type of lithograph that could make his Vision real. Lithography is a partnership between the Artist and the Artisan — he who creates and he who executes the vision. When looking for a replacement for his lithographer, he discovered that the BEST he was offered by other lithographers was the ability to create five-color lithographs in editions of, at most, 50. Rather than compromise his vision to these lesser parameters, he found that the computer and *giclée* technology could provide him with a different means to share his Art.

If you liked Michael Parkes' stone lithographs, you'll probably like his giclées, too. They depict similar subjects with similar skill. They are printed on comparable papers with comparable inks. Only the method of putting that ink on the paper has changed. Both methods produce beautiful prints. In neither case is there an "original" that can be held or sold. Is anyone prepared to argue the case that, because one was produced on stone by the artist wielding a crayon and the other on a monitor with the artist wielding a graphic tablet pen, one is Art and the other is not? Both represent, to the best of his ability, Michael Parkes' vision. If that vision produced Art in one medium, who can say it doesn't produce Art in the other? The answer can be found in that Latin phrase *cui bono?* ("Who benefits?"). To proclaim that Pixels can't produce Art is disingenuous, especially when put forth by those who make their livelihood selling only what THEY designate as Art. They may argue that there is just too many bad computer images for it to be Art. They're deliberately missing the point.

The computer has provided the opportunity to manifest and share visions to more people than ever before. If Theodore Sturgeon were alive today, he would probably re-state "Sturgeon's Law" to proclaim that "99% of everything is crap!" Bad computer art merely demonstrates the creators' lack of artistic vision. They may have a way to say something, but they either have very little to say or not enough skill to say it. You only need attend an amateur art show to see similar results in paint. The level of painting skills may be higher simply because it takes more effort and practice to manipulate liquid paint. The artistic vision, generally, is similarly limited.

Yet, an artist like Dave McKean is part of the blessed one percent. He uses the computer to bring forth challenging, beautiful images. Before the computer had developed into a useful tool, McKean created *tableaux* in three dimensions and then lit and photographed them for print. Those staged arrangements were not kept. The pieces were reclaimed and reused to manifest other visions. There were no "originals" beyond the photograph that captured the vision. What was being "sold" was his vision, not an assemblage of objects. With the computer, McKean can come closer to the *tableaux* in his head because the inherent limitations of the three-dimensional world have been removed. His control over the light and the mood is precise and the physical size relationships of reality are eliminated. The computer has actually set his mind free and allowed him to envision more. McKean obliterates the same barriers in the medium of film. His vision extends seamlessly into another transitory art. Film has no "original" to sell. Film is simply a means of bringing an artistic vision into a form that can be shared. No one cares that a lot of modern film is based almost totally on "pixels." What matters is whether or not the film is any good.

In the "reproducible arts," the printed image is what matters. The computer has opened the way for a new art form. Modern art sensibilities suggest that everyone is an artist, and the computer is a willing accomplice in that deception. More people are now able to generate a reproducible image and most of their work is certainly grounds for this discussion. It isn't only that the ratio of art to Art has changed, but the sheer quantity of the output has increased dramatically. All of which should reinforce our appreciation of those few artists with both the vision and the skill with which to share it with us. Since it's what is inside their heads that matters, why should we care if they utilize paint or pixels to show it to us?

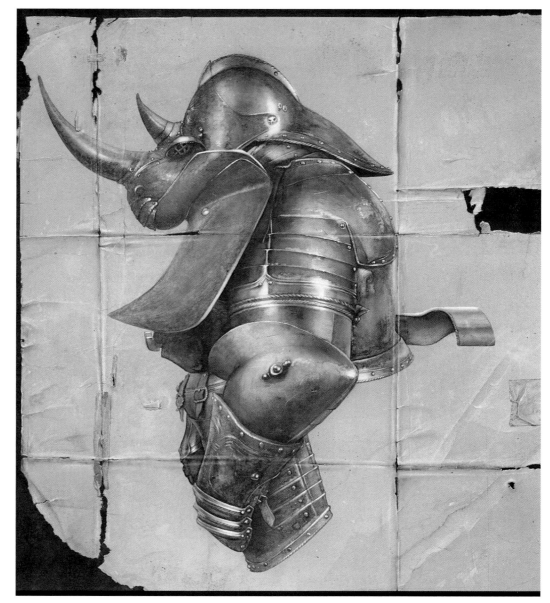

Rhino Armour *II by John Howe,*
watercolour on paper, approximately
40 x 60 cm, unpublished 1983

Jim Vadeboncoeur, Jr. is an ex-technical illustrator, an ex-graphic designer, an ex-bookseller, and an ex-art dealer. Now retired, he devotes his time to writing, researching comic books, and to publishing *The Vadeboncoeur Collection of ImageS* — a magazine devoted to illustration art of a century ago. See www.bpib.com/images.htm

THE latter half of the 20th century has ushered in the Computer Age, and with that a Pandora's box of new opportunities, taking the world utterly by surprise. This new technological era was as instantly different to the times before as the first steam engines ushering in the Industrial Age were to pastoral, agricultural yokes that preceded it. The digital realm strikes us as entirely different because there is no immediate physicality. An intermediary is required — the computer — to decode its secret language and transform the mass of unintelligible kipple into something that is familiar to our hairless, mammalian selves. In the early days of the computer, this translation was difficult and was relegated to a secret international cabal of mostly introverted, inquisitive, technology-obsessed … um … nerds. In any case, today is a different story. Computers are an intrinsic, Borg-like part of our everyday lives, invading every form and shape of our human culture, to the detriment and benefit of all. Art is no exception. Many artists today use computers in some way during their creative process, whether to research a prospective project, access source imagery, or use the computer as a creative tool in itself. This brings to light the impact and influence which digital technologies and media are having on our society. As the curator of a modern, non-traditional museum, my major function is to distill simplistic narratives from complex historical or cultural threads, and it's obvious to me that digital is here to stay, so we had better figure out how it fits into our creative *Weltanschauung*. The place that digital works have now and will attain in our culture may hinge on four main considerations: why we enjoy art, digital or otherwise; the historical processes of artistic creation; the concept of origination with regard to artistic works; and how digital works are being accepted by the societal arbiters of cultural importance — museums.

First, we enjoy art because the creative urge is universal to us all, and our affinity for that small subset of humans with the talent to express that urge (artists and their creative process) seems to be a human constant. As far as I can tell, the enjoyment of art, traditional or digital, has two distinct levels. The first is in the direct and immediate emotional pull that you experience when seeing a piece of art that you enjoy. You may know nothing of a piece, the artist, the context, or anything, but for whatever reason, the art speaks to you. And you enjoy it. This is the primary way that people appreciate artwork. The second and more sublime phase of art appreciation is the knowledge that there is a creator of that work. This meta-appreciation goes beyond the direct sensory contact between audience and the work, and enters an entirely different level of connection — a kind of Six-Degrees-of-Kevin-Bacon, where the artwork acts as an intermediary between the appreciator and the creator — allowing a moment of shared meaning, even if it is entirely within your head. It's a powerful epiphany to realize that you and the artist share something, even if it is only the fact that you possess something in which the artist, and by extension her creative magic, has touched.

Inevitably, societies translate that appreciation into cultural values. The emotional and financial value of artworks is intrinsically linked to the artist. The artwork is an abstract expression of the creator — a living being with experiences and life decisions perhaps similar to our own. For works created by non-living beings — machines, mathematical equations, or universal constants, the same still applies, but in a different sense. A Mandelbrot fractal-scape or music created by the background radiation of the solar system implies order. And order reveals purpose (such as a higher power or a guiding force) or stability, giving us a sense of continuation and knowledge that there will be a future. In the end, we value art because someone or something created it and we yearn to access, or

A Curatorial Perspective:
Digital Media and its Place in the Arts
Jacob McMurray

at least bask in those generative powers. Jacob Covey, the art director at Fantagraphics Books (one of the leading underground comic publishers in the U.S.), and an accomplished artist and designer himself, has commented to me, "it mostly comes down to one fact. We, as a society, enjoy art because it is infused with the artist's vision and immediacy. Art has no undo function. Art depends on vision and the passion of the artist to execute it. It's completely anti-scientific, but the most important facet of art is *soul* — the hand dipping into pigment and forming an inescapable form."

Second, an exploration of the progression of artistic processes in the past shows that artworks cannot be divorced from the creative processes in which they were created. Those processes form a clear historical path that mirrors the technological development of humanity. For most of human history, the artist directly created art, and each instance of art existed as a unique human artifact. Whether it is cave paintings at Lascaux or oils of the Renaissance masters, each creative artifact was unique and directly showcased the immediate connection to the artist. Unique artworks, because of their individuality, are undeniably appealing. According to Covey, "there is soul in the inking line, in the brush stroke, in the mistakes and smudges, or the absence thereof. It is unquantifiable and indefinable. The less sensitive viewer would never know the difference until they saw original art compared to prints. Beautiful." Nevertheless, the singular method employed by humanity for most of its history was changed forever with the appearance of processes enabled by duplication. By the sixth century woodblock printing appeared in China, followed there by the use of moveable type in the 11th century. Europeans came along late, with Gutenberg's press appearing in the 15th century. By the early 20th century, lithography, intaglio, and screen-printing had all become methods by which art can be created, in duplicate or multiple editions. The concept of the "original" now becomes fuzzy, and the connection between the appreciator and the artist is now more tenuous than before.

The development of photography in the 19th century further thinned the connective tissue between the audience and the artist, and brought — along with its potential for expanded artistic innovation — a significant increase in "fuzziness" *vis-à-vis* uniqueness, adding to the audience's confusion. The printing techniques discussed above require active composition and the result is only limited by the artist's skill and imagination. Photography is similar, and certainly does afford the artist a myriad of methods of controlling the outcome, but in the end, it is about capturing the artistic image, versus composition. Printing is active, where photography is reactive and is limited by what you can put in front of the lens. Digital works are the new kid on the block, and provide the most dilemmas. "Computers have," muses Jacob Covey, "in a sense, democratized art. More people are able to utilize the computer as a tool and that tool has opened doors for many emerging artists, but it also has flooded our society with innumerable sub-par talents, which have the unfortunate effect of lowering for all the societal bar of artistic talent. This is especially true with art in commerce, such as graphic design." Equally problematic, art today is often created by a combination of processes. Designers create graphics, which are then etched into polymer plates and printed on antique letterpresses. Photographers develop prints, which they then retouch and color by hand, creating unique art pieces. Illustrators use hand drawn sketches, which are scanned into the computer, manipulated with Photoshop and printed as lithographs. The primary issue with digital media is the inherent insubstantiality of the works (unless they are transferred to some other media), which brings us to the concept of "origination."

A digital artwork made tangible has the unique attribute of always being a copy, and hence, less valued. For, what is the actual, original piece of art? As argued earlier, within the artistic spectrum, appreciation leads to value. And the value of artworks is greater when the piece in question has a solid connection to its creator. The only reason there's any discussion of the validity of digital works is because we are having difficulty answering the question "what is the original work?" Value is assigned by the knowledge that the work you have is the original, or as close to it as possible. With unique artworks, this is apparent. The artist's hands or tools created that particular piece of art. With a photograph or any kind of print, often the only indication that an artist had a physical hand in creating the piece is his signature upon the sheet. This certainly isn't an original, but it's as close as you will get for these media, and often, this is enough to satisfy our inner gauge of artistic worth. This can be taken a step further with numbered editions. Editions with a lower number feel more valuable, because a lower number implies that this particular print was created earlier (and thus is more original) than its higher-numbered fellows.

The problem of valuation with regard to digital works of art is compounded by the fact that digital artwork and media are quintessentially ephemeral, and therefore have little relative worth, compared to their physical cousins. What is the original with a digital work of art? Like photographs and prints, there isn't one, but with digital works, there isn't even anything physical to appreciate. There are as yet no famous digital-only artists. Name me one. If some have attained any sort of recognition in the art world, it is because their works have been translated into physical objects that can be purchased and collected — digital Giclée prints, spreads in magazines or books, or limited edition lithographs. Perhaps the closest gauge to the future worth of digital works is the path that the video medium has taken. Film is similarly ephemeral, but through time and commerce, it has attained the sheen of artistic worth. This same exercise in determining origination can be expressed with records, books, posters, or most other iterative forms of creativity. Beyond unique works of art, which are easy to categorize, there are no absolutes, only gradients of merit — the closer a work is to the artist, the more original and valuable it is as a work of art.

Finally, we come to the issue that is perhaps the most concrete and tangible: how artistic works created in a digital medium are maintained and presented in the modern museum. Museums have long been repositories for society's cumulative cultural achievements. They have progressed from mere curiosity collections of the rich and scholarly, through ages of unfortunate cross-cultural plunder, to today, where most institutions have concrete missions, rigorous collections foci and appropriate staff to care for their myriad objects.

I am employed by two sister institutions, the Experience Music Project and the Science Fiction Museum and Hall of Fame, in Seattle, Washington. Both museums share staff and facilities, and only differ in the content they explore. The Experience Music Project (EMP) has a permanent collection of over 120,000 objects. A little more than 2,000 are currently on display. The Science Fiction Museum and Hall of Fame (SFM) has taken a different tack — it only has a permanent collection of around 200 objects, and perhaps 70 of those are on display. All in all, SFM itself displays over 700 objects — the other 600-plus come from various lenders, the primary one being the institution's founder and benefactor, Paul Allen. Asset management and care for collections of this size require permanent skilled staff. We currently have a collections manager, an A/V preservationist and a registrar employed full time to take care of our collections. We also have excellent fabricators and a preparator that allow the artifacts to be safely displayed. Although we haven't as of yet had much of an opportunity to deal directly with digital works, we are well aware of the issues at hand. The primary digital works that we do deal with consist of conservation photos of physical objects, digital photos of events at the institution, digital video or audio files for content in our exhibitions.

Caring for digital assets brings up many challenges that differ from care for physical objects, ranging from storage, preservation, and documenting, to display. "One of the reasons I find digital images a bit difficult to deal with," according to Angie Battalio-Bunker, registrar for EMP/SFM, "is that since they must live on a server somewhere, their life and safekeeping is out of my hands. I must rely on other departments, namely our Tech department, to safeguard my digital image 'artifacts'. This is obviously not the case with physical artifacts — I can control entirely where they are stored, how they are stored, and who has access to them." Angie continues: "I find that physical artifacts are easier to deal with from many angles: you can physically track them to a box, you can look at them to establish condition. They're tangible and accessible and 'real'. But digital images in our collection are 'real' too and are becoming more and more part of our permanent collection. We take digital images of all the physical artifacts: mostly to help with identification and to document condition. These digital images are then linked by our photographer to the artifact's record in our database. Digital images are not only important for future identification and for determining a condition baseline, but also help curators to 'see' the piece without the artifact enduring excessive handling. So, digital assets have in fact become a way to preserve the physical artifact and ensure the collection lasts longer." At the same time, while digital assets may pose certain challenges for categorization, "storage" is a whole different issue. Storage costs for physical objects vastly outweigh digital storage costs, but then again, digital storage is perhaps more susceptible to damage than a well-cared-for physical collection. Angie agrees; "It would be interesting to do a cost analysis of storage of physical artifacts vs. storage of digital information. Physical storage is very costly — paying a professional staff to handle, move, and track the pieces. The physical space demands a tightly controlled HVAC system that is constantly maintained and monitored. Archival storage boxes, tissue, tags, and other materials are all needed to properly store physical objects." As for the concerns related to displaying digital media, intellectual property rights, while certainly being an issue for physical objects, is paramount with the ephemeral nature of digital media. While the Fair Use doctrine can be considered as an option for exhibition or educational use within the walls of a museum, states Battalio-Bunker, when digital images are being graphically reproduced, "the IP issues are complex."

Although the two museums have little on display that truly could be considered a traditional work of art that exists solely in the digital medium, the exhibition of digital artworks is becoming increasingly more common with museums that showcase modern or contemporary art. Perhaps the closest we have come to showcasing digital works is with our *Art of Modern Rock: The Poster Explosion* exhibition. This is a show that I co-curated at the EMP, which explored the modern rock concert poster phenomenon. In addition to installing physical rock poster work on the walls, we featured several large monitors and projections which displayed, at a rate of one per second, single images of 40,000 different rock posters. The images weren't being displayed as part of an exhibition video, or as support material for other physical objects, but as pieces of art themselves. And our choices, given the varied methods of presenting these works, suggest that our display method and exhibition intent played a heavy role in the reception of these digital works as art. Digital works appear to be more susceptible to subjectivity than other media. Kirsti Scutt Edwards, a former colleague of mine who is currently the exhibitions manager at the Berkshire Museum, theorizes: "like any work of art, digital works rely solely on being exhibited in order to exist and affect meaning. But digital works rely on an individual to complete this connection in a far more intimate way — there is far greater involvement with how a work is presented that can ultimately affect how an audience perceives it. To what degree an artist or a curator controls the presentation of an installation piece can alter a work of art far more easily than a work of art created in a more traditional medium."

It is clear that the discussion of the digital as an artistic medium is ongoing and the debate is important to the formation of the genre. The difficulty that we have in contemplating the place of this medium within the spectrum of our larger human artistic history is due primarily to the relative youth of the art form, but it is also complicated by the ephemeral and ethereal nature of digital works. As an art curator, I tend to look at historical trends, and certainly the most confident I can be that something is a lasting trend is when I can witness it from a significant temporal remove. Only through time can you discern what will be the next Beatles versus the newest flash-in-the-pan. In art terms, digital media and processes have been around just long enough for its audience to realize that they are a valid medium, but not long enough for that audience to fully grasp the extent of digital art's merit. We've put a simple framework on the issues surrounding the medium through the examination of our reasons for enjoying art, the history of artistic processes, the idea of origination, and how museums deal with digital art, but only time will tell us where it is going.

Todd Lockwood, **Sword of Angels**
Digital media. Cover for the novel
by John Marco, DAW 2005.
30" x 22"

Jacob McMurray is a Seattle-based curator, designer, and publisher; co-owner of Payseur & Schmidt literary publishers, and the screen-printing studio Patent Pending Press. As Director of Exhibitions and Ephemera for the magaziine *Born Presents* he occasionally creates installations and exhibitions. These mostly non-profit ventures are funded by his senior curator position at the Science Fiction Museum/Experience Music Project (Seattle, WA). In his negative free time he delights in printing manifestos on his 1906 Pearl Improved #11 letterpress and waiting for the revolution to come.

F OR those of us involved in illustration long enough to remember the simple advent of the fax machine, the current status of our medium can be bewildering. The fax machine introduced a massive step forward in communication, and it wasn't long before we relied on it … and within a short time it was ubiquitous. The same might be said for the computer, with one important difference: While everyone agreed the fax machine did not alter the way illustrators created their work (it just improved the communication process), the same cannot be said of the computer. It is altering the way artists create their work, forcing them to become more creatively flexible, more productive, and more aware of the role played by "commerce" in the production of commercial art today. From an agent's point of view there have always been two essentials in the agent/illustrator relationship beyond the talent: is the illustrator creatively flexible? Can he/she deliver on time? The answer, now more than ever, must be a resounding "yes" to *both*.

The 40-minute subway ride down to the RCA building on Chambers Street to fax a comp to my associates in London seemed like a worthwhile trip at the time and certainly a step up from the rattling telex machine that was residing in my apartment/office in Manhattan. It was 1981. "Welcome to the modern world," I thought. I had shaved days off the deadline. Twenty-five years later a new shift in technology is upon us and this time it has dramatically altered the creative process.

Having represented all types of illustrators for those 25 years I have found myself at the center of this traditional vs. digital argument many times over. The illustrators I represent range from 22 to 62 years old. They work in diverse markets and with many different mediums, but publishing in its many forms is predominantly the source of our business. Currently 60% of my illustrators use some aspect of the digital tools made available to them. The remaining 40% are traditional illustrators creating work purely by hand. The essence of the debate comes right down to this question: Do we grasp with both hands and harness every new medium that comes our way, or do we look at them as necessary evils that are having a negative impact on the way illustration is created? There's no question that the digital revolution has been — and continues to be — a juggernaut plowing through commercial illustration, nor any doubt that illustrators have to adapt.

The illustration world today is a different place, and illustrators must tackle the challenges before them. Certainly, being the less glamorous sibling to the creative end of the business, productivity is key. The most common refrain amongst illustrators in all parts of the business is how flat fees have remained over the past 10 years. With that in mind, there is no escaping the simple logic that to counter such a plateau, an illustrator has to produce more work. This rationale eventually meets its bitter and twisted end when it's realized that even if an illustrator is able to achieve a 20% or 30% increase in the amount of work produced, it's based on the notion that the work will in fact be there. For a myriad of reasons, none of which are usually personal, some illustrators are not inclined towards working directly with an art director or designer, and prefer working with a representative who simplifies the process, in both a creative and business sense. One of the less obvious responsibilities of the representative is to keep the illustrator abreast of what's happening in the industry at large, which can be like straddling a see-saw. There's that delicate balance between harsh reality and finding the silver lining.

Paint to Pixel: Life Beyond the Canvas
Alan Lynch

One of the not so subtle "happenings" is that clients are increasingly expecting their creative departments to come up with design solutions — with or without use of an illustrator. This in turn means, of course, that designers are expected to create illustration on demand and in-house. Illustrators and their representatives should have seen this coming. We had witnessed fifteen years earlier the virtual purge of typesetters as the first wave of digital media arrived.

So, it's not with pleasure that I report to my illustrators the cold facts of life on the front lines. The single most disturbing one being that anywhere from 30% to 50% of covers designed are produced entirely in-house. The inescapable conclusion is that while productivity is important to counter flat fees, the reality is that there is less work to go around. Therefore, while the digital medium can increase an illustrator's productivity, it does not ensure increased income.

If the illustrator is talented — or inclined — enough to master the medium, then his art can be created, even partially, in a digital format, giving him that rarest of virtues: the ability to change his mind. Not sure that green sunset is working? A couple of key strokes and it's orange. What an unbelievable tool! Trouble is, it works both ways. An art director not only knows the illustrator can do this, but he too can make this change, and not always with the illustrator's knowledge.

This shift in control of the image means that the designer can create multiple versions of any package for presentation, and in turn, this feeds the expectation of the client: "let's see the sunset in green, orange, red, and pink." An argument could be made that the pressure on the designer leads to using the illustration as a means to an end — which of course it has always been; but the illustrator also had a very personal stake in the way the package ended up and a resulting status that came with the more successful efforts. Unquestionably, that has been dulled and I think the illustrators' contribution has been degraded accordingly.

There is indeed irony to the fact that one of the most alluring qualities of the digital medium for artists is the control they have over how and what they produce — and yet this very attribute is the same thing that works for publishers to the detriment of illustrators. *Control.*

The business has changed dramatically with regard to the balance of power, and the process of creating an illustration has changed with it. In some ways creating the illustration has become a much more collaborative effort. In the pre-digital era, illustrators would sit in their studios, wait to receive the material upon which to base the illustration, produce sketch concepts to be approved, and then create a finished piece of art. The illustration was approved, approved with changes or, occasionally, rejected. While I'm happy to report that the rejections have declined considerably, it's at the expense of the illustration being "approved with changes", because there's where the intersection of digital illustration, production, and design meet — or collide. Many illustrators are quick to suggest that this increased collaboration is just a further erosion of illustrations' unique contribution to the marketing effort. While that might sound slightly precious, the facts are clear. There are many more fingers in the creative pie these days and the results are not commensurate with those higher levels of group decision making: six different suggestions about how to change or "improve" one illustration will not necessarily make the illustration six times better.

The more successful illustrators are the ones that understand that the business they are in is a commercial endeavor, and there will be frustrations along the way. For the majority of illustrators their assignments come with certain expectations and requirements regardless of how they create the illustration. The business has always depended on evolving from concept to finished art and success is attained and defined when there is a collusion of great image and great design along with a satisfied client. However, how illustrators maintain that mission while working within this new dynamic, and how their work will evolve should they decide to engage in this medium, is the challenge. For the younger generation of illustrators who are schooled from an early age in digital formats, making the transition is not the issue. It's the older generation of artists who are experiencing the greatest difficulty in adjusting; they have spent their careers developing a more traditional and individual style only to realize that they are somewhat trapped. Some illustrators are just not ready or inclined towards this new medium. The question becomes: at what point does a new market paradigm force them to reconsider their position, and what are their choices?

No matter what line of work you're in, increased productivity is generally considered "a plus." Thus, although it's far from being a magic pill, the digital medium has provided an important alternative for illustrators for whom increased production rates are an important part of the equation, but it's the classic case of double-edged sword: For every good reason why art should be created in a digital format there is also a negative one. Nevertheless, one thing remains true — illustrators who paint or produce work by traditional means generally don't have the ability to increase their productivity. Painting faster is not an option. So, if greater productivity is the new criteria for success, then illustrators have to consider changing, which is the main reason I have usually encouraged illustrators to embrace the new medium and make it work for them. Invest in the new technology, be patient, and ride the learning curve. *Survival is paramount.*

If we abide by the principle that it's all about the image and end result, then we should be less concerned about how the illustrator gets there. In many ways digital illustrators have come full circle in the short time they have worked with the medium: the once heralded shiny neon smooth finishes that these early pioneers developed have given way to the anti-digital look. Many illustrators work with digital mediums but have managed to give their creations the patina of a hand-hewn piece of work. A finish that actually looks digital is so 2002!

Traditional illustration will always have its place. The demand may be lower today, but that decrease was beginning to happen anyway. Like a lot of publishing, cover design is trend-oriented and trends by definition come and go. There is life beyond the canvas and illustrators have and will continue to move into the brave new world using all the innovative tools they can. To discourage or devalue the digital medium is counter-productive. This is but one option an illustrator has at his disposal and, providing he can produce another stunning individual visual interpretation, why should we be concerned about the medium? The commercial illustration arena is a tough business. Getting caught up in process is much less important than the finish.

Moving into the digital medium does, however, come with a price. Once the illustrator makes the transition why would he ever go back to a traditional medium? I represent a few who happily go back and forth but there are also many who haven't picked up a paintbrush in years — and they don't shed a tear. So, in taking their lead, neither shall I.

Alan Lynch was born in England, and moved to the US in the early 1980's where he continues to represent a variety of illustrators from around the world. He is married with three children and lives in upstate New York.

DIGITAL or paint? Canvas or computer screen? It's the hot topic at the moment in science fiction art and there's no right or wrong answers, just opinions. Since I've been involved with this genre for approximately half-a-century — having read my first science fiction novel in 1955 when I was nine years old, and having bought my first science fiction paperback from the Teenage Book Club (TAB) a few years later — I feel as qualified as most to add my voice to the chorus. You might not like what I have to say, but hopefully you'll understand what I'm saying and why I'm saying it. Not that it will matter since I suspect we are already past the tilting point in regards to the creation of modern SF art, but, at least a different viewpoint will be championed — *the science fiction art collector's viewpoint*. A minority view, no doubts about that, but an important one I believe for reasons that will follow.

I started out strictly as a reader in science fiction, devouring primarily Ace and Ballantine paperbacks throughout the mid-to-late 1950's, then moving on to science fiction magazines, beginning with *Astounding SF* in 1959. By 1961, when I was fifteen years old, I began toying with the idea of becoming a writer, and before long I was submitting fiction to *Analog, Fantasy & SF, Galaxy* and *IF* magazines. By the time I graduated high school and began attending engineering college, I had racked up an impressive number of rejection letters from most of the major editors in the field. As almost an afterthought, I also had assembled a collection of several thousand science fiction paperback books and magazines mostly bought at the bargain price of 2 for a quarter in used bookstores in the New York metropolitan area.

In 1967, I sold my first short story to *IF* magazine, attended my first World SF convention in New York, began collecting SF hardcover books, and decided that no right thinking individual could ever support themselves comfortably on the money earned as an SF writer. So I abandoned my notion of becoming a writer, though I kept on collecting. Life progressed in interesting ways. I got married, opened a science fiction and fantasy bookstore, started collecting original science fiction art, and moved to Chicago, all occurring in somewhat reverse order. The first SF painting I ever bought was the F&SF cover for the first installment of Robert A. Heinlein's "The Door into Summer," painted by Kelly Freas, and it cost me $90. It was the beginning of a continuing obsession that has lasted for 34 years and shows no signs of abating. I suspect I will die reaching for a dimly seen painting on the wall of a hospital room somewhere, someday. I only hope it will be something nice.

I returned to writing approximately when I was 40, having made enough money that I could write primarily for pleasure and not to support myself, my wife, and my son. Over the years, I've had 36 books published, ranging from technothrillers to horror novels to *A Biographical Dictionary of SF and Fantasy Artists* for which I won a World Fantasy Award and was nominated for the Hugo. During those same years, I collected art with a passion, buying and selling pieces always with the thought of earning enough money from my deals to help pay for the next masterpiece on the horizon. Over the decades, I estimate several thousand pieces of original art, mostly from before 1970, have passed through my hands. Maybe more.

My own collection, which has stabilized over the past few years, numbers around 450 pieces, fairly evenly split between paintings and pen and ink illustrations. The focus of the collection is on artwork from the 1930's to the 1950's, with special emphasis on the works of Virgil Finlay. I own approximately 100 pieces of art by Finlay. I also own a dozen or more pieces by Kelly Freas, Ed Emshwiller, Hannes Bok, Lawrence Sterne

YOU'LL BE SORRY
Robert Weinberg

Portrait of Robert Weinberg *by*
Jon Arfstrom in watercolor. c. 1985

Stevens, Edd Cartier, Roy Krenkel and lots of others.

I also own originals by Michael Whelan, Don Maitz, James Gurney, David Mattingly, Ron Walotsky, and other important artists from the 1970's through 1990's. The one area my collection is lacking is in modern SF art. That's because a vast majority of the art I like now is digital in nature. For those pieces, there is no original, just a computer file. For those people who need to hang something on the wall, a print is about the best you can do. A print? Next to my original paintings? *Don't be ridiculous.*

Now, with my credentials as a fan, a reader, a writer, and a collector in the science fiction field reasonably well established, let's consider the great debate. Should science fiction paintings be done entirely digital, or should most paintings, with certain exceptions, be done in the usual painted manner?

As a fan and reader of science fiction, I vote for digital art. Science fiction has always been the literature of big ideas. Space opera, a tradition that stretches back to *The Skylark of Space* by E.E. Smith was one of the early driving forces of sf and recently, with the rise of authors like Peter F. Hamilton and the continued fine novels by Dan Simmons, space war fiction is back with a vengeance. Needless to say, the advance in SF films made through digital effects has influenced the book covers we are seeing more and more. Let's be honest. The *Lensmen* novels featuring huge battles between fleets of the Galactic Patrol fighting the legions of Boskone can only be created using digital technology. Sure, the Borg, from *Star Trek, the Next Generation*, were as nasty a bunch of cyborgs as could be found in SF horror stories about robots, but it was digital effects that gave them the spaceship fleets and the armies that made them seem a threat to all life. Digital art, while somewhat cold and impersonal, has also given SF artwork a solid dose of what the old time fans refer to as a "sense of wonder."

Switching over to my career as an author who has written science fiction, fantasy, and techno-thriller stories and novels, I also believe that digital is the wave of the future for SF art. In the 1960s, I wrote numerous short stories on a typewriter. I also wrote two long non-fiction books on a Smith-Corona machine that easily could have been used as the anchor for a battleship. Some of my earliest novels were written on an Apple 2e computer. Every chapter needed to be saved as its own file. Page numbers had to be reset constantly, and changing a name meant making global corrections in twenty different files. However, it still was a lot better than typing.

Now, I write books that never once are seen as pages. The manuscript is a file. The corrections are returned, still in the file. The book is indexed by file. Notes are added by some keystrokes. Typesetting and layout is done electronically. The only time paper is involved in the book is when it is finally published. I don't think I could be dragged kicking and screaming back to a typewriter, even for double the money I usually get per book. So, I understand why a modern artist might not want to fight with a canvas or a color that just does not look right, or a brush stroke that registers too thick. Most writers abandoned paper and pens and pencils long ago. There are no manuscripts for fans to collect. No pages from a partly written story. They are antiques. So are paints and brushes and canvases.

So, the writer and the fan inside me both side with those artists who want to work in an entirely digital medium. What does the collector part of me say? Three words.

You'll be sorry.

As an art collector, someone who buys original paintings and black and white illustrations in the science fiction and fantasy fields, I think of digital artwork as the devil's invention. Fans collect art because the pieces are originals — they are one of a kind items, unique and special and very precious. Originals are personal. They are vibrant, they are alive, they are testaments to the talent of an artist. An original is the true vision of an artist on canvas or board. They are a hundred times, sometimes a thousand times, better than the reproduction of the piece on the cover of a book. Anyone can own a reproduction, even a limited print, but only one person can own an original. If not the creator, the artist, then let it be a collector. Someone who loves the piece and gives it all the attention it deserves.

Besides which, collectors are willing to pay good to extraordinary prices to own particular paintings they want. Selling originals to collectors has always proven to be a lucrative way for artists to make extra money from their paintings. In some cases, the income received by artists for older pieces of their work can be more than what they were paid for the reproduction rights to the original. With digital art, the artist will be able to sell prints forever, but no collector will pay thousands of dollars for a print, whereas numerous original paintings have sold for that price and will continue to do so.

Digital art shatters the entire concept of uniqueness that makes collecting such a special hobby. When art is done digitally, there is no difference between one version of the art and another. A detailed print is exactly the same as the original. It is a copy produced from the same file. It is one of many. It is part of the Borg. The painting itself may be spectacular, but it has no soul.

Leaving philosophical concerns aside, there is another reason why digital artwork will end up being a long-term disaster for SF artists. Because digital art discourages collecting science fiction art, after some years, the science fiction art collectors' community will disappear. Collectors will find other things to collect, or will only collect originals from the early days of SF, leaving the digital artists to fend for themselves.

SF art has always been the poor stepchild of the science fiction genre. While many many fans discuss the latest books, the new ideas in their favorite novels, or the talents of a certain editor, relatively few fans talk about the art that illustrates science fiction. While art is noticed, it barely registers on the minds of most SF fans and collectors. To them, the story is the thing — the only thing.

Without a hardcore base of art collectors, research into science fiction artwork will disappear. While this claim sounds unbelievable, it's not. It was true in the past and it will be true again in the future. During the 1930's and 1940's there were few fans who cared about science fiction art. Thus, there were scarcely any articles written about art or the artists who created it. Try discovering information about artists like Lawrence Sterne Stevens, or Herman Vestal, or even Paul Orban, all major artists in the 1940's and 1950's. There are no interviews with these artists in science fiction magazines or fan journals. There are no articles about their work or how they got interested in science fiction. There is only blank space. No collectors means no fans means no information.

What little history of science fiction art there is, exists because a few dedicated collectors of SF art went out and hunted down information about the artists of the time. Without the efforts of Gerry de la Ree, there would be little known about artist Virgil Finlay. Without Don Grant, there would be nothing available featuring the art of George Barr or Alicia Austin. Without the dedication of fans like Ken Moore and Alex and Phyllis Eisenstein we would know much much less about great artists like Kelly Freas and Ed Emshwiller and John Schoenherr. If I hadn't wanted to know more about the artists whose work I collected, there would have been no *Biographical Dictionary of Science*

Fiction Artists. If Howard and Jane Frank had not been dedicated fans and collectors of many of the great artists working over the past twenty years, the SF Art field would be much smaller and much more ignorant. The fans are the historians of science fiction. Not the academics, nor the scholars, but the fans. The collectors are the ones with the passion who want to know more and are willing to go to extremes to find out what they want to know — and, it's the collectors who save the art that many of the artists would otherwise abandon or destroy.

No more paintings means no more collectors means no more art scholarship and history. The science fiction art field will survive. But it will be a lot less exciting. And we'll all be sorry.

Jill Bauman, **The Story of Noichi the Blind** *by Chet Williamson. Published by Cemetery Dance Publications, 2007. Acrylic on stretched canvas. 14" x 22."*

Bob Weinberg is the author of sixteen novels, seventeen non-fiction books, and several dozen comic books. His work has been translated into 15 languages. Bob is the co-author of *The Science of Superheroes* and *The Science of Supervillains* which separate the real science from pseudo-science in comic books.

INDEX OF NAMES